of
BIRDS
and
BIRDSONG

By the same author:

FICTION
The Tales of Dawood Khan and Other Stories

NON-FICTION
Jungle and Backyard
India's Wildlife in 1959–70: An Ecological Survey of the
Larger Mammals of Peninsular India
Nights and Days: My Book of India's Wildlife

EDITED COLLECTIONS
Nature's Spokesman: M. Krishnan and Indian Wildlife
Edited by Ramachandra Guha
Eye in the Jungle: M. Krishnan – Photographs and Writings
Edited by Ashish and Shanthi Chandola, with T. N. A. Perumal

of BIRDS *and* BIRDSONG

foreword by Zafar Futehally

M. KRISHNAN

edited by Shanthi and Ashish Chandola

Original sketches by M. Krishnan
Reproduced by Soumen Chakravorty

ALEPH

ALEPH BOOK COMPANY
An independent publishing firm
promoted by *Rupa Publications India*

First published in India in 2012 by
Aleph Book Company
7/16 Ansari Road, Daryaganj
New Delhi 110 002

ISBN: 978-81-923280-6-5

1 3 5 7 9 10 8 6 4 2

Printed and bound in India by
Replika Press Pvt Ltd
310-311 EPIP Kundli
Haryana 131028

*The editors would like to dedicate this book to
Indumati Krishnan who painstakingly collected as
many of M. Krishnan's articles and sketches as she could.
Krishnan meticulously preserved the negatives of his
photographic work but did not think much of his pieces, or
the sketches he made to illustrate them once they had been
printed. These constitute the Krishnan archives, from which this
selection and earlier ones have been gleaned.*

CONTENTS

FOREWORD

I think I first heard about Krishnan in 1950, when in his usual abrasive fashion he protested against the policies of the Chief Conservator of Forests of Tamil Nadu. He was furious about the planting of the open downs of Ootacamund with eucalyptus and acacia. He objected not only on ecological grounds but at the aesthetic insensitivity of violating the essential features of that landscape. I wrote to him then about my own appreciation of his outburst, and that established a good bond between us. Later, after getting to know him a little better, we invited him to spend a weekend with us in our home in Andheri and then in Kihim.

Krishnan was a great campaigner for what he called the 'quiddity' of India, its physical landscape—the terra firma as well as its water bodies, marshlands and everything else. If that was done it would automatically preserve its faunal and botanical wealth. This implied that he was dead against the introduction of alien species in our country. The carefully selected exotic flowering trees in the compound of the Indian Institute of Science left him unmoved. He insisted that our native trees would have created a more pleasing environment, apart from being more long-lived and integrating better with local conditions. He made his views clear to the director of the IISc and did not mind the rudeness this involved. He could not restrain himself from expressing his true feelings and was rather proud of his ability to do so. In this he matched Salim Ali, and in Kihim this occasionally led to a confrontation between the two 'greats' while we lesser mortals squirmed apprehensively.

After I became honorary secretary of the Bombay Natural History Society in 1962 I was in regular touch with Krishnan as he was on its Advisory Committee and kept a sharp eye on its policies. When the Jawaharlal Nehru Memorial Fund was established (sometime in the 1960s),

I thought that Krishnan was the right person to write a report about the dwindling state of our wildlife which had become a matter of general concern. While in Delhi, I took the opportunity to meet Padmaja Naidu (daughter of the freedom fighter Sarojini Naidu), the secretary of the Nehru Institute, and enquired whether Krishnan could be awarded a suitable fellowship to enable him to write a book on the status of our wildlife. Padmaja did not hesitate a moment having been a reader of Krishnan's famous column, 'Country Notebook', in *The Statesman*. The book *India's Wildlife in 1959-70* was published by the BNHS in 1975.

From 1973 onwards, for more than a decade, I met Krishnan frequently at meetings of the Task Force for Project Tiger. There was one subject where I disagreed with him.

I was keen that we should take advantage of the research offers from students at universities in the US who wished to work in the tiger reserves. I felt that just the physical presence of these students would be a deterrent to poachers, which had always been a serious problem. But both Krishnan and Kailash Sankhala were not keen on foreign intrusion, in spite of their acknowledging the great work done by George Schaller on tigers and the deer in the Kanha National Park.

Coming now to Krishnan's pieces on birds, so painstakingly collected from various publications by Shanthi and Ashish Chandola, what can one say except to praise their accuracy and elegance combined. Krishnan's extensive vocabulary and wide literary knowledge, not merely in English, but also in Tamil, made his writing of absorbing interest for the general reader. Like Justice V. K. Krishna Iyer, whose judgements were laced with words his brother judges had never heard, Krishnan, too, was fond of the rare word, but these were of course used because they were the most appropriate ones for what he wished to describe. For example, when describing the enormously large nest of the White-bellied Sea-Eagle, he used the word 'faggots' for the material, 'trifid' for the fork of the tree to which the nest was anchored, and 'flotsam' for the source from where the nesting material was collected.

His extraordinary capacity to observe details is revealed in his article on House Crows. While seated in a roadside restaurant, and being dissatisfied with the 'twiggy and garlic spiced' chaklis, he amused himself by throwing them among the assembly of crows which had collected there. While almost all the crows were happy with eating one chakli at a time, retiring from the fray to enjoy the meal after each catch, he spotted one crow which had managed to grab four chaklis in its beak before commencing its breakfast—quite an achievement with only its beak as an instrument. What is remarkable is that Krishnan spotted this one variant among the multitude of *Corvus splendens* which were around. The word he uses for the Jungle Crow—'sapient'—is exactly right because they have learnt to live in cities, even though originally they were entirely jungle birds.

While admiring the exquisite morphology of the Hoopoe so designed as to make it easy for it to probe for worms, grubs and insects underground, Krishnan was able to note that the flicking of its crown feathers open and shut 'express the entire emotional range of the mood of the bird;' during the one minute he spent observing the bird, 'it played with its crest six times.'

Wherever he was, at all hours of the day, Krishnan had his ears tuned to the calls and songs of birds. Once, in Bangalore in early February, he was alerted by the tonking of Coppersmiths at noon—signs of the approach of an early summer. Normally the hot weather commences in Bangalore in April. He avers that no call 'is so sure a sign of summer's onset as the midday voice of the Coppersmith.'

Krishnan seems to have been singularly fortunate in being on the scene when some exciting event happened. For example, when an Indian Roller sitting high up on the edge of a branch lost its balance in a gust of wind, and fell, but managed to right itself before touching ground.

Every piece in this collection has something original even for the seasoned naturalist, and even his description of common events holds your interest because of the writing.

Let me end with a story that has an unusual ending. Once, when Krishnan was watching a Shikra eating a bloodsucker, first one Jungle Crow and then another came close by. 'The hawk resented their covetous glances,' and abandoning its prey, flung itself on the two crows with such good effect that soon the three birds found themselves on the ground. But ultimately the two crows freed themselves and flew away. 'I would much like to tell you,' Krishnan says, 'how the victor returned to the hard-won meal and consumed it in triumph, but in fact this incident ended even more like a story. For, while the hawk was routing its enemies, a third crow made an unobtrusive appearance on the scene, by a rear entrance, and flew away with the dead lizard even more unobtrusively!'

Zafar Futehally

September 2011

INTRODUCTION

An entire wall in M. Krishnan's room was covered with a bank of wooden drawers that were packed full of black and white negatives put in orderly sleeves and labelled in his own neat hand. These were images of India's wildlife made with patience and care by the pioneering nature photographer, often with a camera that he had constructed himself using bits and parts brought for him by friends, or picked up from some obscure shop in Madras, the town where he had his home. Selecting images from this large collection for *Eye in the Jungle*, the first anthology of Krishnan's writings that we edited, was a huge task that turned into an enchanting and rewarding journey of discovery as the selected negatives turned into positive prints under our watchful eyes in his own, long disused darkroom. Krishnan's articles, themselves, were easier to handle. As we sifted through these to select excerpts to go with the images that had been chosen, they cast a gripping, enticing spell on us. We knew, then, that while *Eye in the Jungle* would celebrate Krishnan's unsurpassable work with both the camera and pen, it would be a precursor to another book another day.

Looking through the large body of his work, we found that Krishnan had written extensively on birds. These had appeared in various publications such as *The Statesman*, *The Hindu* and *The Illustrated Weekly of India*, among others. Many of the pieces we were able to date were written in the 1940s and 1950s, and quite a few were accompanied by sketches that, being an accomplished artist, Krishnan had drawn himself. Maybe these were written before Krishnan had fabricated and put together his camera that he famously called the 'Superponderosa'!

The sketches were delightful, some extremely simple, others with greater detailing, and they enhanced the imagery of his inimitable prose.

We spent months in Krishnan's room and darkroom, but came across no original sketches. We checked with the family; and Krishnan's son, Mr Harikrishnan, asked the editor of *The Statesman* about the sketches—but very soon it became apparent that they had been lost forever. However, omitting the sketches was not an option. We just had to find an artist who would faithfully reproduce them from the faded, yellowed, brittle copies that were available.

While on a filming assignment in Corbett some years ago, we visited a jungle camp where the 'Golghar' had two pencil sketches of birds. We asked the owners of the camp who the artist was, and were told about Soumen Chakravorty, who lived in Bangalore. This was too good to be true. Soumen readily agreed to do the reproductions and has done a painstaking and excellent job. *Of Birds and Birdsong* started to take shape.

Perusing the archives over the years, we learnt a myriad things about the man. Born on 30 June 1912 in Tirunelveli, Krishnan, the youngest of eight siblings, went to school and college in Madras. From a young age, Krishnan was a prolific reader, had tremendous observation skills, and above all an enquiring mind. In the 1920s, when Krishnan was around eleven, Krishnan's father, the famous Tamil novelist A. Madhaviah, moved the family to Mylapore, then on the outskirts of Madras where the scrub, paddy fields and coconut groves sheltered creatures such as mongooses, civet cats, snakes and tortoises. Of this period during his childhood, Krishnan says, 'I used to wander around with a catapult in my hand and a jackknife in my hip pocket, feeling every inch a settler in a new land.'

It is hardly surprising that with such distractions Krishnan did not excel academically, even though he enjoyed botany which he studied under the famous plant taxonomist P. F. Fyson. In the 1930s, it was possible to do a BA or an MA in botany. Krishnan spent two years doing a Bachelor's, and another two doing the Master's course at Presidency

College, and secured a third class in both! He was then persuaded by his family to study law and graduated from Law College in 1936.

Krishnan must surely hold a record of sorts for the various jobs he held—working with the Associated Printers, the Madras School of Art, as publicity officer at All India Radio in Madras; then, in 1942, he moved to Sandur where he worked for the maharaja in various capacities— schoolteacher, judge, publicity officer and political secretary! His curiosity and observation never deserted him, and though he found a plethora of interesting subjects wherever he was, it was perhaps during the time he spent at Sandur that Krishnan's fascination and love for nature matured, and he firmly settled into being the extraordinary naturalist and writer that we know.

The foundation of natural history in India makes for a fascinating story set in the late nineteenth and the early twentieth centuries. It is also the story of a bunch of extraordinary people—nearly all officers of the Raj—dispersed along the length and breadth of the country. For them natural history was a productive pastime, and though they came from diverse fields, they were meticulous and precise in their observations. Thus M. A. Wynter Blyth, the headmaster of a school in Saurashtra, Gujarat, studied butterflies, and his book *Butterflies of the Indian Region* remains the authoritative text on the subject even today. Col. F. Wall, an army officer, wrote on Indian snakes and T. C. Jerdon, a doctor by profession, put together the first volumes on the birds and mammals of the subcontinent. A. O. Hume, a bureaucrat, is more often mentioned as the founder of the Indian National Congress, but few are aware that he was also an accomplished ornithologist who laid the foundation of ornithological work in India.

Then there was E. C. Stuart Baker, who has to his credit the remarkable achievement of writing eight volumes on birds for the series *Fauna of British India*. Stuart Baker was a police officer in the Assam cadre, and the story goes that he was twice tossed by a gaur, trodden upon by a rhino and lost an arm to a man-eating leopard 'and yet played a dexterous game of tennis!' Though the work of these remarkable people and others like them laid the basis for scientific study of the flora and fauna of India, it was the books written by shikari naturalists like Jim Corbett that ignited the popular imagination.

Early bird books, like Hugh Whistler's *Popular Handbook of Indian Birds*, were written in an immensely readable style and, in more recent times, Salim Ali also followed more or less the same format. These were well-illustrated reference books or guidebooks, which stoked the interest of readers in birds and birdwatching and established the amateur ornithologist.

Krishnan's work does not fit any of the above moulds. His work stands out as uniquely original, combining acute and systematic observation, depth of knowledge and the understanding of nature. The ultimate freelancer, Krishnan did not just write about birds, mammals, insects, and so on, but also about every aspect of natural history, even addressing issues like conservation and environment well before they had become commonplace. His mastery of English literature, exhibiting a rare charm, is evident in his writing. Such brilliance in nature writing had never been seen before or since in our part of the world.

Acknowledging Krishnan's unique character and talent, E. P. Gee, a tea planter, photographer, wildlife enthusiast and a contemporary of Krishnan, describes him in the following words in his famous book *The Wild Life of India*, first published in 1964:

> I think of M. Krishnan [as] one of the best naturalists of present-day India. He is middle-aged, active and does a lot of writing on natural history for newspapers and magazines. He is an artist also, and an expert wildlife photographer. [...] He is a bit of a 'lone wolf' and does not care for meetings or advisory boards, but as a naturalist he has no equal.

If at all Krishnan can be 'compared' to any of the earlier greats, it would probably be to E. H. Aitken, better known by his initials 'Eha', as he perhaps came closest to Krishnan as far as humour and wide-ranging interests were concerned.

Though partial to writing about mammals and birds, Krishnan wrote on just about any subject—cricket, Indian cattle breeds, native Indian dog breeds, dog shows and even short fiction, not just in English but also in Tamil.

Besides newspaper columns, four books were published during his lifetime. These included *Jungle and Backyard* (1961), a collection of short anecdotes titled *The Tales of Dawood Khan and Other Stories* (1977), and *Nights and Days* (1985), the first book to showcase his photography. When Krishnan applied for the Jawaharlal Nehru Fellowship, Padmaja Naidu, who was on the selection panel, expressed her surprise. Krishnan quipped that he thought he had better apply for the fellowship himself as that would ensure that he would not be put on the selection panel! He was awarded the fellowship in 1968, for a survey of the mammals of peninsular India, at the end of which *India's Wildlife in 1959-70* was brought out by the BNHS in the form of a book.

Krishnan served on the Indian Board for Wildlife after it was first set up in 1952, and was also a member of the Steering Committee for Project Tiger, when it was launched in 1973. He was awarded the Padma Shri in 1970. In 1995 he was included in the Global 500 Roll of Honour by the United Nations Environment Program (UNEP), for his contribution to natural history and conservation.

In 1950 he began writing 'Country Notebook', a fortnightly column for *The Statesman* of Calcutta. This column ran without a break for forty-six years, with the last piece appearing in the paper on 18 February 1996, the day that Krishnan passed away.

In an article titled 'Interviews With the Great' and published in 1958, Krishnan describes how he not only got the break to write on wildlife for newspapers and magazines, but also a free hand to write as he pleased:

Oddly enough, I have never interviewed a celebrity for a magazine or a newspaper, though I have been a photojournalist for years. The reason for this is not that I am superior to such assignments: it is simply that no editor so far has had the courage to trust me with the commission. Once, I very nearly got commissioned to interview several well-known people. But when I explained how I wanted to do the job, particularly the photography, the editor hastily retraced his steps and offered me, instead, free scope for features on India's fauna and flora.

When it came to birds, Krishnan wrote on everyday birds, birds found in every garden both in the city and in the countryside. The more common the bird, the more he wrote about it—he wrote multiple articles on the House Crow, the Rose-ringed Parakeet and the Common Mynah, to name a few. And yet, even though he wrote about the same subject, there was almost always a different perspective to it. And while he might have been a reluctant magistrate, he infused extremely apposite legal titles to some of his articles. 'Forty Days S.I.' are his observations about a Rose-ringed Parakeet that he rescued and nursed before releasing! Another article titled 'Avian Courts Martial' talks about—

> The 'lynching' of one of their kind by Common Mynahs and Jungle Babblers, and the execution of a crow by crows, have been reported in the correspondence columns of *The Statesman* recently, and an explanation invited. The resigned passiveness of the victims has been remarked, and a comparison to courts of justice suggested.

I have read similar reports of avian tribunals, but shall not refer to them as the 'court of justice' explanation is bad, both in fact and in law. I do not object to the comparison because there is no considered justice in these assaults by birds on one of their feather. No serious student of jurisprudence will pretend that rabid injustice has not been dispensed at human judicial tribunals. There have been many bloodthirsty courts in our history where the procedure was a farce and everyone knew the verdict before the trial opened, but they were content to pronounce the sentence—its execution was left to others.

'I'll be judge. I'll be jury,'
said cunning old Fury:
'I'll try the whole cause,
and condemn you to death.'

Lewis Carroll tactfully refrains from adding what Fury did to that mouse. It is as one interested in law, not as a naturalist, that I object to the comparison.

Krishnan's language and description of some of our most common birds are a delight to seasoned birdwatcher and amateur alike. Describing the Jungle Owlet, Krishnan says:

The Jungle Owlet, in spite of its name, is common enough in the garden. It is a little, mottled brown bird, no bigger than a mynah, but more stockily built. It sulks all day in some dim recess, but when it is dark it comes into the garden and sits straight-backed, and rigid on a post or paling, or on some dead and withered branch. It likes to perch in the open, where it can have a look around, and so it avoids the foliage and obscurity of the treetops. How like the very top of that old casuarina post it looks as it sits bolt upright in the dusk, mottled and brown and scarred! By and by a moth goes flittering past, and the very top of the post detaches itself from the main section and swoops after the moth on soft, soundless wings. It is back at its perch in a moment, once more a bit of bark and wood, so still you can hardly believe it was ever anything else. That is the way the owlet hunts, and it is as good a way as another.

Writing about the White-headed Babbler in a piece titled 'Birds of a Feather', a Krishnan perspective on the appearance and behaviour of these 'frowzy birds' is enlightening:

What do you suppose would happen if you and half a dozen of your cronies were to dispense with all privacy for a week and spend the time together, each hour together, awake or asleep? Well, murder could happen, anything could with no decent interval of aloneness, but this is certain: at the end of the week, if you survived it, you and your fellows would have acquired an abandoned laxity of dress and conduct. Bristly chins and loose, amorphous clothes are inevitable, and your conversation would have changed to a babble. Prolong it to a fortnight, and you could never change back to your fastidious selves thereafter.

This is just what has happened to the White-headed Babblers. They live too much together to keep up appearances, and they care no more.

M. Krishnan

Some descriptions are so exquisite that they transport the reader to the rural countryside and literally bring it alive:

> The millet stands nine feet in the fields, and the heads are ripening in the sun. The scrub has a fresh newly washed look after last week's downpours, the skies are clear and the air crisp. Each morning the brave, resounding calls of partridges answer one another in the fields around, and at sunset they call again. November is here.

Krishnan's description of bird calls is equally compelling:

> The Large Grey Babbler or 'Gangai' is a bird of open hillsides and wooded scrub, and by no means a *rara avis*... It loves the open, and does not skulk in the undergrowth or hide in foliage—you cannot miss this bold babbler, because of its size and blaze-edged tail; and even if you do, no matter, you will notice its fellows. For it is highly sociable even for a babbler, and goes about in parties invariably, in a loose string whether on the ground or bush or in

the air. And then, of course, there is its voice. One would need to be stone deaf, and almost blind, to miss this bird where it occurs... There are many birds in our country with compelling voices, but they pass. Spring and the monsoon resound in the countryside with the voices of cuckoos and rollers, and even the hot weather at its peak stimulates certain birds, notably the barbets. However, these voices are stilled when the seasons are past—even the Koel is silent for six months.

But rain or shine, the *quey, quey, quey* of the Large Grey Babbler is heard in a chorus that persists right through the day. Only the night brings relief from their loud, insistent calling.

And of course he found birds wherever he looked and shared this with his readers. In 1939, Krishnan wrote:

If you travel all day in a train and have no one to talk to, and if you are not one of those who can read or sleep while moving, you stare at the passing scenery and feel bored. Naturally. The passing scenery is dreary and unvaried, on the plains at any rate—the spiky, grey migration of agaves by the rails, and casuarinas and palms beyond. But lean back a trifle more in your seat and shift your gaze to the telegraph wires outside, and you will find something to amuse you and keep you amused—you will see almost all the birds of the countryside go streaming past the windows on these 'never-ending perches'.

Krishnan wrote inexhaustibly about birds—he described them, their hunting techniques, their courtship displays, he wrote about their song, bird language, birds in the rain, sleeping birds, bird flight—the list is endless.

Keeping in mind the exponential growth of cities today, one would suppose that urban wildlife would have been better off in the 1950s. But according to Krishnan it was not so, and he laments the march of 'civilization' and the toll it was taking on local fauna. In an article interestingly titled 'Non-Reclamation', he says:

In the old days urban gentlemen lived in bungalows with large, tree-filled compounds, and it was part of their gentlemanliness not to bother overmuch about the further reaches of their domain. Today the urban rich, when they do have a bit of garden space, have flowering trees near the road and rectangular lawns in front of the house in herbaceous borders; cannas flank the drive and crotons in pots decorate the portico, and if there is a plot in the backyard they grow anaemic tomatoes in it.

Our public parks display a hideous and patent symmetry: wide, hard paths intersect one another at right angles, rows of flaming cassias and poincianas stand stiffly at attention, there are sandpits and short-mown lawns for the children and concrete benches for older visitors. There is not enough under-shrub and bush anywhere to tempt a mongoose to stay or a warbler to nest. There is no *Lebensraum* for the lesser fauna even.

Off and on, during the past thirty years, I have watched the bird life and lesser beasts of a city area dwindle and vanish, and I know at first hand how our extensive agriculture can drive out wildlife in rural areas.

Even now it is not too late if we follow a sensible plan of non-reclamation in the countryside and encourage gentlemanly neglect in city gardens and parks, to bring back the charm of wildlife to these places. What many people (including enthusiasts for our fauna) do not realize is the power of nature to recoup, left to itself.

The noted historian and biographer Ramachandra Guha points out in a biographical note on M. Krishnan, that one of the important traits of his writing is that 'Krishnan never talked down to his readers, assuming in them a knowledge and range of interests equal to his own.' He wrote for the common man and if his readers did not understand his references, Krishnan expected them to go to the library and find out for themselves. Krishnan's extensive vocabulary and his use of antiquated words often had us scrambling for the dictionary, an exercise which left us amazed at how appropriate the usage was.

In 1952, Krishnan called for the effective protection of the Great Indian Bustard: 'I have reason to believe that in a dying race the reproductive instinct is exceptionally strong, but unless sufficient living space, food and protection are provided (artificially by man) this last minute resurgence cannot save the species.' He goes on to ask: 'Can we save it? I think it is possible if governments will enforce protective measures without too long deliberation. ...A fine will not deter a gourmet. ...Something must be done, harshly, effectively, to make the flesh of the bustard have a bitter taste to the man with the gun.'

The 'man with the gun' was very much a part of the 1950s landscape and though that 'officially' changed in 1972 with the passage of the Wildlife Protection Act, the Indian Bustard is no better off today than it was at the time Krishnan wrote. If anything, its future is even more precarious. Sadly, the grassland habitat of the bustard is not only under pressure from industry and agriculture, but even forest departments—custodians of our wildlife—consider these as wastelands, and intensive tree planting across these grasslands still goes on.

A 1953 piece entitled 'Nature Study' gives us an insight into the importance Krishnan attached to the understanding and knowledge of nature:

> One of the chief defects of our education is that it fails to stir or inform the natural curiosity of every child in the life around. This failure is so sustained, so gradually asserted and insidious, that no one notices it—and then one is through with school, through with college, and wholly preoccupied with a life that is blind to the rest of creation. Few people realize how complete this lack is, for it is a lack not only in our education but in our culture as well.

Krishnan's prose transcends age and is timeless, as this collection shows. It is natural history, literature, wit and humour all rolled into one. It is this 'wealth' in Krishnan's writing and not natural history alone that inspired us to make this selection. On the whole, interest in wildlife and nature has increased in our country, but the emphasis remains on megafauna. We, ourselves, were drawn to birds because they are all around us wherever you go. Maybe in lesser or in greater numbers depending on where you are, but they are there. Watching, identifying and observing birds is worthwhile, satisfying, and time pleasantly spent.

Krishnan's writing will appeal to readers of all ages, and while dipping through these at leisure some will rediscover, and others discover, the dictionary! As Krishnan himself suggested, education is incomplete without encouraging 'the natural curiosity of every child in the life around.' Besides, Krishnan's writing is literature at its best. And so this collection is aimed at a vast audience who, we trust, will see through the eyes of Madhaviah Krishnan that birds are our everyday companions. They are to be found in cities and villages, in the countryside and in the great forests where tigers and elephants, the gaur, the leopard and the rhino roam. Enjoy their company, for like so many small things, they are what may 'make all the difference.'

We have attempted to break up this collection into sections to make it reader-friendly, although it is not easy to classify a bunch of articles that appeared in newspapers and magazines, under appropriate headings. Each is a stand-alone piece, so the reader is free to pick up this volume at any point and put it down at will. We think Krishnan would have agreed with that even though he would not necessarily have admired our attempts to slot his articles, just as Krishnan can never be fitted into a narrow slot himself!

We leave you to read this book with a quintessentially Krishnan description:

Life moves, in India, to the accompaniment of certain immutable things, the suffocating architecture and traffic noises of cities, the chatter of bazaars, the earthiness and cattle and creaking wells of villages. And we live, wherever we are, amidst poverty and the cawing of crows. Not that the two go together, in any way. In my mind crows are associated with sleep, though all crows are silent and in bed long before I go to sleep. The raw proximate cawing of crows is among the first sounds one hears on waking, and on those few, delightful occasions when one gets the time for a siesta, the last sound one hears, on the brink of sleep, is the faraway voice of some crow, so strangely soothing in its tone.

Shanthi and Ashish Chandola
1 January 2012

A NOTE ON STYLE

Many bird names in the Indian subcontinent, both common and scientific, have changed since Krishnan wrote these articles; we have, therefore, provided the common and scientific names prevalent then and in use now, side by side, at the end of the book for purposes of standardization and for the benefit of the curious reader. This has also been done to bring the requisite scientific accuracy to the text. We have capitalized the names of birds belonging to individual species, all other bird names are lower cased. It should, however, be pointed out that wherever Krishnan used a now-outdated common name for a bird, we have elected not to change it to its contemporary name as we felt it would be too intrusive. The notes at the back of the book provide all clarifications that might be required.

The book has been divided into eight sections. 'Those Were the Days' gathers together early pieces written between the mid 1940s and 1950s, and focuses on Krishnan's reflections on bird life in that period, including his thoughts on age-old practices such as falconry and pigeon post. 'Splendour in the Wild' focuses on birds of spectacular plumage and birds exhibiting flamboyant behaviour. 'Fond Recollections' is a motley bunch of pieces, which takes its name from an eponymous one in the section, and records Krishnan's everyday encounters with birds, whether at the breakfast table or in a zoo. 'Bird Life in a City', again, takes its name from a piece within the section, and sketches the life of birds within urban settings. 'Jungle and Backyard' takes its title from his own 1963 book, and collects his impressions on some birds found in the wilderness and others that have comfortably established their own wilderness in someone's backyard. Krishnan's ability to enter compassionately into the cultural habitat of birds well enough to characterize them as social beings without anthropomorphizing them, is evident in this section. 'Birds From the Countryside' groups together pieces on birds that one would encounter in rural India. 'The Ear that Hears' includes his observations on bird language, bird calls and birdsong. 'Bird Flight' is self-evident. That said, these sections structure the book only nominally. Readers are urged to find their own method of navigating through the book. Each of the pieces in this selection stands alone, and is masterful in its own right. The reader will not be disappointed no matter on which page he or she lands.

THOSE

WERE

THE DAYS

THE POOR MAN'S DOG

In one of his books Konrad Lorenz tells of the affection for its keeper that a starling, hand-reared from infancy, develops. Let me give you his own words: 'An extraordinarily understanding friend used to describe him [the starling] as "the poor man's dog". That is entirely appropriate. He has a point of character in common with the dog, namely, that he cannot be bought "ready-made". It is seldom that a dog, bought as an adult, becomes really your dog... It is the intimate personal contact that counts. So you must feed and clean your nestling yourself, if you want a really affectionate bird of this species.' Lorenz suggests that the nestling should not be more than two weeks old when taken in hand.

Elsewhere he explains how and why an infant bird, secluded from its own species, tends to regard its human keeper as its parent, its fellow and even, on occasion, its mate. Other biologist-naturalists have also studied this 'imprinting' process, but probably no one has understood it more personally than Lorenz or explained it so well, which is why I quote him.

The starling is a *rara avis* in peninsular India, but anyone who has brought up a fledgling mynah will know the truth of what Lorenz says. Such birds lose all fear of their keeper, get deeply attached to him, and may safely be allowed full liberty. Every mynah fancier (I was one as a boy) knows, empirically, that for success he must get his pet really young, say, when it is about ten days old. When full grown it is apt to fly away, but till then it makes a most confiding and inexpensive pet.

However, it is not about starlings or mynahs that I write. I wonder what Lorenz would say if he were to see the most fearless and confident of all pet birds, the common partridge of our country, trotting demurely behind its master, coming up at once when called and entering its cage on invitation, answering his most softly sibilant whistles in its ringing voice. No finer poor man's dog exists.

Not every poor man can keep this pet, for it needs much understanding and patience, and those who spend their spare time in the more conventional relaxations and in social pleasures cannot find the time for it. The middle class, of course, can never afford it, for in addition to the constant pursuit of a living such folk are hopelessly preoccupied with keeping up appearances—but some day I hope to break clear of the traditions of my class and go in for a partridge.

Among the poorer people, there are some who spend all their spare time in some fancy, which holds compensations for all their lacks. In other countries such men have bred hardy breeds of dogs or new varieties of cage birds—here, such men sometimes keep partridges. These pursuits often go by local and family traditions, and in the South it is usually working-class Muslims who sustain the fancy.

The point about partridge keeping that will interest naturalists is the fact that the birds are rarely reared from the nest. Occasionally a quail-sized nestling, that will take a year to 'furnish' fully, may be seen with a fancier but often enough it is a three-quarter-grown bird that is taken on hand, wild caught. I have heard fanciers claim that they have tamed and trained full-grown wild-caught birds. Still they make the most confiding and attached pets.

Only the cock is reared, for the prime function of the pet partridge is to fight. Devoted patience, fond care and solicitude and hours of complete freedom are the captive partridge's privileges; in exchange for these its master asks only one thing of the bird, that it shall annihilate all opponents in its fights, win him his wagers and justify his pride in it.

I shall say nothing about partridge fighting here. The way the birds fight is interesting and, so far as I know, no adequate description of a fight has been written, not even by Lockwood Kipling, who had an eye for such things. I have seen a fight only once. I should like to watch it again, and secure photographic support for my account, before I write of it. But I may say that the loser in the battle, cut by the victor's spurs and buffeted by its wings, is rarely blamed by its master and never ill-treated. It is some defect in its conditioning for the bout or in the poor quality of the feed that that rascally grain-merchant has foisted on its owner that is blamed for its failure. The true partridge fancier is far too fond of his bird and knows it too intimately to be wholly utilitarian in his fancy.

The training of the bird takes up much time. It needs regular walks, fine seed (it likes grass-seed especially) and termites, besides other food. Most of the exercise it needs is provided during walks abroad, along roads and footpaths, with its master. The fancier carries a round cage with split-bamboo bars and a brass hook and cone on top, and 'speaks' to his bird, trotting behind him or just ahead, from time to time—and it answers his softest calls and runs up to him. Sometimes two friendly fanciers may go out together, but on such occasions one bird is invariably carried in its cage (usually with a dark cloth cover, fashioned in the manner of a teacosy, drawn over it) and only the other bird is turned loose, for otherwise the birds would go for each other at once. It is usual, when training a new bird, to take a well-trained one in a cage on walks—the soft cheeping of the confined bird, which cannot see all around because of the hood, ensures the free bird following closely, for there is no sound that excites and holds a cock partridge like the voice of another of its sex.

When I was a boy I have often seen a lanky, lantern-jawed Muslim fancier with two unhooded cages, one in each hand, and a pair of partridges trotting at his heels. It is likely that these birds were a mated pair; in a feral state partridges always go about in braces. That man was a noted fancier and as one specially privileged I have sometimes accompanied him on his walks, and helped him to locate termite mounds for his pets, but in those days I could not tell a cock partridge from a hen. Every subsequent expert I have consulted has pooh-poohed the idea of anyone taking two loose partridges along on a termite seeking expedition.

Partridge keeping is more of a suburban than a rural fancy. It is truly indigenous and a pastime that calls for the traditional Indian skill and patience with wild creatures—not that I suggest that we are, as a nation, fond of wild creatures, especially the more civilized and educated among us.

THE DYING GLADIATOR

By a twist of fate the one time I had the chance to acquire a gamecock official prestige barred me. I was a magistrate then, and my fondness of livestock had already drawn comment. My Racing Homers had been invested with the aura of respectability by the local Boy Scouts using them for their pigeon post (a post suggested and mainly run by me), but the goats were less easily justified.

There had been emergencies when I had to herd my goats myself, and however unostentatiously a magistrate turns goatherd news of the event gets abroad. I had a polite, unofficial note from my chief which said that rumours (which, of course, he discounted) had reached his ear that I had been seen in the scrub jungle piloting a number of goats with bucolic shouts, and that while he appreciated my right to do what I liked outside office, such capricious behaviour on the part of a First Class Magistrate was, nevertheless, ill-advised.

There had been a pompous paragraph on the official proprieties and the dignified and unbending countenance of justice, and, evidently pleased with the etymological aptness of the description, he had repeated the words 'capricious behaviour' several times.

So, when a case of betting on a cock-fight came up before me, and a magnificent bird was produced in evidence, I resisted temptation firmly. My clerk, whose adjective law was superior to mine, assured me that the thing to do was to confiscate and auction the fowl besides fining the owner—I still doubt the legality of this procedure, but it had been followed by my predecessors in office, and who was I to try to act wiser? There were people present in the court who would gladly have bought the gamecock at the auction and, after a discreet interval, sold it to me at a formal profit—and somehow they had sensed my interest in this piece of evidence.

But I was firm. I contented myself with sharing my lunch with the haughty bird during the afternoon recess, and with admiring it. The iron spurs, which were also filed as 'material objects' by the police, were interesting, about an inch long, made of mild steel, and really sharp. They were encrusted with blood and had already begun to rust, but I wanted to keep them—as a souvenir of my triumph over temptation. I was denied even this satisfaction. My learned clerk said the rules decreed that such objects, which could be used again to commit an offence, had to be destroyed.

Only once, as a schoolboy, have I seen a cock-fight, and have confused and almost staccato recollections of it—the crowd in the bylane, people squatting and standing in a ring around two gamecocks, the earnestness of the men, the indifference of the birds to each other; then, unexpectedly, the spontaneous flare-up of combat, the incredibly swift and savage attack, flailing legs and flying feathers and blood; and then the sudden collapse and death of one of the combatants in an unrecognizable shuddering mess of dishevelled plumes and slashed flesh. I have seen dog-fights, ram-fights, partridge-fights, even a brief tussle between two circus camels, but for sheer shock and impact and savage fury that cock-fight was unapproachable. Blake must have known its violence and gore at first hand, to have written:

> *A gamecock clipped and armed for fight*
> *Doth the rising sun affright.*

Naturally the law takes a grave view of cock-fighting. It is a rather horrible sport, but even I, who feel revolted by its carnage, realize it is a sport: the kind that stimulates speculation and betting. Once zamindars and other rich, leisured people were much given to patronage of cock-fighting, but those days are past. The gamecock is a rare bird today, and getting rarer.

M. Krishnan

It is said that domestic poultry originated in India, and our junglefowl go a long way towards proving this claim. However, it is in other countries that fine and specialized breeds of domestic poultry have been built up and stabilized. True, we have no native breeds to compare with those tender-fleshed egg-layers, but in our gamecock—purely the product of indigenous breeding skill—we have a bird second to none in looks and power. The gamecock is essentially the same all over India, a tall, hard-muscled, brown-and-black bird with a long, graceful neck, a broad keel, and great, columnar legs—the legs and spurs are the features of the breed, and are most impressive. The hen, as in all gallinaceous birds, is smaller and much more modest in looks.

The reason why this superb and wholly indigenous breed is almost on the point of extinction is that it is of no use except in a fight. Obviously its flesh would be too tough for the table, and the small eggs have no appeal to the poultry farmer. However, a gamecock would make a grand pet, and the race can be saved if only people would keep it for its looks and its temperament. After all, utilitarian worth is as out of place in a pet as in sport, and the gamecock is a bird of real quality. It is capable of deep attachment to its keeper, and intolerant of strangers and intruders. A gamecock parading one's compound lends more than picturesqueness to the place; it lends it security for, believe me, it is a formidable watchdog.

PIGEON POST

Pigeon post is based on the homing instinct of birds, strongly developed in certain breeds of pigeons. In many other birds also, swifts for instance, this instinct is urgent; but then they are not domesticated and so cannot be pressed into man's service. Not all breeds are suitable for pigeon post. It is true that practically every kind of homer, and even Dragoons and High-flying Tumblers, will come home from varying distances, but for any serious project only one breed, the Racing Homer, need be considered. The carrier is not a suitable breed in spite of its name: today it is a show bird, pure and simple.

Pigeon post is an ancient institution, but by no means an outmoded one. During all recent wars, homers were used for delivering messages from ships out at sea and aircraft in difficulties, where wireless would have betrayed the messages to the enemy. I should explain here that I do not write of such long-distance emergency post, or of pigeon-racing, in this elementary note—those are highly specialized avocations demanding expert skill and knowledge, and the very best birds that can fly over hundreds of miles. But for pigeon post on a modest scale, say under a hundred miles on any flight, any good working strain of Racing Homer will do: and the running of it is something that most people can do, after a brief probation. Incidentally, no pigeon outside the pages of romantic poetry will convey a message to a person and bring back a reply—not even a postman does that!

The basis of pigeon post being the birds' natural desire for their home, a roomy, comfortable loft is of prime importance. It is not enough to provide one's homers with sufficient food, breeding lockers and perches in this loft—every detail that makes for comfort, cleanliness and security should be carefully studied and utilized. The loft should be so made that cleaning and disinfection can be carried out regularly and thoroughly; therefore, have a concrete floor to it, and avoid nooks, corners and cracks as much as possible in the arrangement of the nesting-boxes and perches. A constant supply of clean drinking water should be available, preferably in wells of the type that the birds cannot soil. A trough of water for bathing should also be provided from time to time. Whether the birds are hand-fed or from a hopper, strict regularity in feeding is essential. Feed your birds at the same time morning and evening, and give them just as much grain (sound, clean, mixed grain) as they will consume at each meal, so that they will be in good condition and still have a sharp appetite for the next meal. A grit-box and a lump of rock salt should be available to the pigeons always, and finely chopped green vegetables should be given to them occasionally. The loft should be airy but free from draughts, and it is important to ensure a dry, damp-proof interior. Fine-mesh expanded metal is best for the side walls, as it is easily cleaned and allows light to enter, but is rat- and snake-proof and prevents cats and other predators from snatching at a bird sitting close by the side wall.

It is wise to have a smaller loft installed by the side of the regular loft, separately, so that sick and seedy birds can be isolated, and breeding pairs be kept apart if necessary.

When the birds are settled in their loft and at home in it, their training can commence. The first thing they should learn, both squabs and adults, is to enter the loft through the trap. This trap is usually an arrangement of vertically hung wires, hinged to a top cross rod of an open window, the free lower ends of the wires resting against an outer crossbar at the sill, so that the pigeons can walk into the loft raising the wires, but not out of it again. A convenient landing board is provided just outside the sill of the trap, so that the birds can fly right on to the board and walk through the trap into the loft. Of course the trap should have outer shutters, to close the trap when not in use. The best way to train the pigeons to come quickly in through the trap is to let them out on hungry stomachs, clean up the loft and place their food inside it, allowing them only the trap to come through inside to feed.

Squabs strong on the wing and flying freely around the loft (say, about three months old) and adult homers can both be trained for the post. However, they should never be flown together. The birds are taken in baskets some distance away (about a mile) and tossed individually. At each subsequent toss the distance from the loft is increased, a little farther away for the first few tosses, then in longer laps. Always train your birds in the same direction, and on empty crops, so that they will have an incentive to get home quick. Of course, they can be trained to come home from any point of the compass, provided they have been trained over the course separately in each direction, i.e. trained to fly in from the north, then the east, then the south, and then the west. Over hilly country, or where flying conditions are poor, training should be gradual, especially for the first thirty miles or so. Over flat country or water, the training can be done quickly.

A certain percentage of losses is inevitable during this education, through accident or incapacity. In areas where they are common, there is no wholly satisfactory method of eliminating losses from hawks, particularly in the case of young birds. Flying speeds depend upon head-winds, visibility, and individual capacity, and also on the familiarity of the pigeon over the course. Over short distances the birds take a longer time comparatively than over longer flights, because the time spent in circling to gain height and bearings on release, and in getting down to the loft, has to be added to the actual flying time from toss to loft in each case. Pigeons do not fly well in poor light and when there is foggy weather, and they do not fly at all in the dark.

And what are the uses of pigeon post in peacetime? Apart from the allure of the pastime (life has few things more satisfying to offer than the sight of one's homer volplaning down to the loft from a far flight, dead straight like a bullet, on stiff, swift, unflapping wings, gaining size and definition with each moment), pigeon post can have real and varied uses. Over countrysides where the roads are not of the best, homers are faster than fast cars, and wherever news needs to be reported from the outskirts of such country to a centre from time to time, they can do the reporting cheaply and expeditiously. Even where messages need to be conveyed and reconveyed from depots and outposts to a central station and back again, all that is needed is a loft at each outpost and at headquarters, with the birds of each loft ringed to mark them—a pigeon from one loft can be kept in another for days safely, with the certainty that it will fly straight home on release, provided it is kept apart by itself. Where industrial operations are being carried out over a large rural area, and wherever there are outposts with a central station (rural police, for instance) pigeon post can help substantially. Unfortunately, its possibilities are unknown in our country except to men of the fighting forces and a few others. I believe that pigeon post offers a truly valuable and interesting addition to the activities of Boy Scouts, and the police in rural areas, but it is hard to get people to realize the advantages of anything that is new to them. The work of setting up lofts and training birds (a simple job where the facilities are made available) seems too great an initial handicap to them, and they do not see that the routine can be established soon, and that thereafter the project will be richly worth the while. If people will look solely at the difficulties in the way—well, they can have the melancholy satisfaction of seeing everything in life black and unpromising, including pigeon post.

THE BRAHMINY KITE

An elderly gentleman from the borders of Hyderabad (Deccan), who has lived as a gentleman should, spending his ample leisure in open-air pursuits, assures me that he has known the Brahminy Kite to be successfully used in falconry, that, properly trained, the bird can bring down middle-sized quarry both in the air and bush.

Now, the Brahminy Kite is powerfully built, more like an eagle than a kite, and if size is the criterion, it is large enough to bring down a pigeon or a partridge. Moreover, I went into the matter not only with my landed informant but also with his equally elderly, equally sporting tenants, and there was good evidence that at least one local falconer had trained the bird successfully for hawking. Falconry is no longer practised in those parts, for the landlords are now preoccupied with depriving legislation, and their camp followers with that hateful thing, working for a living.

But in my many talks with these old-timers I felt satisfied that the sport had flourished there only twenty years ago. The country is ideal for it, being dead flat and bush-clad. Red-headed Merlins, kestrels, Shikras, Tawny Eagles, Short-toed Eagles, harriers, a buzzard or two, and an occasional passing Laggar, represent the local raptors, but I was told that in the old days Peregrines were imported, and a big, bold, peafowl-killing bird which, to judge from hearsay, was nothing less than the Bonelli's Eagle.

I am no falconer. In fact, my acquaintance with birds of prey has been from the other side entirely, that of a man who kept racing pigeons for years, and so had to watch the skies anxiously and get to know their killers. But thinking it over it seems to me that, heavily built as the Brahminy Kite is, it lacks the dash and speed of wing to provide anything more than novelty to the sport of falconry, especially when there are many nobler birds available.

Mind, I do not say that it lacks the heart. The Brahminy has been called a coward by many ornithologists, a chicken-raider that will not face the mother hen, a snatcher of small fry from the basket of the fishwife. That opinion, I feel, is not scientifically sound. We rarely make allowance for avian values and individual variations in judging a bird's 'character'. Many of the eagles, which this kite resembles in miniature in build and flight, also live mainly by scavenging and piracy. Moreover, the Brahminy Kite can be quite aggressive on occasion.

Once, feeling curious about the contents of their nest and trying to get a closer look, I was attacked with such determination and persistence by a pair of these birds that I had to beat a hasty and undignified retreat, though I knew I was being critically watched by three small boys. And though it is true that this kite gets its living picking fish and other things off the surface of the water, and by robbing successful but smaller hunters, it can and does kill snakes; I have seen one with a four-foot rat snake in its clutches, but it could be that the snake was killed by some villager and later picked up by the bird.

That brings us to the question: is this the Garuda? The Garuda (omit the terminal 'a' for most North Indian languages and add 'n' after the terminal 'a' for Tamil), according to mythology, is the most feared enemy of the snake tribe, the bird whose very name strikes terror in the heart of the denizens of the subterranean Naga-land. Throughout South India the Brahminy Kite is called 'Garudan', and even in paintings (paintings of no great antiquity, say, about a century or two in age) this bird is shown in depictions of the mythological Garuda. However, the Crested Serpent-Eagle, the Short-toed Eagle, and some hawk-eagles are much more given to snake-slaying than this kite, and are much nearer iconographic descriptions of the Garuda.

Be that as it might, I find an unforced occasion for quoting here an old Sanskrit verse that has always appealed powerfully to me (in spite of

my comprehensive ignorance of Sanskrit!), so tellingly does it expound
the power of circumstances:

> *Do not associate with the lowly:*
> *If you must, with the mighty make friends:*
> *For the cobra, having Vishnu's protection,*
> *Inquired fondly after the Garuda's health!*

SEEN THROUGH A CARRIAGE WINDOW

The traveller by rail from Peshawar to Madras, says Dewar, 'should, aided by a good field-glass, be able to distinguish fully one-third of the commoner birds of India.' Even the ordinary *Passenjare*, unarmed with field-glass, and with no formidable pilgrimage to make, can see quite a number of these. For wherever the railroad goes the telegraph wires follow—interminable perches, specially designed for their convenience, according to a certain community of birds.

Now this is a large and varied community, though its members never reach any size. A bird as big as a kite, or bigger, would find the wires too thin for its feet. It is true that a considerate government has provided poles and insulators for their express benefit, but the larger birds are not much given to perching, and the few that do, prefer less open country than that our trains run over. For the same reason flycatchers, barbets, cuckoos and similar foliage-loving birds avoid the railway; they keep to their groves and gardens. The 'tele-fauna' is made up of the perching birds of the open, especially of those birds which like to sit on high, keeping a sharp lookout for any movement on earth or air—the birds which hawk flying insects and which pounce down upon creeping things. However, it is wiser not to be too exact on such matters. I once saw an undoubted quail planted squarely on a passing telegraph wire. What business can any quail possibly have atop this unnatural perch? I do not know, but I am almost sure that the quail did not either.

On the Wires
Barring the ubiquitous crows, the commonest bird of the railroad wires is the King Crow.

You will find it wherever you go, a bold bird with a forked tail, sitting alone and in pairs always on the alert. King Crows are amazingly clever on the wing, and care little for trains and such man-made things. I have seen one almost brush against the windows of my compartment in an attempt to snap up the fleeing quarry. Bee-eaters, beautiful little birds, which perch in rows and make sallies into the air after insects, can be seen all along the line. Bee-eaters wear an emerald green and turquoise livery; shot with bronze over the wings, and the two middle feathers of the tail prolonged beyond the rest. When they fly they sail about on stretched, triangular wings and you can tell them apart from other birds by these tokens. The roller is never lacking from these perches. It is a thickset, lubberly bird, somewhat smaller than a crow, which looks a dull, nondescript red-and-blue, and very sleepy, in repose. In flight, however, it is transformed into a striking 'study in Oxford and Cambridge blue'. It feeds with equal ease from land and air, and is, in fact, keenly searching the scrub for a young lizard or a nice, fat grasshopper, while you think it has gone to sleep on its feet. A bird of similar habits, the White-breasted Kingfisher, is almost as frequently to be seen. A fisherman by birth, it is much more at home on land, hunting its prey much as the roller does. In fact a certain naturalist has predicted that in course of time this kingfisher would cease to fish altogether and become a regular land-lubber! The Common Kingfisher, a much smaller, orange-and-blue bird, can be seen wherever there is water. This is the 'Halcyon' of the English poets, but it never reaches the same dimensions in our country, in the absence of people to boost it. Passing a river or backwater you may see the Pied Kingfisher, the finest fisherman of them all. It has

M. Krishnan

a spangled, black-and-white plumage, and is quite as big as its white-breasted cousin. It hovers over water, scanning the depths for fish, and when it has spotted one makes a most determined plunge, straight down. Late in the evening, you will see a number of tiny, dark birds with forked tails, sitting in orderly rows, and perhaps you will note a metallic blue glint as the slanting sunshine touches their plumage—these are swallows, resting awhile after their strenuous flights. Later still, the squat, cubist forms of Spotted Owlets will make their appearance on the wires. They may even be heard above the puff of the engine, for they are very noisy after the long day in bed.

The Shrike

No account of the 'tele-fauna' would be complete without the butcher-birds or shrikes. If you see a grey-brown bird, the size of a mynah or smaller, with a longish tail, bull-head, strong hooked bill, black eye-stripe and a sturdy, business-like air about it, you may put it down as a shrike. The shrikes of the telegraph system sit independently apart, but at some times of the year, and in some places, you come across flocks of the Ashy Swallow-Shrike, a kinsman of the butcher-birds. This bird is an ash-grey all over, smaller than a mynah, with a square tail and long, triangular wings which cross over and project beyond the tail in repose. When it flies it sails about on taut wings, looking very like a large, grey, short-tailed bee-eater. It is a rare bird, but when you meet it, you meet it in large numbers, crowding the wires and hawking insects on the wing.

These are the true habitués of the telegraph lines, the professional hunters which use them as lookout stations from which to chase or swoop down on the quarry. A number of seed-eaters and ground birds can be seen on the wires in addition to these birds which sit on these perches because they like to take the sun and air. These vary, to a large extent, according to the nature of the countryside over which you travel. Where there are trees or large bushes, doves can be seen, preening themselves fussily, or even courting, unmindful of the passing train. Parakeets are common where the vegetation is at all dense, especially towards sunset. They roost in small flocks along the wires and indulge

in screeching matches. The Pied Wagtail is invariably present near stretches of water, a black-and-white bird, larger than a sparrow, with a long horizontally carried tail which it wags about incessantly. This bird has a sweet song, and will often sing while perched on a wire in this fashion, but its tinkling voice is quite lost in the rattle and squeak of the train. Sparrows and parties of the White-headed Babbler are common in the neighbourhood of stations, and the Red-vented Bulbul can be seen everywhere, a small, sooty brown bird with a black crest and a cheery whistle, that sports a crimson patch under its tail and a white one above.

Railroad Neighbours

Besides these there are the birds of the countryside, birds which are not particularly addicted to the telegraph wires but which are nevertheless found near the rail-track, often quite close by. The common brown mynah and the smaller Brahminy Mynah, a grey and cinnamon bird with a black crest, are found in large flocks over level scrub and fields. Hoopoes and Cattle Egrets are essential features of pasturelands—this last is a stately white bird, which follows the droves, snapping up the insects that fly above the crunching hooves. Its cousin, the paddy bird, which 'sits all dingy brown and flies all white,' is very fond of wayside pools and drenched paddy fields. It is quite a common bird, but you have to look for it, for it is inconspicuous except in flight. Bush-chats and robins (the robin, by the way, is a little black bird in India, and wears no red on its breast) affect the agaves which flank the track on either side and even ascend to the wires above at times.

Kites and Scavenger Vultures are all that the traveller is likely to see among the birds of prey. The Pariah Kite is found over every type of country, and the Brahminy Kite over wetland. Scavenger Vultures—

better known, perhaps, as Pharaoh's Chicken—can be seen wherever a heap of foul refuse has collected by the wayside. They are repulsive, yellowish-white birds with black flight feathers and the most objectionable habits imaginable.

Watching Birds

These are the birds usually seen through compartment windows. Many more could be listed by the painstaking naturalist, though these would be of local or unusual occurrence. One can convert an otherwise tedious journey into a pleasant trip by watching out for the friendly little birds outside. They go past you very quickly especially when they are perched on the wires close by; but they appear and reappear so often within the frames of the windows that you can have little difficulty in spotting them. The great advantage of seeing a bird from a train is that you see it unobscured by foliage, and more or less on a level with the eye, or from above—an advantage best appreciated by men who have carefully stalked their bird to a tree and can see just the tip of its tail peeping out of the leaves. You move round slowly and catch a glimpse of its abdomen, and then it puts a branch between your eye and itself and flits away unseen to some other tree, leaving you to wonder whether it is *Oriolus kundoo* or *Oriolus melanocephalus*, or *Oriolus* at all!

Naturally, there are seasonal variations among the birds of the railroad. Some of these are migrants, and others only come into evidence with the advent of the monsoon. Even the time of day affects their numbers. The heat of the noon drives most of them to shade and foliage. And on a really dark night, I venture to guess you will see none at all.

THE SHAWK

A few miles from Mahabalipuram, celebrated for the richness of its carvings, is a shrine no less celebrated among the pious. Tirukkalukunram (I follow the spelling of the railway guide) is one of the sixteen (or is it sixty?) holy places of the South.

It is a temple perched on top of a small, rocky hill, lacking the rugged grandeur of other Southern hilltop shrines. But every day it is graced by the visit of two saints in avian garb.

Rain or shine, shortly after the noon invocation, a portion of the sweet, opulent prasad, of jaggery and milk, ghee and rice, is brought out by the priest and placed on a shelf of rock. And two large, white birds materialize from the skies and partake of the offering. They are, of course, not birds at all but saints in feathers, most rigorous in their penances and rites.

Each morning they wing their northern way to the Ganges, for a dip in its purifying waters, then they fly all the way back to Rameswaram, for a further dip in sanctity, visiting Tirukkalukunram in time for lunch. Local traditions give the names of these two punctilious saints, and further particulars.

Unfortunately for those with romantic inclinations, these birds have no claims to looks, in spite of their whiteness and the sail-like spread of their black-pinioned wings. They are not even kites, as the railway guide calls them, but are Scavenger Vultures, perhaps the least prepossessing of our birds. On the wing they look handsome enough, circling with effortless ease or swooping along the skyline at a terrific pace, breeze-borne. But the weak, yellow beak and face, the dirty hackles and the clumsy, waddling gait proclaim their ugliness when they are on the ground and near. In their youth they are less hideous, a decent, dark brown all over, but even then you can tell them apart from kites and other brown birds of the sky by their wedge-shaped tail. I do not remember the saint-names given to them at Tirukkalukunram, but can give you their other aliases—the neophron, or, more specifically, *Neophron percnopterus ginginanus*, Pharaoh's Chicken, the Lesser White Scavenger Vulture, and, according to 'Eha', the bird known to Mr Thomas Atkins as 'The Shawk'.

The last name, I think, is derived from the bird's habit of frequenting heaps of garbage and ordure: if I am right in my etymology, it is a name truly indicative of this vulture's disposition. Wherever there are mounds of manure or other assorted filth, offal and refuse lying around, you are likely to find the neophron. It is commonest outside the city and industrial centres, where there are broad acres of what the engineers call 'rubbish', and around hilltop shrines and country marketplaces. It is a very useful bird indeed, and no one who realizes the public good that scavengers do will ever dream of looking down upon it.

Incidentally, it is not only at Tirukkalukunram that it is held sacred: it was venerated in ancient Egypt. Unlike most other birds of its profession, it is not gregarious, but usually goes about with its mate, in a close pair. Like all vultures, it is long-lived and has wonderful powers of sight and flight.

It is likely that the pair at Tirukkalukunram have long been in residence, and it is a fact that they are most punctual in their attendance at the shrine. But there is nothing remarkable in all this. Many birds have an instinctive sense of time, and these vultures deeply appreciate regular provision of food. I have seen several pairs of these birds in and around Tirukkalukunram, so that it is quite conceivable that when the seniormost pair dies, their territory and 'prasad' are taken over by the pair next in the order of precedence among local neophrons—that way one can understand how, for generations, these birds have been attending at the shrine each day, and set up the tradition of immortality. Irrelevantly, it occurs to me that the phoenix must be some sort of vulture.

I can even testify to the fallibility of the daily visits of the pious birds. One day, in the winter of 1935, no birds turned up at the feeding rock, in spite of the priest's loud invitations and widely waved arms. No vulture of any sort was visible in the skies, and I concluded that a cow must have died on the hillside beyond, that day. The priest made no comment, beyond pointing to the slight drizzle that there was, but an elderly gentleman by my side volunteered a complete explanation. He was a native and assured us that the absence of the birds was most exceptional; in fact, they were absent only when some major sinner, who should never have been admitted to the precincts, was there. And I must say I did not like the rather pointed look he gave me.

VEDANTHANGAL: OLDEST BIRD SANCTUARY IN INDIA

Vedanthangal is in the Chinglepet District, a little village not shown on the smaller survey maps, some fifty-five miles from Madras and six by road from the nearest place to which bus or train can take you. And perhaps the oldest bird sanctuary in India lies here.

There is a small seasonal lake here (or a large tank—call it what you like) seventy-four acres in extent excluding outlying low land. In summer, and till the rains arrive in August or September, the lakebed is dry—a shallow mud basin with little grass or other small growth on it, but with about five hundred barringtonias growing in massed clumps near its middle and singly along the inner edge of its palmyra-topped bund. The trees (all *Barringtonia acutangula*), except for a handful of thin acacias, are mature and stout-boled, with spreading, evergreen crowns, but they are not tall—not much over twenty feet in height, some not even that high. When the rain-fed lake is full, it is about ten feet deep in the middle and the trunks and lower boughs are submerged, with only the leafy, much-branched crowns showing above the thick, green water, in darker green mounds. And thousands of birds come here, to nest in these crowns.

Village Protection

From time immemorial they have nested here, and been effectively protected by the villagers. The motive of these good people in protecting the birds is not wholly altruistic but I do not believe it is wholly selfish either. The droppings of the mixed assemblage of parent birds and the rising generations, enrich the lake water endowing it with manurial potency. It is this water that is used for the neighbouring paddy fields.

Both the Indian and Madras wildlife boards have accorded recognition to Vedanthangal, but it was a sanctuary for centuries before the boards were there, and officially recognized long ago. The records of such official cognizance are interesting.

Late in the eighteenth century, Mr L. Place, collector of Chinglepet (1796-98), appears to have given an original 'cowle' to the local inhabitants, who asked for official recognition of their age-old 'prescriptive right' to protect the birds against all comers. This document stated that no birds might be shot or snared in the Vedanthangal tank area.

On 7 January 1858, George G. Tod, chief assistant magistrate of the district, renewed the sanction at the request of the villagers, who had lost the original given them by Mr Place. Mr Tod's 'cowle' is in rather quaint Tamil and runs as follows:

> Whereas it has been represented that in the kadappai trees of the lake of your village of Vedanthangal a variety of birds nest and live freely and that the Hon. Placesaheb had long ago given you a cowle prohibiting the shooting or capture of these birds, which document has been lost, and whereas you have now asked us to give you another in replacement, this has been issued to you.
>
> Should any persons, Europeans or hunters or such people, come to the lake and attempt to shoot or capture the birds in contravention of the above-mentioned order, show this to them and prevent them from doing so.

More than three-quarters of a century later, this order of 'Todsaheb', carefully preserved by the villagers, was produced before *another* 'Todsaheb' for renewal—only, this second saheb chose to spell his name with a double 'd'.

On 10 February 1936, Mr A. H. A. Todd, collector of Chinglepet, issued an order which says:

> Vedanthangal tank is a bird sanctuary and has been kept as such by the villagers for over a century. Notice in English and in Tamil in bold characters should be painted on wooden boards

and set up at each end of the tank bund. The form of notice to be put up is enclosed. The expenses should be met from office contingencies.

How Many Trees?

I saw no wooden boards carrying prominent notice when I first visited Vedanthangal in June 1954, nor during four subsequent visits made late last year and early this year. But I saw the lake area dry and birdless, and later water-filled and teeming with nesting birds, and was able to collect sufficient observation material for this note.

Asked to guess how many trees grow in the middle of the lake, people would be hopelessly out in their estimates. Most would put the figure around fifty, the more reckless might even go up to hundred. No one who did not know the actual number would think some three hundred trees stood there, so closely are they massed and so confluently do their tops run into one another, when seen from the bund. A clump that from the bund looks as if it were made up of two or three trees actually represents twenty. I have taken no census of the trees, but on a rough reckoning I made out there were three hundred in the middle.

The trees, as I have said, are old. During summer the seedlings that sprout in the shade of their parents are grazed or trampled down by cattle, but I think they would need transplanting to the periphery, some distance away, to develop into vigorous new clumps, even if they are otherwise protected. So much for the history and topography of the sanctuary. Before going on to the really interesting feature of Vedanthangal, its nesting birds, we may briefly consider the probable origin of its name.

'Vedan' in Tamil means 'hunter' or 'fowler', and 'thangal' is an old Tamil word that has two relevant meanings in this context, viz. 'tank' and 'the act of protecting or guarding'. Those who construe the place name to mean 'fowler's tank' must surely realize that they have hit on a singularly inapposite rendering. Vedanthangal having been a bird sanctuary for so long, it seems reasonable to presume it was named so because its birds were protected against fowlers.

Now for the bird life. I list the species I noticed nesting here during the latest breeding season, still 'on' as I write. But first I must point out that I may have missed a few species that go about the business of securing posterity unostentatiously, that my observation was limited to the few clumps I could watch through binoculars and the fewer clumps I could get near to, and that sustained observation over a long period (not half a dozen random visits) is necessary for any appraisal of the species, numbers and priorities in a large mixed heronry, and the nesting habits of the birds.

No Migratory Birds

I found no migratory birds here excepting a few teal I saw on the afternoon of 12 February flying over the lake. That afternoon I also saw a pair of pelicans here, but these are not migratory birds, and are common near Madras where there are broad sheets of water, for example at Pulicat Lake to the north of Madras (Vedanthangal is more or less to the south). However, I heard persistent reports from local inhabitants of the occasional visits of large, swan-like birds that rode easily on the water—not pelicans, surely. What I heard strongly suggested Barheaded Geese to me, and if they have visited Vedanthangal during certain seasons, that would mark the southernmost point of their migration.

Hundreds of Openbilled Storks were nesting in the barringtonias, but no other storks—I was rather surprised at the absence of the Painted Stork. All the egrets were here, the Large Egret, the Smaller Egret (which G. M. Henry so rightly terms Median Egret), the Little Egret, and a few Cattle Egrets on the periphery—I don't know if the last nest in the lake, but perhaps they do. An interesting point I noticed was that though the first three were breeding actively and there were nestlings and even eggs in their nests, some of the Large and Smaller Egrets were not in breeding condition.

Night Herons, Pond Herons ('paddy birds') and a few great gaunt Grey Herons were prominently in residence, as also White Ibises. Spoonbills sporting full nuchal crests, the tokens of their breeding condition, were nesting in large numbers. Apparently, they breed here right from November to March.

Little Cormorants and Darters ('snakebirds') complete my list of breeding birds, somewhat incompletely! I thought I saw a few shag, but could not get near enough, and am not sure I saw Dabchick near the shore, and was told that some sort of moorhen or waterhen also resides here.

Unnumbered

Common grey-necked crows and Brahminy Kites were very much in evidence over the lake; common kites, neophrons, and an occasional bird of prey were also to be seen. In any large nesting colony, a few eggs and nestlings fall into the water while their parents dispute territory, nests may be left unguarded momentarily, and opportunities for scavenging, thieving and fishing are not lacking.

I can give no estimate of numbers. The Little Cormorants, Smaller Egrets, Spoonbills, Openbills and Night Herons were the most plentiful. Thousands of birds nest here, and their young survive the hustle and crowding of the breeding enterprise to continue the species, thanks to the protection they enjoy.

Soon after the first rains, sometime in October, the birds start arriving in small flocks, and rainfall being normal, they keep coming till January! The nesting species do not descend on the lake full strength, in sky-obscuring flights, but arrive in small, successive flocks. Many of these start breeding at once, colonizing some tree of their choice before the

next flight reaches Vedanthangal, so that once breeding has commenced, young at various stages of development may be found at any inspection. The position, however, is not quite so simple, for while some species (and possibly flocks) arrive ready to breed, others are not in breeding condition on arrival, and may take their time nesting.

Breeding Time

Breeding goes on for almost five months, from November to March, and many of the birds raise more than one clutch. They nest here, as they do elsewhere, in mixed companies. However, there is a tendency for birds of a feather to keep together in locating their nests, one part of a treetop being largely utilized by one species, another part by some other species. White Ibises sometimes run their nests together, as observers have already pointed out, and at Vedanthangal I saw large, machan-like platforms consisting of the communal nests of this ibis—there were no eggs, but the young on them served to identify the machan-builders surely.

Openbills, the smallest and almost the most awkward-looking of our storks (the palm for such looks must surely go to the largest, the Adjutant!), and Spoonbills, tend to occupy special trees of their own: the Openbills build their nests pretty close, on a sort of flat system. Incidentally, they are capable of the most dexterous turn of wing; not only do they soar, stork-fashion, but they also dip and shoot off in the air at acute angles, at dizzy speed. Young Openbills have no gap between their mandibles (it is this gap in the adult beak that gives the bird its name); they have comparatively short, gapless, wedge-shaped beaks.

Paddy fields around and sheets of water not too far away provide the parent birds with feeding grounds, a most important factor in the communal breeding of waterbirds, for the quick-growing young have insatiable appetites. This, the shade provided by the barringtonia foliage (even the young of most diurnal birds cannot stand the sun), and, more than all, the protection they enjoy are what make the birds arrive here in such numbers soon after the rains. The great Madurantakam Lake is only a few furlongs away, there are minor sheets of water close by; and

M. Krishnan

I observed egrets and ibises feeding in paddy fields eight miles from Vedanthangal, a negligible distance to a bird.

However, the potentialities of Vedanthangal Lake itself as a feeding ground appear to have been overlooked by observers. On the village side the water is shallow and merges into cultivation—flocks of egrets and Spoonbills, and paddy birds, may be seen feeding here all day. Cormorants and Darters fish in the lake, though the former sally out to feeding grounds and return to their nests in large, thick, quick-winged flocks, from time to time. I saw Openbills prodding the shallows at Vedanthangal, not far from their nests, and from the manner in which they threw up their necks and gulped, every now and then, the occupation seemed rewarding. Undoubtedly the regular feeding grounds of the nesting species lie outside the lake, but the water below their nests, rich in algae and aquatic insects and other small fry, is not a larder despised.

Cruel Slaughter

Vedanthangal is one of the most picturesque and interesting breeding grounds of waterbirds in our country. A naturalist can spend a lifetime here, profitably observing the local avian life, but even to the layman the lake during the nesting season is fascinating, the compact field of observation, the teeming colonies in the water, the constant passage of birds to and fro, and the rural setting, combining to capture and hold his eye. It is perhaps just as well that the sanctuary is off the beaten track but it deserves to be much wider known than it is now. Used to a village within a furlong, the birds can take no fright, or other harm, from being observed. Unfortunately, though they are safe on their nesting ground, they are ruthlessly shot all around, when they set out to find food for themselves and their young. The Madras Government, interested in the sanctuary, will no doubt devise means to prevent such cruel slaughter. Vedanthangal can do much to stimulate now apathetic public interest in our bird life, and I hope that more and more people will get to know of its charms and that it will soon develop into a centre of national and international interest.

BIRDS FROM A FAIRY TALE

A dozen coconut trees stand around the house I live in now, and to them come creatures that like straight, twigless boles. Bloodsuckers climb them in clumsy-legged corkscrews, squirrels race up and down the columnar trunks, and there is a squat, mottled gecko that is very much at home here.

Naturally, few birds ever come to the palms, except to perch on the great leaves; but recently a pair of Goldenbacked Woodpeckers have taken to visiting their trunks. They do not stay for long on any tree, but fly from one coconut to another, settling squarely on the vertical boles as casually as other birds hop on to boughs. I find these woodpeckers fascinating. They look so ornate and outlandish, like birds out of a fairytale; and as they run easily up the sheer surface, or slip down it, with no change in their rigidly held pose but for quick, sideways transpositions, they do not look like birds at all. Their movements have that quality of change of place, without obvious, free use of limbs, that suggests clockwork. But whoever heard of clockwork birds that also call to each other in long, harsh, chattering laughs, and have the plumage and mannerisms of the creatures of the fantastic Brothers Grimm!

Actually, these woodpeckers represent no exotic, romantic survivals, but only extreme adaptation to a way of life. Their chisel-tipped beaks sound bark and crevice for grubs and wood-boring insects most efficiently, and their stiff tail feathers serve as props in their precarious stance. At first it may seem strange that things as flimsy as feathers should bear body weight, but the weight of these woodpeckers (like the weight of most birds) is surprisingly little, and the tail feathers only help, in an adventitious manner, as a third leg. Woodpeckers are so used to vertical surfaces that movement along them is normal and easy for them—they have even been observed asleep, stuck on to a tree trunk.

The woodpecker clan is much given to contrasty colour, but no other member of this specialist family has the barbarous splendour of plumage of the Goldenback. The gold of its back is deep and glints in the sun, its crest is a pure crimson, and its bib of white-dotted black and dark wings set off these rich tones emphatically. And its broad-winged, dip-and-rise flight, direct from tree to tree, is not what one would expect from a bird of its size, almost a foot long. Twenty-five years ago, when I was a schoolboy in these parts, there were many spacious, rambling gardens here and tall trees, and Goldenbacked Woodpeckers were common in them. Those gardens are built up now and the woodpeckers are gone. Highly specialized birds need much scope for their limited ways of life, and the Goldenback is, perhaps, the most specialized among the woodpeckers. The pair that visits my compound now represents the last of these birds here, so far as I know. There is nothing surprising in this. With the disappearance of broad belts of trees from an area, birds that need extensive sylvan feeding grounds can no longer find a living in the place. No doubt the woodpeckers said to themselves, 'Tomorrow to fresh woods and pastures new,' and flew away on broad, undulating wings.

But did they find them? There are plenty of wooded tracts within a few miles of this place, but with resident birds like woodpeckers that get used to a particular locality one cannot say that a change of environment can do no harm. They do not take kindly to such changes, and ousted from familiar grounds especially suited to their extremely specialized way of life, they may not even survive the change. A woodpecker of another country, the Ivory-billed Woodpecker, now practically extinct in America, is an example of this rigid adherence to habit and habitat. Surely there is woodland enough not too far from its original homes, but this bird was unable to adapt itself to new territories when driven out of its own, and so perished. I do not suggest that the Goldenbacked Woodpecker is threatened with extinction, or is a rare bird today, but I apprehend that it is one of the birds that will suffer by our progressive civilizations, and I think that I have been a witness to the passing of these quaint and splendid birds from one of their strongholds.

WAGTAILS

Wagtails remind me of a post-impressionist painting, famous in its day, of a dachshund out for a walk. This picture conveys the gaiety of the occasion in a remarkable way. The dog is, for the best part, much like the usual representation of dachshunds, a trifle more zestful perhaps, but otherwise ordinary. Its tail, however, and the length of lead between swivel and owner's hand are shown, not as split-second records of moving objects, but in series—there are numbers of swishing tails and twirling lengths of lead, all combining to give one the unmistakable impression of eager joy.

Wagtails move their tails in the same token of *joie de vivre*. There is nothing in their tail-wagging of the fidgety nervousness of robins: they move their tails up and down, and a little from one side to the other, in a quick shake, and you see dozens of blurred tails wagging.

Common in the Plains

The Grey, the White and the Pied Wagtail are the common wagtails of the plains. There are divisions among the first two, which are migratory birds, and these change colour with summer, so that it is not always easy to place them exactly. However, these niceties do not puzzle one in the valley of Sandur, from where I write. The Grey and the White

Wagtails come in little parties and large flocks soon after the September rains, not only to my hills and valleys, but to all the flat country around. They leave us when the hot weather begins, but I have seen the White Wagtail in Sandur in April and even in May, and would not be surprised to learn that a few of these birds stay on through the summer within the seclusion of these hills.

It is quite easy to tell these two wagtails apart during their winter stay on the plains. Both are grey birds, about the size of a sparrow and with typical long tails; but the grey of the White Wagtail is a pure, clear French grey, whereas the Grey Wagtail has a murky slate back, and the whole of its underside, barring a black bib, is white. In the Grey Wagtail the belly is gamboge in colour. Both birds run along the grass in parties, the White Wagtail being the more gregarious of the two.

It is a pretty sight to see these birds arriving soon after the rains, flying high and dipping and rising in the air after the manner of all wagtails. Their skimming flight seems weak, but in fact they have come from a thousand miles away and will fly back all the way when summer sets in. Having arrived, they add at once to the bird life of the place— one sees them everywhere, on footpaths and fields, even on one's roof. But though they have pleasant voices, they do not sing during their stay with us.

The Pied Wagtail is a bigger bird, and stays all the year round in the same place. It is never found in flocks and in parties. It goes about in pairs, running along the rocky, shingly miniature beaches of the riverbed pools that it loves. Pied Wagtails are never far from water, and they are not shy of human associations.

M. Krishnan

Regular Visitors

When I was in Madras, I knew a pair of these wagtails that would come regularly every morning to take the air on the roof of my house, before going on to a neighbouring pond. The cock sings a charming little song during summer. I have often heard it compared to the Magpie Robin's, but I must say that I have never been able to spot the resemblance. The wagtail's is shriller and less clear and its song more set and patternized. And it never loses itself in the ecstasies of song, nor swells its chest like a pouter pigeon, as the robin does.

It is all a matter of tails. If it could jerk its tail right over its head, and fan it out as the Magpie Robin does, no doubt it would sing as wildly and wonderfully, but being only a wagtail, it is content with its modest, sweet little song.

SHOWER BATH

I came here early in April to keep my annual date with the Southern summer. For a week all went well: slowly the budding heat burgeoned. Then suddenly massed clouds rolled up overhead and the rain came down in torrents. A passing shower, I said to myself, while it rained three inches, and it passed. The sun burned fiercely in a clear sky the next day, and the heat was all the more apparent for the interlude. But since morning it has rained again today, the sky is overcast, the air cool, and it looks as though I must wait for my assignation.

Sitting on my leaky veranda I have been watching birds in the rain. I happen to have Dewar's *Birds of the Indian Plains* with me just now—he has a chapter on 'Birds in the Rain' in the book, and perhaps he wrote it not far from here. I would like to observe something original about the reaction of the birds around me to the shower, but such things do not go by preferences and I have to confirm Dewar largely. He says that birds

enjoy the rain acutely, and that in India it is rarely that they are forced to take shelter from it. 'They know naught of rheumatism or ague', they sit in the rain or splash about in puddles, delighted with the opportunity for a shower bath, and afterwards there is a great shaking out of feathers and preening of wings, and they are smart and fresh and glad. Dewar also comments on how the first monsoon brings feasts of termites and other insects for birds and nestlings, and softens terra firma for the probing bill of the Hoopoe.

All this is true. An odd group of three Common Mynahs have been parading the gravel path outside for the past hour, wading into every puddle and splashing about, as if trying to drown themselves in the knee-high water, and still they are not drenched—their well-oiled plumage seems waterproof. I can hear the neighing call of a White-breasted Kingfisher, and know where it is—on top of a casuarina pole in the backyard. Far out, in a field beyond the road, a flock of Cattle Egrets alight on dazzling wings, surprisingly white in this grey atmosphere, and quarter the wet grass. There are crows on exposed perches all around, determined not to miss a drop of the rain. The only birds I can see that do not seem too keen on a shower bath are a party of White-headed Babblers, sheltering under a mango.

Watching these birds, it is obvious that Dewar wrote about their reaction to rain from accurate observation, but I cannot help feeling that he assigned a wrong motive for their behaviour. It is no craze for originality that makes me say this—it is that I can see no patent signs of joy in these rain-bathing birds. The lives of birds are ruled by instincts mainly, and their responses and emotional expressions follow set patterns. There is a crow sitting on a dead limb of a neem not twenty yards from me, and I have been observing it closely for the past half-hour. It has been sitting there dully, unmoving except to fluff its plumage or caw in a sad undertone from time to time—the illustration is from a leisurely sketch of this obliging model. Now, if this crow is enjoying the shower, I must say it takes its pleasures sadly: Poe's raven could hardly have made a less sprightly picture, had it been out there on that branch.

Nor can I note any tokens of jubilation in the other birds out in the rain. Dewar says that the normally sedate mynahs shed their reserve when it rains, and go mudlarking in abandoned enjoyment. I am alive to the tonic properties of slush and downpour—it does one's soul good to get drenched and splashed with mud, for all ponderous unlovely notions of self-importance and dignity are shed at once, and this sudden jettisoning and the feeling of lightness that follows move one to frisk about and find life joyful. But I think the mynahs I see are undignified only because they are bathing, bathing vigorously in two-inch-high water—few beasts or birds (bar all cats) look their best at their toilet.

Birds are wonderfully equipped for extremes of climate and weather. And they enjoy dust baths. But that is not saying that they may feel no discomfort from clogging dust and secretions in their plumage. Is it not likely that their addiction to rain is an unreasoned response, an instinctive utilization of an opportunity to wash away dust and water-soluble accumulations from their feathers and skins? That would explain their 'non-enthusiastic' but sustained insistence on exposing themselves to the first rains after every spell of dry weather.

SPLENDOUR

IN

THE WILD

THE NATIONAL BIRD

Years ago, when the National Bird was chosen and announced, there were dissenting voices. Some thought our largest bird, then feared on the verge of extinction, the Great Indian Bustard, should have been selected. Fortunately, this magnificent fowl is now conserved in some of its habitats in Western and Northwestern India, and a population of it has even been found recently in Andhra Pradesh. Others thought the Brahminy Kite, the Garuda that is the vahana of Vishnu in our mythology, should have been preferred; and then there were the habitual scoffers who remarked, cynically, that the common crow would have been the only correct choice.

However, the peacock—no less the vahana of a god (Subramanya), with a wider distribution over the country than the other contenders, typically Indian, and unquestionably one of the most arrestingly beautiful of all birds—was rightly chosen. In the past few years, I have had opportunities to observe wild peafowl in many different parts of the country, and to realize how remarkably versatile they are, and how popular notions about them can be mistaken.

Though it is among the largest of our birds, it is much lighter than what most people think it is. The long, profuse and dazzlingly decorative train of the cock suggests a heaviness that feathers do not have. Actually, the train is not the tail but the elongated plumes above it, and is so light that the bird has no difficulty in carrying it well clear of the ground when on the move. It is the Great Bustard that is our heaviest bird. Reliable records put the weight of the adult cock bustard at from 11 to 12 kilograms; the hen is smaller and lighter. A peacock will not turn the scales even at 5 kilograms, train and all.

While on this question of the weight of birds (which, size for size, are much lighter than other animals), I think that as a rule birds that live mainly on terra firma and do not undertake long flights are heavier than those of similar size that are aerial. Both the Great Bustard and peafowl are not birds of the air but of the ground. It may be asked if the larger vultures, as big in the body as a peacock or bigger, are not at least as heavy, though given to soaring on high for such long periods. Other big birds are also fond of soaring—Adjutants and other storks and Spoonbills, for instance—but since wingspan and thermal currents sustain their bulk and mass in the air, no active flight is actually involved. Moreover, I would not venture to assess the weight of a vulture. That would largely depend on whether or not it has gorged itself recently.

There are peafowl in the sub-Himalayan forests, as in Corbett Park, and in the sal-clad hills of Mayurbhanj (which gets its name from their presence); they are there in the mixed deciduous forests of the Western and Eastern Ghats, and also in the Deccan Plateau, as around Gajendragad. There are peafowl in the coastal scrub jungles and in the hill-dotted plains, in sandy Ramanathapuram and sandier Rajasthan, even in the Thar desert where there is some water source and some sparse vegetation. Few other birds favour such widely different settings.

The plumage patterning and colouring of peafowl is much more complex than observation of the live birds from not too near might suggest. Actually, in the wild even a peacock with a resplendent train does not stand out flagrantly against the ground cover. The train is compressed and dark, and noticeable more by its length than its brilliant colouration. Only when it is fanned out and erected does it display its many-eyed scintillating iridescence.

Close Scrutiny

But even a hen has an intricacy of plumage patterning that is evident only on close scrutiny. Some time ago, I came upon the remains of a peahen that a leopard had killed and consumed: the head, neck and legs, and a litter of assorted feathers on the bare, dark earth. Looking closely at the feathers, I was impressed by their diverse and detailed patterning. Each soft brown little forehead-feather was tipped bright green, the off-white ear-coverts were tipped dark brown, and the breast feathers, grey-brown in colour, were edged with white with a purple teardrop beneath the edging. The plumage of the back and wings was no less elaborate.

White (albinotic) peafowl lack colour entirely, but still are as beautiful in their way as the normally coloured bird. The long, sinuous, graceful neck with its sleek cover of short feathers that can be fluffed out at will, the crest on top of the slim head and the magnificent train sustain the looks of such birds. Incidentally, this albinotic variety is not what horticulturists term a cultivar, but has also been recorded in the wild. Evidently, like the white tiger, it is a rare and local phenomenon and has been exploited in captivity to breed true. G. P. Sanderson reports a white peacock from the forests of Masinagudi (in the Mudumalai sanctuary), and almost a century later late in the 1970s I saw a very blonde peahen in this same forest, not quite white, but so pale as to be colourless, and describable only as ash-white.

THE SARUS

We have only one indigenous crane, the Sarus, and that, too, limited to North India (it is not found south of the Godavari), but then it is one of the largest and most notable of all cranes and, moreover, our very own. It is a stately, French grey bird standing as tall as a man (a little over 1.5 metres high), with the head and upper neck bare of feathers and a scarlet-vermilion in colour—the long legs are a pinkish red, the plumage of the base of the neck is whitish, and the profuse plumes over the tail, pale grey.

All over its range in India, the Sarus is protected by popular sentiment. It is usually seen in a pair, and mates for life; it is noted for the attachment of the mated pair to each other and is the 'Crounchapakshi' of Indian classics, celebrated for its deep conjugal attachment.

Unlike most cranes, the Sarus is not gregarious. It does not go about in large flocks but only in a pair, though there may be several pairs in an area; and till the twin young are adult, they usually go about with their parents. Occasionally a dozen pairs or more may assemble briefly, but never form a regular flock. It is strong on the wing, taking off with heavy flaps but flying fast with a rhythmic wing action thereafter, but seldom soars on high or covers long distances, as other cranes do. In its feeding, too, it is much more omnivorous than most cranes, and feeds by itself or in a pair, not in a crowd like others of its tribe—besides gleaning grain from stubble and feeding on the tender shoots and tubers of waterside plants, it takes in quite a good bit of animal food, fish, small reptiles and the like. Once in a while, a pair or two might invade a gram field to feed on the seeds and seedlings, but it is not a determined crop-raider like the migrant cranes.

All cranes are noted for their fantastic courtship dance, but since all other cranes in our country are migrants that come here only after breeding in their cold, northern homes, they do not indulge in courtship displays here. It is the Sarus that can be observed here, dancing with its mate in a spectacular ritual, fluffing out its lax plumes, leaping with a buoyancy and grace astonishing in such a big bird, and coming out with its trumpet call from time to time—this call is always made with the beak pointing skyward, and is invariably taken up by the mate of the calling bird within a split second, so that it is what is termed a unison call. The pair calls together, whether both birds are near each other or separated by a distance. Sarus breed in many places in the North, usually on the periphery of a lake or sheet of water. The nest is built on the ground, a large circular nest of reeds and similar material, and two eggs are the rule.

SILVER HACKLE

South of the river Godavari, roughly speaking, the Grey Junglefowl replaces the Red Junglefowl all over India. It is there in the southernmost reaches of the country, but not in Sri Lanka. And whereas the Red Junglefowl is also there in Pakistan, and has close relatives in Burma and Sri Lanka, the 'silver hackle', as the grey is known, is exclusively Indian, not being found outside the peninsula.

The northern areas of its range overlap the southern range of the Red Junglefowl in places, and in these the two interbreed and hybrids between them are known. Except for plumage details, it is much like the Red Junglefowl, but is slightly larger, no heavier, but standing slightly taller on its legs. In overall appearance it is a streaky warm grey, the hackles of the cock forming a brightly spotted mantle over the neck and upper back. The cock has no elongated lanceolate plumes over the rump, which is a feature of the Red Junglefowl. When not breeding, the cock loses the long, sickle-shaped glossy black central plumes of its tail, and its comb shrinks, but even when in breeding livery, its comb seems less full than the Red Junglefowl's.

Each hackle is black and marked with metallic pale yellow spots and streaks—some also a waxy, shiny white. It is because of its distinctively coloured hackles, with the faintly glistening spots, that the bird has long been known as the silver hackle. Anglers much fancy these hackles for fly fishing, and there is a heavy demand for them. Further, all jungleside dwellers hunt this bird—it is one of the most hunted forest birds of our country. Formerly it was there also in the plains country, but perhaps because of human pressures and occupation of the plains forests by men, it is now mainly to be found in hill forests, from the lowest to the most elevated hills in the South.

The hen is smaller than the cock and quite inconspicuous, much like the Red Junglefowl hen but boldly patterned in black and white on the lower breast and flanks. The cock's crow, heard before dawn and soon after, and sometimes late in the evening, is quite distinctive and unlike that of other junglefowl, or the barnyard rooster—a sharp, not too loud *kuk-ka-kurra-kuck* that is somewhat shrill in tone and carries far. The cock crows both from elevated perches, and from an anthill or low mound on the ground. The bird needs better protection than it gets now, and has long been celebrated in the classical poetry of the South.

THE PAINTED STORK

The term 'painted' in a bird's name denotes an elaborate patterning of its plumage in rich, contrasting colours. The Painted Snipe (which, incidentally, is no snipe), the Painted Partridge and the Painted Sandgrouse all exemplify this trend, and the Painted Stork is no less ornamental in its looks, in spite of its ungainly build.

It is a bird of fair size, standing almost a metre high and strongly built. It is white, with an intricate lacing of short black bars and curved markings over the wings and in a low, broad necklace above the abdomen, with the pinions and the short tail feathers black glossed with dark green.

The skin of the naked head is an orange-pink, and the stout, long bill, curved at the tip, is yellow ochre; the legs are a dull reddish colour. Over the tail is a rich pile of plumes completely covering it, crimson plumes edged with white—even when the bird is seen from near, the crimson and white of these plumes blend in the eye to a vibrant beautiful rose. The illustration, based on photographs, shows the plumage patterning, but cannot even indicate the opulence of the bird's colouring. No wonder it is called the Painted Stork!

Its old name, 'pelican ibis', is also apposite and descriptive in its own way. Though long-legged and a stork, the stout, long bill and somewhat squat build do suggest a pelican, and the curved tip of the bill an ibis. Moreover, in the South, it is much given to nesting in colonies along with the Grey Pelican—it also nests along with other waterbirds in large mixed heronries, as at Bharatpur. As with all indigenous waterbirds, the nesting season varies with locality, for the onset of the rains differs in different regions, but it is almost invariably after the Southwest Monsoon.

Like the Openbill, it is also highly gregarious both when breeding and in the off-season, and has a wide distribution over India—outside our country, it is also there in other Southeast Asian countries.

Like other waterbirds, it builds an elementary, untidy stick nest, rather small for so large a bird, and its fledglings are covered with a whitish fuzzy down and have wedge-shaped, dark bills.

It is strong on the wing, alternating wingbeats with spells of sailing, and like many other storks is given to soaring on high in company, rising so high in the air that a flock of Painted Storks resembles circling specks.

The Painted Stork has a voracious appetite and feeds on a variety of small creatures: frogs and tadpoles, fish, molluscs and crustaceans, and at times even on small mammals and land insects. When breeding, it feeds in and around spreads of fresh water, but when it is through with breeding and has only to fend for itself and not also for an insatiable, clamouring brood, it often resorts to shallow lagoons and spreads of saltwater in small parties.

THE PINTAIL

The Pintail is probably the widest ranging and most abundant of the duck visiting us with the onset of the Northeast Monsoon. It breeds in spring in the cold North, and afterwards shifts to the warmer South, sojourning in many countries, in the southern part of North America, in Africa and in Southern Asia. Here, it virtually has an all-India range, and frequents both spreads of fresh water (jheels, tanks and even lesser waters) and shallow saline lagoons and estuaries.

It is nearly the size of the village duck, which the female Pintail resembles in its streaked and speckled brown plumage, but is slimmer and more elegant; the Pintail has a more elongated build than most wild duck, a build accentuated by the comparatively long and slim neck, and pointed tail-tip. The drake, in breeding plumage (which is retained for quite some time afterwards), is unmistakable—the chocolate brown head and darker nape, the white stripe on either side of the neck descending to the neat, white bib of the breast, the finely lined grey back and pale grey sides, and the two black pin feathers extending far behind the tail are distinctive.

In eclipse plumage (after the moult when not breeding), the drake loses much of its fine colour and turns somewhat like the duck, but even the duck (which has no pin feathers) has a pointed tail-tip; in both

sexes, the beak, legs and feet are lead-grey, which serves to distinguish the drake in eclipse plumage and the duck from other somewhat similar birds of the same genus, such as the Mallard.

Pintail may associate in all-male (or all-female) flocks, and crowd small pieces of water in packed numbers. They are usually seen in sizeable flocks, but at times also in little parties, especially in small waters. The wings are long and pointed, and a bronze-green speculum (a patch of distinctive colour in the middle of the pinions) is noticeable in flight. Pintail fly fast, with rapid wingbeats, usually in a regular flock, sometimes along with a party of other fast-flying duck like the teal.

They feed on grain, seeds, grasses and other water plants, but also take in some animal food, aquatic insects, molluscs and worms. They are largely nocturnal, and may raid paddy fields at night. Pintail are surface feeders in the main, but in shallow water are much given to up-ending, that is, to plunging their head and most of the body almost vertically into the water to seek food, with only the tail showing above the surface. Though wary and vigilant, and so swift on the wing, they are much shot and trapped, being highly fancied for the table.

THE SPOTBILL

The last of the native duck to be noticed in this column is the Spotbill or Spotted-billed Duck or Grey Duck, a bird all of the names of which are descriptive. It is considerably larger than the Cotton Teal or the whistling teals, but not so big as the Nukhta, with a typical horizontal duck build, tubby in the body and broad in the bill, standing low on its short, thick orange legs.

Seen at hand, the dark bill which is a bright chrome yellow over a third of its length (at the tip-end) and with an orange-vermilion spot on top of the upper mandible on either side of its median line, the grey body patterned in a scale-like plumage-pattern, and the orange legs are wholly distinctive and unmistakable. In flight, apart from these tokens, a conspicuous metallic green patch on each wing bordered with a black and a white line (the speculum) is diagnostic.

The Spotbill is mainly Indian, but also has a distribution outside the country to its northeast. It ranges all over India excepting Kerala and a few other locations, and favours large spreads of fresh water and open pools. It is seldom seen in a regular flock, but only in small parties, or even in a pair or two. It is given to local migrations as seasonal needs dictate within the country. It feeds both on aquatic vegetation and on water-insects and similar aquatic small fry, and occasionally raids paddy fields.

It is a strong flier, though rather slow in its initial start, gaining momentum slowly from the take-off. In flight, the tertiaries (or the third and last flight feathers) which are largely white are conspicuous.

Unlike the Nukhta and the Cotton Teal, and like the whistling teals, the sexes are practically identical in plumage, though the female is slightly smaller than the male. And unlike all the other native duck, it is said to be excellent eating, and so hunted wherever and whenever it can be. And unlike them again, it never nests in trees, but builds a neat pad for its eggs in the grass or other vegetation bordering the water.

THE SEA KING'S EYRIE

High up in a towering casuarina, a hundred feet above the ground, the sea-eagles had built their ponderous nest. It was wedged firmly into the trifid, ultimate fork of the trunk, a firmly knit stack of thick twigs and dry branches, looking more like a pile of faggots than anything else. It was hollow on top, though I could not see the depression from the third-storey terrace of the building from which I watched, for the eyrie was well above the level of the housetop, but the way the big nestling disappeared from view every time it waddled to the centre from the rim of the nest showed a hollow.

The sea was not a mile away, perhaps not even two furlongs by air. One of the parent birds mounted guard on the treetop, a few yards from the nest, while the other sailed away on a foraging expedition. These were White-bellied Sea-Eagles, almost as big as a vulture and much more shapely in build, with slaty brown backs, the head, neck and underparts white, sail-like wings broadly edged with black, and a short fan tail. The adults looked strangely like overgrown gulls, the grey and white in the plumage and length of wing suggesting a gull, but they sat in the manner of eagles, upright on the treetop, talons gripping the bough firmly. The wings projected beyond the brief tail in repose, their tips crossing.

Through my binoculars, the bird was startlingly near and clear; I could see the grey, hooked beak, the powerful talons, even the dark, apprehensive eyes. It was watching me intently, with obvious distrust. Thereafter I took care to do my watching from the shelter of a pillar or the parapet, not too obviously.

Off and on, for a fortnight, I watched these sea-eagles, and learned not very much about them. One of the adults was slightly the larger; I thought this was the she eagle. This one it was that stayed near the nest, watching, most of the time. Much of the scouting for food, for the entire family, fell to the lot of the other eagle. Sizeable fish seemed to form the staple diet, though once the forager returned with a long, dangling prey that looked like a sea snake—but probably it was only an eel. The grown birds fed by turns, after parting with a large piece to the offspring. There was a patrician lack of haste about the feeding and flight of these eagles that was impressive: who would believe that it is these same birds that flogged the air above the sea with untiring wings and chased each other in giddy flight, clamouring raucously all the time, earlier in the year!

The youngster was about three-quarters the size of its parents, and much more cognizably eagle. The feathers on its head and neck were not white and sleek as in the grown birds, but streaky, pale brown, and they stood out in hackles. The body was a dark, mottled brown—the colour one associates with raptorial birds. This fledgling progressed rapidly during the fortnight, and when I saw it last (on 1 May), it was standing on the edge of the nest-platform and flapping its wings gawkily, though it had not yet essayed flight.

The food-laden return of the parent bird was the signal for crows to gather around the nest, or fly over it. Not once did I see them profit by this watchfulness: they never dared to get on to the nest, to try to snatch a morsel, though they would sit all around, close by in the tree. At times one or the other of the adult sea-eagles would leave the nesting tree and sit in a neighbouring one (also a casuarina), and when this happened the crows mobbed it immediately. Apparently, away from the location of the nest, they were not afraid of it. Frequently, they forced the big bird to take wing and fly away from their attentions with a harsh, metallic, reiterated call, but once I saw the eagle dive at two crows that were annoying it and send them scattering for dear life.

I was told, by the gardener of the house, that these sea-eagles had nested here for years, that every year they reared their progeny on this same nest, that he did not know what happened to the youngsters when they grew up, but that the old birds remained there right through the year. The nest looked as if the accretion of many years had been added on to a structure that was originally no small thing. We estimated that it was a rounded cube, about four feet each way. Even allowing for interspaces and the hollowness of its top, it must have contained over a hundred sizeable pieces of wood, and have weighed about 200 pounds. How did these seafaring birds acquire the large, dry branches that formed the crossbeams of the eyrie? Did they pick them off the backwaters, or did they wrench them clear from greenwood, as Jungle Crows do? I cannot answer these questions, or find someone who can, but it seems reasonable to suppose that much of the nesting material was, originally, flotsam.

FOND
RECOLLECTIONS

BREAKFAST COMPANIONS

Breakfast was sometime between half past seven and nine in the morning, depending on diverse factors, but was always alfresco, in the tiny open veranda outside the tiny kitchen, at the lone chipped stone table there. And it never varied: crisply toasted and often slightly charred bread, a pungent vegetable curry and a pot of excellent tea. Though neither the rest-house cook nor I could tell when precisely breakfast would be served, till it was, the Jungle Babblers knew it. They were never there, nor anywhere near in the surrounding scrub at other times, but as I broke the first slice of toast, there would be thin squeaks and rustles in the peripheral bushes, and small, low grey figures would come streaking along the ground to the table, and the crumbs would be expertly picked up and consumed as they were formed.

Jungle Babblers

I was struck by the speed and efficiency of these commensals. Much has been written about the loose, lax, untidy plumage and frumpy looks of Jungle Babblers, their witless, weak-winged flits from bush to bush one after another, their pale-eyed, sidelong scrutiny of all things, and their generally scatterbrained behaviour. But at my breakfast table, they were impressively purposive and neatly swift. They came hopping along at such speed that they were just grey streaks darting in, and they wasted no time in preliminaries. Every little crumb was picked up at once, and there was never any need to wipe the table clean when the meal was over. There was always enough bread for me to be generous with scraps, but the curry, which I liked, was doled out inadequately in a small, shallow dish: when I had wiped the dish clean with a piece of bread, there would still be a slice left, which I crumbled into tiny bits and gave to my breakfast companions. Once I did offer them a gob of the curry, to see if they, too, fancied it, but after inspecting it closely through their pale eyes, heads tilted one way and then the other way, they left it alone. Tastes differ.

In recent years, during short trips to open scrub jungles, I have had many opportunities of observing these birds, and their almost identical first cousin, the White-headed Babbler, is a regular habitué of my wild, untended backyard. All these babblers form a clan, with its members unmistakably alike, and are close to the laughing thrushes. They are all gregarious, going about and relaxing in a party of from half a dozen to almost a dozen, which is why they are loosely called 'sat bhai' or 'the seven sisters', names which properly belong only to the Jungle Babbler.

Babblers of all kinds are noisy birds. Some, like the Large Grey Babbler, have an irritatingly reiterated creaky, whining voice; some others are almost musical in their calls. Sat bhais have thin, squeaky voices. I think it is Edwin Arnold (in *The Light of Asia*) who has the line, 'The seven sisters chattered in the thorn'—I cannot conceive why he wrote that, if it were he that did, for the seven sisters never chatter. Other birds do, but not they. Their voice is best described by what Shakespeare wrote (in *Julius Caesar*) of the ghosts that 'squeaked and gibbered' on the Roman streets.

These gregarious birds have a strong bond with their comrades, and as many observers have pointed out, they will rush to the rescue of any member of the fraternity in trouble. I saw such a rescue by my breakfast-table companions. There were two half-grown youngsters in their party, and one morning a Shikra appeared from nowhere, pounced on one of the juveniles, and carried it away shrieking its protests. Immediately, the rest went off in a body in hot pursuit, squeaking and gibbering and flying as fast as their short rounded wings could propel them, in such a furious and determined mob that the raptor dropped its captive and flew away! That youngster, I noticed, seemed none the worse for its near-fatal experience.

Flat Nest

Jungle Babblers build a rather flat nest, usually neatly lined with fine roots, in bushes and small trees, often fairly low. I suppose the successful rearing of the brood depends partly on the vigilance of the parent birds and their companions, for the nest is seldom hard to get at. As one might possibly expect of these grey, untidy, zany birds, the eggs (in a clutch of four) are a beautiful, glossy turquoise blue in colour: sometimes, on close scrutiny, one of the clutch appears slightly different in shape, though not in colour, and this will hatch not into a Jungle Babbler, but into a nestling Pied Crested Cuckoo!

THE HONEY-SUCKERS

This morning I had an unusual visitor. A Yellow-breasted Honey-sucker flitted gaily in through my bedroom window, perched jauntily on top of the old Chinese clock that stands above my head and began to twitter in a shrill, small voice. I rolled softly off the edge of the bed and shut the window, for this honey-sucker had long been scoring over me and I meant to get on even terms with him. I had spotted him first in August, hovering round the hibiscus bush outside the bedroom, sucking the nectar from its flowers and playing hide-and-seek among its leaves with his lively little wife. Of course, they had built their nest somewhere in the garden—they never left it—but all my patience and vigilance had been wasted, and I had never found this nest. Moreover, a honey-sucker in a room is a thing that calls for investigation. Now a sparrow will come freely into our houses and the thieving crow will come sneaking in search of titbits when we are not there; but the little honey-sucker keeps himself to himself, and to his garden and to his hibiscus bush. Not that he is a shy bird, but like most birds, he distrusts the roofed and walled and closed-in spaces of our dwellings. Well, anyway there he sat, on my clock, imprisoned in my room, and I must confess that I felt a grim sort of satisfaction in the thought that he was at my mercy at last.

'*Tweet, tweet,*' he said cocking his head to one side and ruffling his feathers, '*tweet, tweet, tweet*': he seemed utterly unaware of the fact that he was in the enemy's camp. 'Tweet, tweet,' I said in imitation, 'tweet, tweet, my dear little fellow, but how are you ever getting out of here?' He left the clock and hovered casually about the room, inspected a cobweb with great interest, and then flitted out—out through a crack in the windowpane that I hadn't noticed! I told myself later that I'd have thrown the window open in a few minutes anyhow, and that it was the curiosity of the naturalist that had made me close it at all. Really, that's so. And you must know—but let me tell you something about honey-suckers, for all this is about honey-suckers and not me, though you may not have guessed it.

Tiniest Birds in this Country

The honey-suckers or sunbirds are perhaps the tiniest birds in this country. Some people will persist in calling them hummingbirds, but the two are quite distinct. Hummingbirds are natives of America, and they get their name from their peculiar buzzing flight. The honey-suckers, on the other hand, never buzz like that. You may find one hovering on quick invisible wings, hung in the air in front of a flower, sipping the nectar of which he is so fond. The normal flight, however, is a curious alternation of long, low swings and jerky stops. The bill of the honey-sucker is thin and curved and he has a long tongue to reach the nectaries of the flowers, placed deep within the corolla tube. Sunbirds look as if they fed entirely on nectar—they are such bright light things. But all their sprightliness and exuberance is the result of an excellent digestion and an appetite that mere nectar cannot satisfy. Spiders and small insects form the main part of their diet, and it is amazing what a number of spiders a little bird no bigger than your thumb can eat in a day.

There are two main divisions in the sunbird family. The Purple Honey-sucker which represents the more aristocratic branch of the clan, is clad throughout in a scintillating blue and purple livery. A tuft of flame-coloured feathers at the angle of either wing adds further to his claims to superiority. He looks a glossy, jet black from a distance, but wait till he comes nearer or a shaft of sunlight catches him, and you will see him in all his sapphire and amethyst glory. The Yellow-breasted Honey-sucker has a shorter bill and a less gorgeous plumage. The back, wings, tail and head are a glossy, dark purple, and his breast is a pale yellow. As in the case of his cousin, distance and the shade do not improve his looks and he is a plain black and yellow till he comes quite near. These descriptions, by the way, apply only to the cock birds. The ladies dress in a sober khaki with pale yellow aprons. The cock Purple Honey-sucker is no doubt the handsomest member of the race, but a sad fate overtakes him when the breeding season is over—he loses his brilliant purple and blue and even the flame-coloured tufts under his wings, and becomes very like his drab mate except for a streak of purple down his cheek. His yellow-breasted cousin, on the other hand, wears an all-the-year-round suit. Now if I were a prig, I would go on relentlessly to point out the moral of this to you, but I am not. And so I shall spare you that.

M. Krishnan

THE PIED CRESTED CUCKOO

Of all our cuckoos, I think the Pied Crested Cuckoo the most attractive. Others, the Koel and the 'brainfever bird' for example, are commoner, but though the Koel is an interesting bird to watch, it doesn't like being watched and flies away the moment you try to get a little nearer. The Coucal and the Sirkeer are both furtive fowl, even more given to privacy and skulking, and the Red-winged Crested Cuckoo (perhaps the handsomest of all cuckoos) is a shy, jungle-loving bird. We have quite a few other cuckoos, more often heard than seen, but the Pied Crested Cuckoo is the only one that is delightfully unselfconscious in the presence of men.

The Pied Crested Cuckoo is by no means common in these parts, though it is not rare in the open country in summer. One afternoon, last May, I found assorted trees growing close and tall around a well. The shade here was deep and delightfully cool: beyond, the sun beat fiercely down on the parched brown grass and the cracked earth. I was hot and tired, having spent the past hour carrying an outsize gadget bag through the shadeless scrub: I sat beneath a tree and felt instant relief. I was thinking that by contriving to place the wretched bag in a hollow I could fashion a pillow of sorts, and that a siesta in that secluded spot would be a memorable experience, when I noticed the Pied Crested Cuckoos.

Perfect Picture

There were a pair of them, a dozen yards away, sitting side by side on the swing of a thick creeper hanging from a tamarind. A perfect picture—and inside my ponderous bag was my ponderous camera. What quickened my photographic pulse was the fact that few men, so far, have succeeded in getting a good picture of these birds. Bird photographers have a nest-side bias, and Pied Crested Cuckoos build no nest, being parasitic on the babbler tribe. Here, then, was my chance.

I spent the next three hours stalking these confiding birds with my uncouth camera—a contraption (largely designed by me) that looks more like a machine gun than anything else. Prompted by a false impulse, I had just fitted a new viewfinder to it whose reliability was not yet known. My object was to get to within three or four yards of one of the birds, and then take the picture—time and again, I succeeded in this, and when evening came and the cuckoos flew away to some other grove (what had kept them there in spite of my attentions was, evidently, the glare outside), I felt I had all the pictures I wanted. Developing the precious roll that night, I discovered that my viewfinder and lens had had a difference in outlook, and that I had superbly crisp studies of the foliage and creepers well to the left of my subject, though in one frame I had the tail and in another (a long shot taken from ten yards) a minute image of the bird itself. I, too, had failed—like other photographers.

Plaintive Calls

However, I had an excellent opportunity to observe these birds. The two rarely kept together in a close brace, but were never far apart either, and frequently called to each other with a variety of pleasant, somewhat plaintive, brief calls. It is said that the sexes are alike in this cuckoo, but one of my birds was distinctly blacker—the other was a very dark brown on top rather than black—though both were of a size. Of course, it could be that both were cocks, or both hens, but if they were a true pair, I think it likely (considering the general trend in birds in such matters and the trend of the cuckoo tribe) that the black-backed bird was the cock.

Both birds flirted their long, graduated, white-tipped tails upwards not frequently and with a nervous jerk right over the back in the manner of robins, but straight up—I thought they did so because the limitations of the space they were in did not permit the tail being held horizontally. The crest was frequently erected, and then stood up in separate, sharp-pointed plumes.

They searched systematically for insects, working steadily up or down a bough or bush, and were on the move most of the time, though occasionally one of them would return to the swing in the tamarind for a brief rest—I never saw them together on the swing again. Quite a lot of their hunting was done on the ground and in low bushes. They hopped when on the ground, but hopped along with ease, and were very rapid in their movements when chasing and capturing some running quarry.

In the South, this bird (unlike the Koel) does not figure in the folklore and lyric poetry of the country, but I believe that elsewhere in India (particularly the Northeast) it does—probably as a harbinger of the rains, for in the North it is a migrant and arrives with the monsoon.

FORTY DAYS S.I.

At midnight on 26 June last, I was awoken by the angry, terrified voice of a parakeet. I had just dropped off to sleep, but knew at once that it was a parakeet screaming—a few seconds later I heard the scream again, then every few seconds it was repeated. I knew from the sound where the bird was: on top of a clump of coconuts in my neighbour's compound, some twenty-five yards away. It was too dark to make out anything and my run-down flashlight was unable to shed much light on the situation, but I suspected the bird was being attacked and that was why it screamed.

I heard no sign of its attacker—as I said, it was too dark to see what was going on, especially what was going on behind the screen of the great coconut leaves. The screams ceased and I returned to bed. Presently they broke out again, apparently from ground level this time: I heard the flap of wings coming towards me, then there was silence once more. With the aid of the flashlight's glimmer I located the parakeet in my compound. It was lying on its side on the ground, bleeding profusely. When I picked it up it lay inert in my hand, too exhausted to protest.

It was an adult male, as shown by its black-and-red collar, and it had no tail feathers except for two freshly sprouting pins—clearly the attack on it had nothing to do with its taillessness. There was a deep wound on its left side (the kind of wound described as a 'stab injury' in medico-legal books), and it was also bleeding from injuries to the left wing and the crown of its round head. I put it into a roomy cardboard box where it would be safe from further assaults till morning—if it lived that long.

I had a glimpse of the attacker as I conducted the rescue. A single caw came from the foot of the coconuts, then a crow flapped up and showed in darker silhouette against the gloomy night sky momentarily before disappearing.

To my surprise, the parakeet recovered. For the first few days it could hardly stand on the sawdust flooring of its cardboard box. It leant against a corner in a comatose depression, and there seemed little cause for hope. It had to be fed with an ink-filler or teaspoon every few hours—it was amazing how quickly it grasped the idea that the spoon meant nourishment. Every time I picked it up (a thing I had to do with the utmost care because of its injuries), it would bite my fingers till I had it flat on its back in my left palm, then it would stretch out eagerly towards the spoon, beak open, neck long and thin with extension.

I fed it glucose-and-water, milk and tomato juice for the first few days: it would not or couldn't take even well-mashed semi-solid food, probably because one side of the neck was also injured. So quickly did it recoup that on 2 July, I had a packing case converted into a large cage with an assortment of perches, and my bird was able to clamber about and perch.

It lost its two tail pins soon afterwards—birds in an enfeebled condition often shed growing rectrices. It grew wilder with each passing day, and noticeably stronger, and no longer required to be fed by hand. On 4 July it escaped, when the lower door of the cage was opened for cleaning the floor, but obviously it could not use its wings yet. It flapped along, a yard above ground and came to earth within twenty yards: as I was about to recapture it, it flew away again, crossed the road and landed in the miry ditch.

I feared it would soon meet its end if allowed liberty while still so weak of wing, and so ran after it, plunged into the ditch and grabbed it before it could essay flight again. A highly refined-looking gentleman happened to be passing that way, and he watched me as he walked. He said nothing, but his eye spoke his contempt for hulking, grown-up bullies who pounce upon poor little birds.

I released my bird, after inspecting it to make sure that it was fit, on 6 August. I had to wait a couple of days for bright weather, and during this wait abandoned my original intention of ringing it, so that I would know it again if I met it. A child, who visited me to see my parakeet, and the servants warned me that it was cruel to give the bird its liberty:

Speculation Anger Contentment Forty winks

UP — DOWN — climbing silhouettes AND UP AGAIN!

for, sensing the taint of its human confinement, somehow, other birds would mob and kill it. I was also advised to liberate it near a temple, if I insisted on being so cruel. That was sound advice, for a parakeet can find just the kind of natural retreats it would seek against attack in a temple dome.

I had a suspicion (I have it, still) that my bird was an old and frowzy parakeet that I have sometimes seen on my neighhour's coconuts. So I released it in my backyard, from which it could get to the coconuts if it wished to, and sure enough it made a beeline for the trees. It disappeared behind the leaves, and though I watched for nearly two hours, I could get no further glimpse of it. Perhaps I will see it again.

During the forty days it spent in my prison, I gained the impression, slowly, that it was a very old bird. It quite refused to make friends with humanity and was idiotically scared if anyone went near its cage, but it was indifferent to the cat—curiously enough, the feline was equally indifferent to the cage.

Parakeets fly swiftly, but they are essentially climbing birds. Since my bird had no tail, there were no feathers to obscure its legs as it clambered about and I was able to study its climbing technique closely.

Most birds have rigidly set feet, with three toes pointing forward and one behind, but a parakeet can reverse its third toe and most often its feet have the toes in opposed pairs, the better to grasp with. Moreover, its upper beak is not firmly joined to the skull as in other birds but is

M. Krishnan

capable of a certain play—this gives that massive, curved, overhanging hook-bill a measure of delicacy and 'feel' that is invaluable to a climber. A parakeet always goes beak foremost, whether climbing up or down.

It is said that when a parakeet goes to sleep perching on both feet it is a sign of poor health, and that a bird in good health will perch on one foot. I can testify to the truth of this from observation. After the first two weeks (when it used both feet) my bird slept perched on one foot. I have the definite recollection that whenever I saw it asleep it was perched on its left foot, with the right foot drawn up, but I cannot say that it never used its right foot for perching. Had this occurred to me yesterday, I could have verified my suspicions, but you know how it is with these things—this has occurred to me just now, five hours after releasing my bird!

LITTLE CORMORANTS

One way and another, I have been seeing quite a lot of the Little Cormorant in the past few months. Not that it is a rare bird or shy. If you know its haunts you may see it in hundreds, for it is highly sociable, and goes about its most personal affairs quite publicly unlike most birds. Only, it is so very much a waterbird, and I am so terrestrial, that I have had limited opportunities for observing it, till recently.

Of course it is not little. Its name does not refer to its diminutive size, but only to larger cousins. I should think it is heavier built than a kite, though on the wing it looks smaller because of comparatively short wings and a short stiff-feathered tail.

In the evenings the cormorants would come home from feeding grounds to their nesting trees in the water, in wave after wave of close, quick-winged flights. Most of them came from the west, at sunset. A thin, black, pulsating line would cross the flaming horizon, then another and another. By the time the first flight had passed overhead with a swish of stiff pinions, the next would be halfway across, rapidly resolving itself into birds from a quivering black line, and then a pattern of rhythmic black dots, shrinking and growing in unison as the wings were moved in perfect coordination. Even when the birds were right above flying low, one did not see them as so many cormorants, but only as a formation—there was that sameness of looks and matched movement in them that makes it so hard to pick out one soldier from a company at a march past.

Isolated flights would come in from time to time throughout the day. Most of these went straight to the nesting trees, and vanished all at once as the birds settled. Occasionally a flight would come hurtling into the tank, hitting the water over a wide area like a scattering of heavy missiles from some old-fashioned cannon. These 'water-crows' (an English name that is a verbatim synonym of the Tamil name) swam and dived and fished with easy speed, but were less effortless in taking away from the water, splashing along for a few yards before being airborne. When they left the tank for their feeding grounds they went singly and in small parties, so that one hardly noticed their departure, though their return in packed company was almost dramatic.

In the evenings they roosted on the topmost boughs in hundreds, darkening the trees before the night. In flight and repose they kept so much together, in such numbers, that one could not see the birds for the flock.

The young were almost grown up, and sufficiently by themselves for close study—but I knew better than to try anything so messy. Cormorants work hard, frequently flying to distant waters, to satisfy their voracious children, and the young are usually chock-full of the small fish. And when they are closely studied, there is a convulsive movement of their thick necks and the contents of their bulging crops are shot out in a stream on the observer beneath!

Incidentally, in nearly two dozen nests I saw there were only two young per nest (often on the bough supporting the nest, for the juveniles were now well able to clamber about) except for two nests which each held three. The pairs, and the sets of threes, kept close together when they moved out to the ends of their boughs, seeing me approach. Yet the *Fauna of British India* says the number of eggs per clutch is from three to five, and, earlier in the season, I saw at least three eggs in nearly every nest I was able to inspect.

☙

It was as I was watching the paired young from a safe distance, that the great idea came to me. I had a loaded camera, and by sheer chance two flashbulbs in my pocket—earlier that day I had to photograph a human infant and had used the flashgun to catch a fleeting expression. Here was opportunity, to be seized by forelock, mane or tail, for a truly unique photograph. What I had to do was to creep near a pair of young birds, without alarming them, then move in quickly and focus before the rising lumps in their throats reached their beaks, and record the reaction literally in a flash. I gave much thought to preliminaries. Reluctantly I set the shutter to the fastest speed it had, though that meant a wide stop and loss of depth of field—else I could not freeze the shower of small fry as it fell.

I selected a pair of young on a nest low enough for my purpose—the water round that tree was waist-deep and singularly filthy, but one does not get record pictures by sheer cleanliness. I turned my face the other way and slowly, ever so slowly, backed my way till I was near enough for the part demanding rapid action. As I adjusted the focus in a preliminary way before entering upon this second part of the plan, I noticed a leafy twig, directly between me and my subjects: this twig, just above reach, had not seemed obstructive earlier. However, I also noticed a simultaneous compensation. About three yards from the perch of my original pair, actually standing off their nest in another and lower branch of the same tree, was another pair of juvenile cormorants, better placed for my picture. Only, I should be quick, for they were already alarmed and stretching their necks.

I took one long, splashing, underwater step to get near enough, focused rapidly and squeezed the trigger just as the gaping mouths opened to discharge their regurgitated shot. And as the flash flared up, a glittering little fish hit the lens of my camera with a smack, completely ruining the picture. I had forgotten all about the original pair of young birds, now directly above, and they had been a split second earlier in their reaction than their fellows. I am afraid I will have to wait till next year for my remarkable picture. I am still cleaning the eye of my camera with tender care, a little area at a time and in gentle instalments, so as to remove all foreign matter without damaging the coating.

ESCAPE OF AN ADJUTANT

One of the most vivid recollections I have from my boyhood is the escape of an Adjutant stork from a zoo. I knew that large, ungainly bird well. It enjoyed a measure of clip-winged freedom, stalking solemnly around the sunken pond beyond the antelope paddocks, or wandering stiff-legged and aloof through the gardens, its ugly pouch swinging at each measured step. It disliked the too near approach of men (probably with good reason), and being a wary bird it usually managed to keep its distance, but at times I have almost run into it, turning an abrupt corner, and its frantic, uncouth retreat then was at once both comic and pitiable.

One fine afternoon, while the Superintendent was berating a keeper for something he had done, or hadn't done, the Adjutant suddenly took wing. No one had noticed that it had shed its clipped flights and grown fresh, serviceable pinions but it had. It stood on the tips of its toes and flapped its great wings, it took a lunging step forward, and then, to everyone's surprise, it was airborne. It flew over the pond, just above the dark green water, each laboured wingbeat producing a gasping noise (this sound, by the way, is not due to any clumsiness of wing, but has something to do with the forceful manner of take-off, and the elasticity of the pinions—Rock-Pigeons, surely among the finest fliers of the bird world, make a sound like rhythmic laughter with their wings, every time they take off).

Ability to Turn

That stork flew straight and low across the pond, and towards an outlying clump of trees, so undeviatingly that it seemed inevitable that it must crash into the treetops; somehow it managed to clear the treeline, then, as if demonstrating its ability to turn, swung round and came towards us—by this time it was some twenty yards above us. It flapped on with vigorous beats of its wings, rising steadily in the air; then, unexpectedly, it spread its wings and sailed easily around in spiralling circles, still gaining height—apparently it had found a current of air that could sustain it on still, spread wings. We stood there, gaping, rank and duty forgotten, while that heavy, clumsy old stork was transformed incredibly into a thing of power and grace, sailing effortlessly on high, neck indrawn and the great beak jutting out in front, spiralling higher and yet higher till it was a mere speck in the heavens.

I do not know where that Adjutant went; it never returned to the zoo, as the Superintendent confidently expected it to.

In many parts of North and Northeastern India, the Adjutant acts as a scavenger, being found frequently at garbage heaps along with kites, vultures and jackals. In the South, it is sparingly represented by a smaller species, which has no pouch. Both species, I believe, have a red, fleshy pad just above the shoulder and below the nape, the function of which I do not know.

Graceful Flight

The Adjutant is probably the largest, though not the tallest, of our storks, and unquestionably the ugliest of the tribe. It is amazing with what easy grace this huge, clumsy bird can soar, once it reaches a certain height. All storks can soar, like vultures, and are capable of undertaking long flights. However, it is the smallest of our storks, the Openbill, that can claim to be a true aerial acrobat.

Another surprising thing about the Adjutant is the softness and richness of its under tail coverts. Bald-headed, naked-necked, boat-billed and stiff-legged it may be, but the plumes on its underside, just above the tail, are a pure white, wonderfully soft, and exquisitely fine in texture. These plumes, known to the trade as marabou, were once in great demand, but with the decline in feather ornaments in feminine fashions, the Adjutant, the egrets, and other plume-bearing birds have gained a less harried lease of life.

M. Krishnan

BIRD OF SURPASSING BEAUTY

Three peacocks parade the gravel path outside the palace of an Indian state. They are tailless, bedraggled but still undoubtedly peacocks. And to think that generations of men have admired this gawky bird for his 'surpassing beauty'! I must confess the peacock fails to impress me. His jerky, high-stepping gait betrays his affinity to the lowly domestic fowl, though he tries to hide this under cover of his flamboyant feathers. And even his colouring is displeasing. The train and neck of metallic green and blue and purple are thrown discordantly into contrast by the back of sports tweed and the flight feathers of chestnut.

He is like the creation of some vigorous and second-rate poster artist. Why then should this bird have appealed so strongly to the popular sense of beauty? But perhaps the answer to this lies not in the peacock, but in the popular sense of beauty. After all, is it not the creations of the second-rate poster artist that most readily catch the eye of the people? But let us not stray from the peacock to the even more glaring topic of popular aesthetics.

There are nearly thirty peafowl living about the gardens and out-houses and gables of the palace. They wander all day as they please, pecking at the grass and herbs, or else lie spread out on the ground basking in the sun. And at sunset they fly heavily up to the treetops or roost on top of the gables, and there they stay all night, still and asleep. Not all of them are tailless, or rather trainless, for it is this long and obviously splendid train of feathers that spring from above its perennial turkey-tail that the peacock sheds. There seems to be no defined moulting season for these peacocks: some have been trainless, some have been resplendent in their trains and some have been sprouting fresh trains over the past two months. It seems this is a peculiarity of the local birds. Other peafowl, elsewhere, shed their trains regularly each year in the moulting season, and lead orderly lives.

Useless Creatures

I cannot think of a more useless set of birds than of these peacocks. Their ornamental qualities are doubtful and undoubtedly they are a nuisance. They ruin the lawns with their droppings and by scratching up forms in which they lie comfortably curled up, like a dog. Each morning and evening they pollute the air with their harsh, piercing calls. They are not even good for food, for in these parts they are not eaten. It seems the eggs are, at times, but never the bird. And as everyone knows, it is not the peacock that lays the eggs!

I can write more enthusiastically of the peahen. The peahen is a sober, matronly sort of bird. She does not greet the light and darkness each day with raucous cries. 'Her voice is ever soft and low, a most excellent thing in women'—at least it often is unlike her mate's. And a more devoted mother is hard to imagine. A few weeks ago, a peahen with two chicks appeared on the veranda of my house, and this family reappeared each day for I encouraged them with odd handfuls of rice— something about the intense affection of the mother towards her chicks touched a generous chord in me.

And what comic things those peachicks were! They were about the size of a tennis ball with a thin, vertical crest at the end of their scraggy necks, like crested partridges. They would peck industriously at the rice while their mother stood on guard ready to claw the life out of the expectant peacocks that stood idly around. And when the little ones had gorged themselves, she would cluck softly to them to come away; but sometimes when I went too close, the cluck would take on a more urgent and menacing note. And then they would walk straight towards the compound wall, and almost into it, before rising vertically to settle on top of it. Next evening the family would present itself again at my door and wait, clucking with patient insistence for the rice.

M. Krishnan

The Chicks Grow

A truly idyllic scene this—Tennyson could have written half a dozen stanzas of sleepy, sonorous verse about it. But alas! this pastoral ritual came to an abrupt end. The peachicks grew amazingly, almost visibly, and very soon they lost their quaint, partridgey appearance. They rapidly acquired shape and bulk till they were almost as big as their mother. Their crests widened out and the feathers of their necks took on a metallic sheen. One evening I noticed iridescent blue patches on their necks and the fact that they walked with a strut—they had grown into unmistakable peacocks. I chased them away with shouts and I have saved my rice since. The thoughtful man will see a moral in this. Oh no, it is not that man is essentially selfish and petty, and ready to dislike things that have ceased to amuse him. It is that the most quaint and lovable of peachicks may grow into peacocks.

GREY-NECKS

Crows are sitting in pairs on treetops, late in the evenings. They choose a foliage-free bough high up, and for an hour before dark they sit close, indulging in caresses with their bills and saying low, sweet nothings to each other (of course crows have a language—Seton claimed to know a bit of it!). I have seen dozens of these courting couples in the past week, and there is no doubt that the local grey-necks have exchanged a communal life for a connubial one. Shortly they will nest, and rear their young, and the young of the Koel, with loving care—incidentally, I have yet to hear Koels here (where they are plentiful) in spite of the premature onset of summer; apparently their love follows the love life of crows.

The grey-necked House Crow is the commonest bird of town and countryside, and so varied in habit and intelligence that it is always interesting to watch. More than one observer of Indian bird life has devoted an entire book to it, and still how little we know about it! Does it pair for life? Nothing definite seems to be known on this point. The one sure way of finding this out would be to ring a number of crows with distinctively coloured rings, and watch them over years—strong metal rings would be needed, as these birds have powerful and clever beaks and will peck at and remove celluloid or similar material. Both birds of a pair must be distinctively marked—I used to know a white-flecked crow and watched its nest in successive years, but could never be sure if its mate was the same each year. Grey-necks live in a flock in the off season, when not nesting, and roost in company. It may be thought that this sociable winter habit would be conducive to promiscuity in pairing when the breeding season comes again, but this need not be so—there are monogamous birds with a gregarious habit.

One thing I am fairly sure of, after watching House Crows and Jungle Crows for years, is that the former are far cleverer on the wing. They are less clumsy in build and movement, though less powerful, and on the whole I think they are more intelligent than their jungly cousins. It is in flight, however, that their superior skill is obvious. When the termites swarm and both kinds of crows are feasting, the grey-neck's comparative air mastery is clear.

A House Crow will shoot up from its perch, chase a fluttering insect on quick flapping wings, and take it surely—it is more given to hunting winged prey in this manner than most people think, especially in the fading evening light. Moreover, some grey-necks are noticeably more expert in this art than others. Recently I had occasion to verify the truth of this.

I was sitting at a table in an open-air café on a beach one evening, and was offered a plate of 'chaklis'—which I thought unfit for human consumption after sampling. After my usual thrifty habit, I looked around for human habitués to whom I could donate the burnt, twiggy, garlic-spiced dish. There was a thin dog with soulful eyes watching me, and further away there was a pair of casual grey-necks, apparently more interested in a tête-à-tête and the seascape than in me. I turned my back on the dog, for I find yearning canine eyes beyond my will power, and tossed a bit of the 'chakli' into the stiff crosswind. The crows jumped into the breeze and one of them caught the morsel deftly in its beak—they never take things in the air in their feet—and swallowed it in mid-air. I tossed another bit high, and, as if by magic, five crows shot up after it.

Presently there were well over a dozen grey-necks. I kept on tossing the twiggy inducements into the breeze, and when the plate was empty I ordered another. I learned much from this brief spell of flighted offerings to the crows. In spite of their packed numbers, they never collided in the air, and only once was one of several fragments thrown up together allowed to land. One crow—I am certain of it as I never took my eyes off this bird—was far cleverer at the game than the rest: its interception of the parabolic trajectory of the morsels was sure and easy. It did not swallow its first catch, but went for the next bit as well without dropping the first one, repeating this astounding performance till it had four bits crosswise in its beak. Then it was forced to retreat for a brief spell of swallowing.

All the crows there were grey-necks—Jungle Crows don't care much for the strong crosswind on the beach. I would much have liked to prolong this tossing experiment, but when the second plate of burnt offerings was finished I noticed that everyone in the café, including the waiters, was staring at me in undisguised amusement, and this forced me to call for my bill and leave in a hurry. Perhaps, some other day when I can summon a less self-conscious mood, I may complete the experiment.

M. Krishnan

INDIA'S KING CROWS

Everyone knows the King Crow, the jaunty little Black Drongo. It is one of the most familiar birds of the Indian countryside and open forests—only inside human settlements are crows, House Sparrows, and feral pigeons, at places, even commoner. The King Crow has an all-India distribution, and names in all our regional languages, in some more than one—'kotwal' is its best-known name in Hindi-speaking tracts, and singularly descriptive of its bold, energetic character. In different parts of the Tamil country it has different names, and in classical poetry names no longer current: further, there is a countryside belief that if the King Crow crosses one's path from right to left when setting out on a mission, it is an augury of success. Long, long ago, when I undertook to provide natural history quotes for the Tamil encyclopaedia of Madras University, I did quite a dissertation on diverse references to the bird in that language, but what the King Crow brings to my mind now is no literary or traditional allusion, but my first meeting with the doyen of Indian ornithologists, Salim Ali.

On the Bund

It was an encounter rather than a meeting, on the bund of the Vedanthangal waterbird sanctuary, which I was surveying for the Government of Madras (as it was then). We differed sharply on what could, and what could not, be permitted in such a preserve, and since both of us had the courage of our convictions, strong words were exchanged. Then, since further words were pointless, we took a long walk around the tank, talking of other things, and at one point passed very near some grazing cattle with King Crows perched on their backs. He asked me if I knew that there was a white rectal spot at the base of the King Crow's beak, and looking at the birds close by I said there was not. 'What do you bet?' he asked with a boyish gusto that surprised me in one a dozen years my senior. Wisely, I took no bet, but borrowing his binoculars scrutinized the beaks of the birds, and there, sure enough, was a tiny white spot just at the gape. Salim Ali has made special studies of quite a few birds, but I believe the King Crow was not one of them: nevertheless, in his infective zest for what interested him, which 'age could not wither nor custom stale', he was more like that bird than any other.

King Crows are late to retire for the night, and are up well before the first daylight, an hour earlier, with the 'false dawn' beloved of Anglo-Indian writers of an earlier era. During the day one usually sees them perched on a post or a fence, on a telegraph line or some such commanding eminence, keeping a sharp lookout for prey on the wing: occasionally they do descend to the ground to pick up crawling insects, but most of their hunting is done in the air. They also go riding grazing cattle, to pounce down on the insects flushed by the hooves from the ground vegetation.

In deciduous forests, and also in rural tracts where trees surround human settlements, the harsh, uninhibited, cheery predawn chorus of King Crows is the first announcement presaging daybreak. There is a vivid reference to this chorus in ancient poetry, and those who have heard it will know how remarkably exhilarating it is, in spite of its stridence, a rollicking assortment of rasping calls that taper off into musical whistles.

It is not often that we find that the character attributed to birds and beasts in folklore and countryside legends has a basis in actuality, but there is a truth in the widely held belief that, in its own way, the King Crow is the protector of the poor, though it is not so intentionally, but only incidentally. About this time of the year (about midsummer) King Crows breed, building their nest (a cup of fine twigs) fairly high up a twiggy tree, and during the breeding season will not suffer any possible depredator to come anywhere near: the pair launches a regular dive-bombing attack on the intruder in concert, regardless of its much bigger size, and keeps attacking till they have chased it far, far away.

M. Krishnan

Tree Pies

It is not only crows and tree pies (both inveterate nest-raiders) that come in for this treatment, but even large raptors. In the Anamalais I once saw a Black Eagle reconnoitring an open valley (probably in search of nests, for it is given much to nest-raiding and baby-snatching), and suddenly a pair of King Crows appeared on the scene and began attacking the eagle, besides which they seemed quite tiny. This magnificent eagle can coast along at high speed, sailing on tautly outspread pinions, but that time it fled with frantic flaps of its wings!

Defenceless birds like doves, orioles and bulbuls often build their nests lower down in the same tree in which a pair of Black Drongos have nested, thereby gaining dependable security for their own eggs and nestlings. This phenomenon has been recorded by various reliable ornithologists and birdwatchers. Is it merely a flight of fancy on my part, or do I really see a distant metaphorical semblance even in this to the late savant? A good many younger ornithologists have surely benefitted by the uncompromising integrity and insistence on hard work that Salim Ali brought to his own studies.

FOND RECOLLECTIONS

Black birds, as a rule, are glossy. Look at the King Crow, the Racket-tailed Drongo, the cock Koel and robin—even the homely crows have a shine to their darkness, like a glace-kid shoe. Some black birds are even more fancy, the sheen on their plumage having an iridescence: the Hill-Mynah's black is shot with flashes of purple and green, the little sunbirds have a gem-like purple glow, and many other birds have a watch-spring-blue gloss to their blackness.

But the cock Pied Bush-Chat is not like that. Its black is shine-less and gentlemanly, and sets off the patch of white in each wing and above the tail so neatly, and brings out its stubby little figure trimly. Its mate is even more sober in attire, the colour of sun-baked, brown clay.

It is scrubby country, given to spiky, stony vistas framed by thorn bush, that the bush-chat likes best; and here it will often take up residence, with its mate, around one's home. So will many other birds, but I think that none of them can impart to a modest cottage set in a plot of wasteland the same sense of cheer. I should know, having lived for years in just such a dwelling.

For seven years a pair of Pied Bush-Chats lived close beside me, till I left. Each year they built their nest in the vicinity, in a cleft in the kitchen wall, in the roof of my goat-shed, and once in the axle-hole of an enormous, handleless, stone roadroller that lay permanently unrolling on my wiry 'lawn'—that brood, I remember, came to grief soon.

Robins, many wagtails, sparrows, bulbuls, sunbirds—all sorts of birds would come to the curious low circular wall that enclosed my house or to the aloes and the few hardy bushes that I succeeded in cultivating.

But it was the bush-chats that were the permanent residents and I was glad this was so; they were such quiet, self-assured and confiding tenants, unlike the giddy, fidgety visitors.

During summer and even during the cold weather (especially in December) the cock bush-chat would take his stance atop the terrace, or on a mast-like strip of plank from a packing case that somehow came to adorn the roof of the goat-shed, and sing his glad, brief song—a loud, clear rising whistle ending on a note of untamed sweetness.

Listening to it on a sultry afternoon, I have often felt convinced that there is more to birdsong than scientists know yet, and that there are times when a bird sings merely because it can and feels like it.

I know that scientific-minded people will shake their heads sadly over this little tribute to a lost friend; they will tell me that it is a projection of my own emotions, a sickly and unworthy sentimentality, that is responsible for this note.

No matter. I knew these chats for years and *they* did not— and if science is the elimination of all feeling and perception and an unwillingness to believe what is not printed in a book, then I have no use for it.

BIRD LIFE

IN

A CITY

HOOPOE

I used to know a Mahratta head-mali, with decided ideas on seemliness. He would come to work in a crisply starched khaki coat and a magnificent turban of tiger-striped mull, and was superior to messy digging or work on rough shrubs—such things he left to underlings. Each day he would spend hours on the lawn, quartering it systematically to locate weeds, inspecting each blade of grass with a dignified, critical decline of his beturbaned head. I have never seen a man look and behave more like a Hoopoe.

You will not find Hoopoes away from open spaces. They seem to suffer from a mild form of claustrophobia, for though given to perching in trees and the occasional reconnaissance of shrubs, they will not enter thick cover, and are happiest pottering about some stretch of unconfined turf. What they like is short grass, and just now, with plenty of it in garden and scrubland, Hoopoes are common birds.

Most of the time they are on their feet, looking for grubs, worms and insects in the grass. The zebra-patterned wedge of the horizontal body and tail hides the trotting feet, so that a curious, clockwork effect marks their movements. Other low-to-ground creatures, whose short legs are hidden by the bulk of the body, also convey this impression, but perhaps it is most noticeable in the Hoopoe. The jerky mannerisms of the bird, and its habit of scuttling over the ground in brief dashes, accentuate this illusion of mechanical propulsion.

The very full crest is spread out into a flamboyant fan, then suddenly shut tight into a spike counterbalancing the curved line of the beak, this gesture being repeated again and again as if to relieve the tedium of the long, pedestrian search for food. There are many birds with highly emotional tails, but here it is the head that wears the crown that is uneasy.

The folding and unfolding of the volatile crest express the entire emotional range of the bird, and each passing mood. I have seen a Hoopoe indulge in this play with its crest six times within a minute for no reason that I could discern, but there are rules regulating its conduct on certain occasions. When the bird probes the earth in search of prey, or when it takes off from the ground, the crest is shut close, and just before alighting from flight it is fanned out as fully as it can be.

Some of the most fantastic frills and fancy touches are to be found among birds—great casques, racket-tails, grotesque wattles and spurs, streaming pennants, bright bibs and redundant tail coverts. As a rule these barbaric ornaments are associated with love, and are on during courtship. But the Hoopoe on the lawn is strikingly decorative as any bird of strange plumage, though it is fulfilling a daily need and being useful to us—how rarely does beauty go with routine need and utility! As the bird moves forward on invisible feet, the slanting sun touches it, turning the fulvous sienna of its breast and crest to liquid gold, revealing fully the emphatic contrasts of black and white in the back. Then suddenly the crest is shut and the bird shoots up on slow, fluttering, broad wings, patterned even more rhythmically than its body.

Yes, the Hoopoe has claims to remarkable looks, and like others with such claims it is at its best in public. For its domestic life is a shocking contrast to what one might expect from a bird so richly plumaged and with such a patrician love of lawns. It nests in some recess, maybe in a crevice in the roof of an outhouse: the less said about the foul mess that is its nursery the better. The phrase is often used in a prefatory way, to hold forth at length on an unsavoury topic, but I shall be literal—I shall say nothing at all about that nest.

M. Krishnan

PRETTY POLLY

I do not like things in cages, but if I had to have a cage bird for a pet it would be a Rose-ringed Parakeet. For it has an adaptable nature and bears confinement cheerfully, unlike other creatures. Anyone who has seen a flock of parakeets go screaming across the sky would doubt this—the short, powerful wings of this bird do suggest a love of freedom. But its short, powerful, clever beak, its versatile feet and its obvious zest for life are the tokens of a curious mind, and you cannot confine curiosity. Shut it up in a miserable little tin cage and Polly is still busy exploring the weak spots in its dungeon, twisting a bit of wire here and pulling at a rusty nail there. Who was it who said—

Stone walls do not a prison make,
Nor iron bars a cage

—he must have owned a Rose-ringed Parakeet.

Of course, I do not suggest for a moment that Polly would do well in a tin cage or be happy. Curiosity needs sufficient space to turn in. Moreover it needs light and warmth. A parakeet shut up in a cold, dingy metal cage soon dies a natural death of mental and physical suffocation. My point is that it dies exploring to the last, Scott-like, and does not abandon itself to hopeless, dispirited brooding as other birds do. Polly will live as long as you or longer, if its wants are provided, and its wants are very few considering its complex personality. The cage must be roomy—say, three feet each way—as otherwise the long, graduated tail feathers would get battered and broken. The sides must be of some kind of wire netting, allowing plenty of light and air to enter, and you must fix up at least three round wooden perches of different diameters within the cage. This is very important. If you inspect Polly's feet you will see that they are peculiar. There are four toes as in most birds, but instead of three of them pointing inexorably forward and the fourth behind, the third toe swings on a versatile joint, to join its two fellows in front or the one behind, as the bird pleases. This is a foot made for grasping and climbing, and Polly is a born climber. The perches cost nothing to you and provide it with endless occupation.

Parakeets are remarkable in having their upper mandibles joined flexibly to the skull— the slight play this allows makes their beaks by far the cleverest among birds. There is nothing Polly cannot do with its beak and the adventitious aid of its blunt, sensitive tongue. It can hook its beak on to any support and climb, it can shell a monkey nut with dainty precision, or bite your finger till you feel the bone will crack. Such a beak was made to cope with a variety of things and it is good to remember this. Do not give your parakeet milk and rice and plantains every day—it detests sameness and appreciates hard and pungent things for a change. Guavas, nuts and chillies are always welcome, and a lump of salt, a grit-box and a small container of fresh water take up little room in the cage. Polly will eat an astonishing number of things besides these: all sorts of wild fruits, bread, biscuits, toffee and even tobacco, though I am sure tobacco is not good for any parakeet's health. This supplementary list can only be discovered by experiment; it depends entirely on the vagaries of your particular Polly.

Lastly, remember that it is not every parakeet that will talk. The ability depends, largely, on native gifts peculiar to individual birds and to a lesser extent on the patience of the tutor. There is no doubt that some parakeets can talk with startling clarity—one can make out the words quite easily, especially if one has been told them. Of course the repertoire is limited, to half a dozen sentences in a specially talented bird. Polly never speaks to please you—only to please itself. It will talk

M. Krishnan

incessantly for an hour, and then be sullenly silent when you want it to show off before some guest. Anyway, it is always the casual visitor, and not the owner, who is amused by Polly's powers of speech. Once, years ago, I shared the same house with a parakeet that could say 'Okay, darling!' in the most flippant tones. At the end of two months the words had lost all meaning to me, and I still suspect people who use them of insincerity and vacuity. I must explain that it is only because a parakeet does not know or mean what it says that its repetition seems so pointless and tiresome. It is quite different with us, of course. We are not being tiresome when we say the same thing over and over again. We are being consistent.

FRIENDLY HOBGOBLINS

Other birds fly away. Or else they go about their business, unmindful of you, or sit passively on, not knowing you are there. But the Spotted Owlet resents your prying into its affairs, and takes pains to let you know that it does. It glares malevolently at you from round unwinking eyes, and bobs its round head up and down, the baleful yellow eyes still upon you, and a torrent of gurgling, voluble swearing pours out at you from its squat, softly barred form.

All owls are apt to resent close scrutiny but none so expressively as this owlet, though it is never dangerous as some of the larger members of the tribe can be. The Spotted Owlet's intimidatory display has been called clowning: because it is so small we can afford to feel amused at its impotent anger and bowing, bobbing clock-face. Imagine the bird magnified to the size of its larger cousins, and the demonstration would seem funny no longer; it would serve to scare people then all right.

Everyone knows this little owlet, by far the commonest of our owls and equally at home in town and country. In Madras, mosques and old public buildings, with towers and spires, offer ample hospitality to these birds, and I suppose other cities are not lacking in homes for them. Where there are aged trees, with knots and holes in their trunks, the owlet prefers a nice, dark hole in the wood, sufficiently deep for daytime retreat and siestas. Not that it has the traditional owl's intolerance of light. Spotted Owlets come out at noon sometimes to hunt prey, and it has been rightly said that they are crepuscular because they fear, not the sun, but the mobbing to which other diurnal birds subject them when they show up in daylight.

I have seen these owlets in broad daylight on several occasions, atop exposed perches, and though there were other birds about they took no notice of the owlets. That proves nothing, of course; no doubt other birds do mob them at times. But once I had a striking demonstration of how little the Spotted Owlet minds the glare. I was waiting in a railway retiring room for a belated train on a blazing February day, and just outside the window was an owlet, sitting on a telegraph post right out in the sun. For three-quarters of an hour, from 11.15 a.m. till 12.30 p.m., it sat stolidly on, turning its clock-dial face right over its back to glare at me from time to time, but was otherwise static. When I went out to the foot of the post it flew away, but I remember I had to shade my eyes with my hand in spite of my tinted glasses, so intense was the glare.

Owlets clutch at their prey with their comprehensive talons, and catch them that way. Insects form their staple food, hawked in the air or pounced down upon from a lookout post but they take minor lizards also, and even little birds and mice. I do not know why such a useful bird should be so widely abhorred, but the curse of the owl tribe is upon it, and even today there are quite a number of people encompassing its destruction when it is incautious enough to take up residence near their homes.

A decrepit gateway in a mansion I used to know was a favourite place with these birds, though they were sternly discouraged with a gun. I think quite half a dozen owlets were shot by the sentry on guard there during the four months I knew the place, without appreciably affecting its attraction to the local owlets. The man was always careful to make sure that a bird he had shot was finally dead before he would pick it up, and assured me that the clasp of its feet was a thing not lightly forgotten.

I am afraid we do not know our friends. I find the quaint, semi-cubist looks of the Spotted Owlet charming, and its noiseless flight and bold behaviour interest me. Others may not have my tastes (maybe mine are depraved) but surely a bird so useful about the house and garden, and such an efficient check on obnoxious insects, deserves to be encouraged—and shooting it on sight is no way to encourage any bird.

MINDLESS CRUELTY

A few days ago I had to spend an entire afternoon in a suburban library, and having nothing better to do, browsed through the crumbling old tomes it held. And there, in a British encyclopaedia of natural history compiled in the first years of this century, I came across an interesting theory on the hostility of men to owls. It said that this was entirely due to men being diurnal and owls being night-hunters by nature: if only the birds hunted by day, surely farmers would come to know what valuable allies they were in keeping a check on rats, mice and other crop-destroying creatures, and far from persecuting them would protect them zealously.

After coming home that day and retiring for the night, my wife woke me up at midnight to deal with a situation beyond her abilities. I sleep in a covered veranda on top of the kitchen block, which is separate from the tiled ground floor main house in which my wife sleeps. Some large bird or bat had entered her bedroom and was floundering about, causing the cobwebs and adherent dirt high up the tiles to come down in showers. The main house is one high-roofed long shed, divided into compartments by thin wooden partitions that reach only halfway up, and the electric lamps hang low in wide, opaque shades, so that the roof above is very dimly lit.

Midnight Visitor

However, I could see our midnight visitor was a Barn Owl. On switching the torch on, I had a clear view of it as it sat bolt upright on a rafter high overhead, and the dark patches of dried blood on its legs and part of a broken wing projecting besides the tail showed that it had been grievously injured—probably by being stoned by men—and had sought refuge in my house, which is not unlike an old, dark barn. There was nothing I could do to help, beyond leaving it in peace, and so, telling my wife that it would sit still and not disturb her if left alone, I went up to my cot.

Next morning, it was still precisely where it had been. Climbing unostentatiously on to a table to gain a less upslanted view, I took a few flash photographs of it and then left it alone, after telling everyone not to go anywhere near it. I could not think of a method of capturing it without the risk of the bird injuring itself further by dashing against the rafters in a panic, and I did not know how to set a broken wing. Was there anyone I knew who might help? While I was thinking over this it flopped out of the window, zigzagging its way with lopsided flaps out of my backyard to a clump of mangoes in a neighbour's compound where, deep hidden in the foliage, it would be safe from chivvying crows. I had reckoned without the predatory vigilance and bloodthirstiness of a young hooligan living there, who promptly stoned it to death the moment my back was turned.

Barn Owls are the widest distributed members of their family. They are there in both the Americas, in parts of Africa, in Europe and all over South Asia, even in Australia. They are the only sizeable owls—they are quite crow-sized—that will enter towns and cities, often establishing themselves in a niche in the decorative architecture of a mosque or a temple, along with the 'wild' pigeons to which they do no harm. They can and do prey on small birds like sparrows, but their main quarry are rats and mice of every description—apparently, even city rats and mice do venture into the open at night, to cross from one house to another.

For years I knew a Barn Owl that lived in a deep crevice in the broken side wall of a two-storeyed hostel in a congested city block. Owls regurgitate the bones and fur of their prey in pellets—these do not pass through the birds. One can get a fair idea of what they hunt by dissecting these casts, which accumulate on the ground beneath the diurnal roosts to which they return each day with the sun. The skulls and bones of rats, mice, musk shrews and geckos form the main components of these casts in India.

Specially Feared

It is this owl that is specially feared and hated by people in our country, as a bird of ill omen—probably because it is the owl that resides commonly in and around human habitations. The cause of this intense, uninformed and most unreasonable hatred seems to lie mainly in the bird's voice. It is silent by day, but with nightfall comes out with what has been aptly described as a series of strangled shrieks, varied on occasion with deep, hollow snores. This, the utter silence of its flight, and its pale ghostly appearance, are all against it, and it is an ill omen indeed for the bird to settle anywhere near humanity—for the bird and not for the people who, in spite of their grandiloquent name, 'Homo sapiens', do not even know their friends when they see them.

M. Krishnan

THE BABY SNATCHERS

How right it is that almost the first bird to be specifically mentioned in press dispatches by our National Committee for Bird Preservation should be the common Indian crow: and how too right (as the Australians say) that this mention should be dishonourable!

The Committee has urged urban and suburban municipalities to encourage charming and inoffensive birds like orioles and flycatchers by decimating the too thick crow population. Crows, it points out, raid the nests of these innocents and devour their young.

Commenting editorially on this, a Madras paper offers its sympathies to the municipalities appealed to by the National Committee. The utility of crows as scavengers in municipal areas is stressed, and their claims to citizenship in our democracy boosted—moreover it is pointed out, with much truth, that it will be no easy job giving these hardened birds the push.

Now, the National Committee is on very firm ground in accusing crows of having an inhibiting effect on the less common and more attractive bird life of any place. All the world lives on nature's provision for unborn generations, on the store of good food set by in eggs and grain but crows are inveterate nest-wreckers and baby snatchers, ruthless and untiring in their methods. They go nest-hunting late into the evening and, when there is a moon, even at night.

No doubt the National Committee means all crows found in urban areas and not the grey-neck exclusively, though its press note refers only to the 'House Crow'. Actually, the Jungle Crow is almost as much at ease in town and city as the grey-neck, and is even more given to the massacre of infants. Moreover, it is more at home in groves and tree-studded gardens—a point that has bearing on this issue as will be seen later.

However, whether only one or both crows were meant, the fact remains that it is hard to discourage these birds. It is not as if they belong only to municipal tracts—they are the most widely distributed of all our birds. Furthermore they are long-lived, sapient, audacious and capable of learning much from actual experience, a thing that only the most intelligent of birds can do. They are strong on the wing and fly long distances each day. Shooting them, snaring them, even the hanging up of a crow's skin as a warning and a moral, are all only temporary measures. The birds are back the minute they realize the danger is unreal.

Apart from all this, even if a municipality could get rid of its crows, that is not enough to encourage birds like orioles and flycatchers to take up residence in the place. Such birds need fairly close tree-growth and plenty of leafy cover—they are very fond of mango groves. The kind of parks that municipalities raise offer little scope for their lives, for these are usually planted with deciduous flowering trees spaced far apart.

Where there is close tree-growth and plenty of foliage, it is noticeable that crows are much scarcer than in more open places. That, perhaps, is the secret to success in the encouragement of the kind of birds that the National Committee wants the municipalities to foster.

I cannot help feeling that though sound in its ornithological advice on this issue, the National Committee has addressed it to the wrong parties. The owners of large private bungalows are far likelier than municipalities to take pride in the presence of beautiful and melodious birds in their compounds—there is no law prohibiting private parties from discouraging crows as much as they like, and living on the spot they can wage this unequal war with less strain and futility.

What the municipalities can and should do is to provide spacious

M. Krishnan

parks with plenty of trees like the mango and the *Ficus retusa* besides the invariable *Poinciana regia* and cassias—in this way they can provide the woodland type of cover beloved of orioles and many other charming birds. In built-up areas where there are no large, rambling compounds with low-to-ground evergreen trees, it is the roadside avenues that sustain arboreal birds, somewhat inadequately. If the National Committee can persuade urban authorities to raise and maintain parks of the type described, it will have done a very real service to the struggling bird life of built-up areas, besides adding a welcome touch of green to these grey localities.

THE NEST IN THE BOUGAINVILLEA

The bird, I was told, was tiny, dark above and yellowish beneath, and the nest it was building hung close to the dining-room window from a bougainvillea trained against the outer wall. I said it was a sunbird; probably a Purple-rumped Sunbird, for it frequently nests early in February.

My informant was sure it was not. She knew sunbirds and this bird did not have the thin, curved beak of sunbirds; its beak was shorter and straighter. I asked if it was accompanied by its mate, in dark metallic purple and green all over, or that colour above and lemon yellow below. Yes, once its mate had come with it, but it was no sunbird either; it was bigger and brighter but otherwise like the hen. I decided to investigate.

One look at the nest, in an advanced stage of construction, showed that it was a sunbird after all—the typical pendant purse of floss, fibre, dried leaves and flowers, bits of string and jute, all deftly held together with cobweb, and with a round opening on one side with a little porch on top. However, I adjusted the window-curtains and made myself comfortable so that I could watch the nest from close quarters.

The specific identity of the nest-builder had to be established. The cock bird would provide it, I explained in patient tones, for it was difficult even for an, ah, expert to tell the hens of sunbirds apart at a glance.

The little hen came to the nest, perched momentarily on the threshold, pecked at the inside wall and flew away. It reappeared at frequent intervals, dipping under the creeper and shooting up to the nest with a thin *tsee-tseep* to add a bit of building material and peck it in place, before flying away. Its beak was rather short and straight, and moreover it was pale in colour, but it was a sunbird.

Then another bird came up to the nest with it, larger, plumper, more greenish above and a much brighter yellow below, but otherwise like the hen. It perched on a twig close to the nest, then flew away. I felt puzzled, and foolish. I did not know this newcomer—and I do not still, after searching through books.

I explained, with a stubborn faith in my recollection of nesting sunbirds, that one should not be hasty in coming to conclusions in one's birdwatching. Yes, it did look as if my original identification was, ah, somewhat inexact (how pompous we are in our less secure moments!), but it was better to wait and make sure that this was, in fact, the mate. It was just possible, I added, that a dark purple and yellow cock might still show up. No one believed me.

And then the cock returned with the hen, not once but half a dozen times, unmistakably a Purple-rumped Sunbird in its trim yellow waistcoat and glistening dark coat, and my reputation was saved. But it was a near go!

The other bird did not return, though I waited patiently. It could have been the hen of some other sort of sunbird, perhaps a Loten's Sunbird (though its beak was not long), but I am not sure. Watching the nesting hen from a yard's distance, the straight, short beak was noticeable—the cock had the typical, dark, curved beak.

Twice, while I watched, the cock came straight to the entrance hole, perched on the rim, and pecked at the inner walls before flying away. Even though I was so near, and watching so closely, I cannot say if it had anything in its beak on these occasions. According to the books, the cock sunbird never helps in nest building.

As I write, the hen is in the nest, sitting on the eggs. Someone told me once that he knew of a pair of sunbirds that had rigged up their nest in one day—I have never known such quick work. This nest (which I have sketched with great attention to details that are unimportant) seems to have taken all of five days to complete, from the start to the first egg, and that seems to be a fair average period for the construction.

M. Krishnan

AN EXCEPTIONAL WARBLER

The warbler tribe is the most numerously anonymous of all birds. There are several hundreds of them, wren-warblers, willow-warblers, tree-warblers, fantail warblers and just warblers, all smallish birds, most of them quite tiny, and all more or less of a dull feather. They are inconspicuously grey, brownish or greenish, much given to playing hide-and-seek in bushes and no less given to warbling, or to feeble call-notes. It is not hard, once you have the hang of the family characters, to know a bird as a warbler when you see it. Further identification, however, is a matter for the warbler specialist, and even he likes to have the bird in one hand and the textbook in the other.

It is surprising, therefore, to find that one of the most familiar and easily identified of our garden birds is a warbler. It is *Orthotomus sutorius*—if that fails to mystify you, I might as well use the common name and call it the Tailorbird. There are few gardens in India, however modest, that are not graced by the presence of a pair of Tailorbirds.

True there are other warblers that look like the Tailorbirds; there is the Ashy Wren-Warbler, for instance, another small, slim, energetic bird with a cocked-up tail and the habit of flitting airily about bushes. It is more grey or dark browny on top, in any plumage, than the olive-green Tailorbird, though both are of a size and shape and both have pale undersides, but it is not by their looks that you tell them apart, not even by the cock Tailorbird's tail pins, for these are shed after the breeding season. The wren-warbler makes a curious, quickly repeated snapping noise, faint but audible and unmistakable—if you hear a Tailorbird making this noise, put it down as the Ashy W-W.

Tailorbirds have many calls, among them a rapid *chick-chick-chick-chick-chick* (I think this an alarm call, or rather, an alert), a loud monosyllabic *Tweet* and a louder two-syllabled *Towhee*. No other bird of that size has such a loud, bold voice. And if you watch a Tailorbird while it is calling, you will see a transverse black bar appear and disappear on either side of the neck with each call.

The beautifully sewn nest is, perhaps, even better known than the bird. One would think that such a work of sartorial art is the true and unique hallmark of the Tailorbird, but at times the Ashy W-W builds an almost identical nest, also slung within stitched leaves. However, if there are eggs in the nest you can tell the builder at once. The Tailorbird's eggs are speckled, and the wren-warbler's are a deep, shiny red.

The very first nest with young that I watched was a Tailorbird's, in a hiptage bush just below the veranda of a house. Sometimes these birds build their nests close to human life, even in a potted plant on the veranda, at times. So bold and confiding are they that they will continue to feed their tiny, wide-gaped young while you sit and watch the process from two yards away, provided you keep utterly still and don't stare too rudely. No other nesting bird is so easy to watch.

Off and on, for the past two years, I have been watching a pair of Tailorbirds that frequent my garden. They are there all day, and I think all night as well quite often, for I have often seen them roosting in a yellow oleander bush late in the evening. They seem to like my neglected and rank garden, and to feel very much at home, but though there is plenty of insect life here to feed them and their broods they have never nested within my compound walls. Where large-leaved creepers and bushes are available, Tailorbirds prefer to nest in them, and there are few such plants in my garden. I have taken great pains (what a lie—it calls for none) to allow the plants here to run wild and fight it out among themselves, and am reluctant to interfere with the perfectly natural growth of many years, but I think that one of these days, when I can find a lusty seedling and the energy, I will dig a big pit by my kitchen wall, fill it with something less inhibiting than the clay soil of my compound, and plant a hiptage seedling there for the Tailorbirds to nest in.

M. Krishnan

SPARROWS

For nearly twenty years, I have lived in a dark, exclusive house where there were no sparrows, and now I am with these friendly birds again. They come in with the air and sunshine, when I open the doors in the morning, they watch me eat my chota and supervise my bath, and when I can see them no more I can still hear their occasional chuckles above me, for the rafters of the bedroom offer ideal lodgings for the sparrows that decide to stay in for the night. A bright, companionable lot, these sparrows are very much at home wherever they are: only, I wish at times that they would observe one less closely.

And watching them, in turn, I feel that of all birds they are the most like us, not all of us, but a certain happy section of humanity. Sparrows are very like the hearty 'objective' type of people, who lead their lives in public and never blush—vivacious, inquisitive, determined to make the most of things, enterprising and wholly insensitive. Other men, who have not the gift of living like that, are fond of calling them 'vulgar' and 'brazen': words, which clearly denote the extent of their envy! The 'objective' types, whether of birds or men, may lack fine perceptions, and even pride, but they are the pioneers of their races, the settlers and explorers. The sparrows are the settlers of the bird world: they go from place to place discovering new colonies, and when they have found a likely spot they establish themselves there. Almost any site will do for them, for their tastes are typically few and simple. A little air, a little sunlight, and a certain lack of refinement and gloom are all that they ask for—anything from a dilapidated hovel to a busy market square will suit them. Where it is necessary, and possible, they drive out the aborigines from the newfound settlement—my house, for instance, bears indisputable evidence of having belonged to a tribe of swifts till recently.

At times they wander far away from their fellows, to some remote village or outpost, and it is then that you see how very human the sparrows are at heart. They somehow feel less cocksure of themselves then, and grow strangely wild and wary, as if they feared the vast spaces isolating them; they never go anywhere except in minor flocks, and in the evenings they crowd together in hundreds and sing little songs to keep up their spirits.

Blitz Breeding

Having settled, they begin to breed, breeding in the same brisk fashion in which they do all other things. The nest is a shallow cup of variable shape and size, built of straw, odd bits of waste paper, rags or anything else that lies handy. Provided the nest serves to lay and hatch the eggs, sparrows are satisfied with their handiwork, for like all true settlers they have no use for formal arches and spires. They leave all decorative architecture to their cousins, the weaver birds, just as they leave all music to their cousins, the canaries, and fine feathers to the Red-breasted Cardinal. Sometimes, when a nest is nearly completed, the pair of sparrows that built it decides not to use it, for no apparent reason, and starts on a new nest. Perhaps it is because their first attempt was not sufficiently sturdy to please them, and they prefer to build anew rather than be bothered with repairs. It is amazing the way the fledgling sparrows grow. Most fledglings mature quickly, but you can almost watch young sparrows grow. In a little while they lose the gawky looks of immaturity, and assume the confident, pert expression of their elders. But they still keep close to their mothers' sides for the world is still huge and unfamiliar to them.

When Flocks Fly Away

And what happens when the settlement grows too big to contain itself? Well, I suppose it is only rarely that this happens, for though sparrows are brisk breeders and have hardy constitutions they have many enemies, and the keen competition within the tribe serves to check its growth. Where food and shelter from the rains are available (almost any large human settlement will provide both) sparrows may stay on for years. When there is overcrowding in the community, it is the younger sparrows that usually leave, whether to some old haunt, with an elder guide, or to found fresh colonies I do not know. Occasionally, the entire tribe leaves in a body, for reasons better known to itself than to me. All I can say about these sudden departures is that they are neither seasonal nor periodical. Sparrows, our sparrows at any rate, are not given to migrations, except in a very local way. However, they are strong fliers and will travel long distances to their feeding grounds, returning home in the evening. At such times they keep together in a flock and fly fast and high, dipping and rising in the air. Being sociable creatures they talk to one another as they fly, and it is remarkable how pleasant and tinkling their voices sound as they go skimming overhead. The same voices, at close quarters, seem so commonplace and repetitious. It is a curious thing, but this trick of voice can be noticed in other creatures as well. I dislike to press a comparison too closely, but surely you must have observed the same peculiarity in those tireless, hearty, 'objective' men and women whom the sparrows resemble in other ways?

MYNAHS

One misty moisty afternoon in September I watched a flock of Common Mynahs feeding in a field. Grass was growing underfoot, and the birds, some fifteen of them, moved steadily in orderly rows right across the field, like grazing cattle, taking over an hour to do so. Every now and then, a pair of stragglers would flap their way for twenty yards to rejoin the front ranks, but otherwise none of them took to wing in all that time. A little boy passing by stopped to inform me that the mynahs were after the tender sprouts of coming grass, and I did not contradict him—but they were looking for green grasshoppers, not grass.

The Common Mynah is a sociable bird, feeding in flocks and couples, and often roosting in company. Frequently the roosting trees are close by a piece of water. In the evenings, hundreds of these birds assemble at the roosting site, from all over the neighbourhood; and for an hour before dark you can hear them from half a mile away. Their voices are loud in their many calls, and capable of variation from the usual *koks*, *kree-keeks* and churring notes. Whenever this mynah takes wing, it utters a soft, gurgling *ku-lulu-luk*—I believe this call and habit are peculiar to the Common Mynah.

All mynahs have a strong, sensible build, short tails, and sturdy legs. They spend much time on the ground, walking about in search of prey, but they are good fliers too. None of them is really small, and they do not have the small birds' habit of dipping and rising in the air: nor do they swoop around in circles and hang in the air like aerial birds. Flying any distance, they keep at a fair height, well clear of treetops, and get straight to where they are going. They are not specially fast in flight, though, their broad, white-banded whirling wings taking them along at a fair pace only. Mynahs on the wing dive for the nearest shelter when attacked by hawks, a tree or a bush or whatever offers. I remember an almost adult Common Mynah that dived for the arch of Connemara Bridge, in Madras, with a Peregrine at its tail. The hawk closed in when almost under the arch, and flew for a few feet with its screaming victim clutched by the back, but the bridge right in front and the watching men made it drop the mynah, which lay with outspread wings on the liquid mud beneath the bridge. We retrieved the unfortunate bird from there, and it seemed all right except for a thin, flayed wound along the back, but it was dead within five minutes.

Hill Mynah

The mynahs are all soberly but daintily plumaged, in black, browns, greys and white, the dignified restraint of their colouring offset with bright yellow or orange on bill and legs, and where the naked skin shows around the eyes or in lappets over the ears. To my mind the Common Mynah, in its suit of black and Vandyke brown, white wing bands and tail edge, and yellow bill, legs and eyepatch, is as handsome a bird as any. The smaller Brahminy Mynah is perhaps the most aesthetically coloured of the tribe. It has a long, silky, black crest, grey back and rufous underparts—but it has a crouching stance and an angry look in its eyes, and is less free and easy in its manners than its cousins. The black-and-white Pied Mynahs have a starling-like slimness of build, and the starling-like habit of going about in large flocks; but then the starlings are second cousins to the mynahs. Mynahs are true friends of the cultivator, their size and large gape enabling them to deal summarily with grassland insects.

Many Common Mynahs are admirable mimics, and other mynahs can mimic too. The most talented of them all is the Grackle or Hill-Mynah, a big, black bird with orange beak, feet and lappets. It is a typical mynah in its looks, but its feet are meant for treetops, and it is somewhat heavily made. From nearby the black of its plumage shows iridescent purples and greens in the highlights, and the strength of its beak is apparent. It lives on a diet of fruit exclusively, and likes heavy forests, but its voice is the voice of a mynah, though richer and mellower than that of others. Hill-Mynahs are much prized in aviaries and bird shops, and you are likelier to see one in a cage than outside it. They are accomplished mimics and can be taught to imitate a variety of sounds. I used to know one that could whistle snatches of a tune, in addition to a repertoire of interesting remarks. This bird could also imitate, to perfection, the anxious clucking of a hen calling her brood, and seemed to enjoy the frenzied performance quite as much as its listeners. Many Hill-Mynahs can reproduce the calls of other birds, and their voices have an amazing range of pitch and volume. Perhaps they are as good mimics and talkers as any bird, perhaps they are the best—but they have the handicap common to all creatures that talk and sing: you cannot switch them off, when you wish to!

BIRD LIFE IN A CITY

Thirty years ago, we moved out of a crowded part of Madras to the house that my father had built in Mylapore. No one consulted me over the move, for I was the youngest of the family, but I remember the occasion and the sense of pioneer adventure it gave me. My father had chosen this spot after much cogitation, as the likeliest to offer peace and space to his retirement.

There were a few bungalows around, and many groves and fields in between. Our road, or rather the section of it that held our house, was the northern boundary of an oblongish area, the other three sides of which were also closed in by roads. I am tempted to draw a map, but words will do. The tramline and a row of houses formed the eastern edge. The southern edge was more or less lined with residences, and a new colony (to which we belonged) was coming up in the north—but the west was still wild.

Former Setting

The triangular, southwestern half of the oblong was a series of paddy fields, coconut groves and pastures, with only two small churches and a 'mutt' to break their continuity. I use the past tense from a regard for accuracy. I live in the house that my father built, and the locality still retains its oblongish shape, but it is chock-full of construction now, built up ruthlessly with just sufficient space between for secondary roads.

In those days I used to wander around with a catapult in my hand and a jackknife in my hip pocket, feeling every inch a settler in a new land. There was a pond on either side of our house and a much larger one on the southern periphery—all these are filled up and built over.

My neighbour's compound was a miniature jungle. In it there were mongooses, palm civets, snakes, tortoises in the pond, even a starry-eyed blackbuck, though I must confess that it wore a collar. Beyond, further west, were the paddy fields, coconut plantations and scrub, which jackals visited after sunset and where quail were not uncommon after the rains: once, I saw a hare here. It is all concrete and metalled byroads now, and squirrels and rats are about the only wild beasts one can find in it.

It is of the bird life of this restricted, oblongish area that I write. The title, with its wide scope, is misleading, but perhaps I may justify it by a brief, necessary mention of the rich avifauna of Madras. It is curious but true that Indian bird lore has grown up around the cities— 'Eha' in Bombay, Cunningham in Calcutta and Dewar in Madras have contributed much to its literature.

It is a mistake to think that cities hold few birds, and that these are mainly dark and metaphorical in character. From a varied knowledge of the countryside, I can say that parts of Madras are quite as bird-filled as the country can be, even today. Adyar is still an ornithologist's paradise; one could name other localities in the city's purlieus, but what I should stress is the fact that the part of Mylapore I live in was not less plentifully favoured with birds, and that even now there are birds here.

Birds, with their wonderful powers of adaptation and airborne freedom, are less immediately affected by colonization than terrestrial fauna. As a boy, I got to know the birds of this area the hard way, with little help, and my recollections of them are trustworthy.

What changes do I notice? With the disappearance of extensive woodland (provided by contiguous, tree-stocked compounds), meadows and inundated fields, certain birds have also gone. Spotted Doves, ioras, Magpie Robins, fantail-flycatchers, the Brahminy Mynah, Hoopoes, King Crows and the Grey Shrike (the thorn fences and the pastures are no more), Cattle Egrets, Pond Herons, the Common Kingfisher (the smallest of the tribe) that used to frequent the ponds—these once common birds have left the place, and few of them come in again, even as stragglers.

Other birds are in the last stages of departure. Orioles and bulbuls, somehow never plentiful even in the old days, and bee-eaters and rollers,

M. Krishnan

belong to this class. For the rest, the birds that were here are here, but in much reduced numbers. I think it would be best to group them in some manner before telling you of them: classification is tedious, but unclassified, profuse listing can be worse.

First, the stray visitors, the birds that come in by chance or mischance. Naturally, it is not possible to be specific about them. Night Herons visit my area occasionally, though they have no roosting tree near here, as they used to have. On moonlit nights I have heard lapwings, but I have never seen them.

A few years ago, my son found and captured a pitta in a recess under the ancient wood-apple tree in my little garden. This was late in April, but obviously the bird was a migrant, for it was in an exhausted condition. Pittas visit Madras during the winter, and have been known to stray into outhouses, but I had never before seen the bird in this locality. We felt quite touched that this beautiful wanderer should have crossed so much outlying construction to find sanctuary in our modest little garden.

Another vague group belongs to the skies. In spite of the law, the skies do not belong to anyone, and have been little affected by our congested architecture. But it seems reasonable to conclude that birds sailing and soaring day after day over a particular locality find the pastime worth their while, that the lesser fauna of the place and its isolated bits of waste provide them with prey.

Abundant Variety

Except for swifts, and occasional intruders, these sky-birds are all birds of prey, that is, birds that live on anything from vegetable refuse to insects, lizards, squirrels and small birds. In this reckoning of aerial fauna, I leave out the early morning and late evening skies, through which many flighting birds pass.

There is surprising variety in the birds of our diurnal sky—besides the ubiquitous kite, there are Brahminy Kites and eagles whose flight suggests power in reserve, Scavenger Vultures on dazzling, graceful wings, hawks, even an occasional Peregrine.

About a furlong from my house there is the last patch of nature in these parts, a small, grassy field, fringed with a wide border of thin scrub, with a strange grove of dead and decapitated coconuts at one end. This is the beat of a kestrel, scanning the mean scrub for insects and small fry, from its hovering stance in the air.

Then there are the garden birds, though the gardens today are few and nominal in this place, and mostly limited to roadside trees. However, a number of birds find the vegetation adequate. There are honey-suckers where there are flowers, Tailorbirds, Coppersmiths (there are banyans along the outer roads), flaming Goldenbacked Woodpeckers looking strangely out of place in this drab setting (building in coconut groves, householders have retained a few marginal trees with thrifty forethought), Spotted Owlets where there are old trees, and Koels and White-headed Babblers. The last two are especially plentiful.

Dewar, writing some half a century ago, remarks on the abundance of Koels in Madras. The babblers are a triumph for the axiom that unity is strength. Most babblers babble, and stick together, but each sect has its own distinctive voice and demeanour. White-headed Babblers are characterized by pale, watery eyes, weak, tremulous voices that grow suddenly shrill in excitement, a certain laxity of plumage and purpose. They go hopping along to some corner, and one bird turns a dead leaf over while its fellows look on with a critical slant of their white heads—then, suddenly, the party dissolves in hysterical squeaks, and whirrs across on weak wings to another corner of the compound, where they proceed at once to turn over dead leaves again.

M. Krishnan

Clearly, the birds are daft, but they are a feature of Madras gardens (however nominal the garden) and will always be. By sheer *esprit de corps* and an inability to take life too seriously, they have prevailed where their betters have given up.

I must devote a separate paragraph to the Common Mynah. It is a highly cosmopolitan bird, and is at home in the bustle of cities, as those who have seen the bazaars of Bombay and Mysore will know. But in this locality it keeps more or less to the roadsides and open spaces, entering dwellings after the rains, when grass sprouts up in the yards and grasshoppers abound.

Two very dissimilar birds, the White-breasted Kingfisher and the Rose-ringed Parakeet, must go into one group, the garden-cum-house group. Thanks to the undependable water supply of the city, many householders here have retained the wells in their backyards, a conservatism that the kingfisher appreciates. This most interesting bird has largely given up fishing as a profession, and prefers to sit up over puddles, water-drains and other places (often far from water), hunting tadpoles, insects, lizards, anything that it can pounce upon and gobble up.

The posts of clothes lines are favourite perches with these birds—these posts are usually just the right height for them, for they like to sit up not too high above ground, being less expert on the wing than other birds that hunt from lookout posts, King Crows for example.

The parakeets are loud and numerous. They perch on coconut trees and promenade the parapets and mouldings of houses. What do they find to eat here? There are still a few fruit trees that no one cares for in our gardens—mine has three mangoes and a custard apple tree, the fruits of which I do not dispute with parakeets and squirrels. But, apparently, these versatile birds are much less dependent on cultivated fruits and grain than I had thought.

Elsewhere, I have seen parakeets taking up permanent residence in terraces and turrets, but here they are not yet our co-tenants. Most of them nest and roost in the grove of dead coconuts; the charred, black columnar trunks there are riddled with holes occupied by the parakeets—the birds lend a fresh, verdant touch to that desolation.

On ledges and parapets, these parakeets assume curious attitudes, which they rarely do when on trees. As they walk clumsily across the flat, hard cement, their backs are humped and their tails trail behind them—sometimes, on a narrow ledge, the tail is thrown up and spread against the wall by the force of friction, as the bird turns. Parakeets in classical sculpture are often shown in these very attitudes—I have heard art critics, with no eye—except for the stone, go into raptures over the rhythmic formalism of such carvings. It so happens that I have a quick sketch of a parakeet on my neighbour's terrace, in this same pose, with tail spread against the parapet wall—the illustration is a faithful copy of this sketch. I do not mention this merely to record my satisfaction at the thought that years ago, maybe 2,000 years ago, another artist was so struck by a parakeet in this pose that he depicted it, more lastingly than I can, in stone. The significant point about this is that parakeets have frequented towns and parapeted buildings from time immemorial, and that our artists have taken their models from these birds on ledges.

Lastly, co-tenants. One of these, the domestic sparrow, can be ignored—for some reason that is beyond me, it has always been a *rara avis* here. The others are very much with us, both the grey-necked House Crow and the all-black Jungle Crow. Crows are such sapient birds, their ways are so curiously dark and daring, that one could write pages about them—(Dewar has, in fact, devoted a whole book to the grey-neck)— and I dare not add another paragraph! But I will say this. I have watched civilization overtake the Jungle Crow, in my own backyard.

It was a rude, uncouth, apprehensive bird in my boyhood, lacking poise, shy and sidling in its approach to the tap for a drink, clumsy and precipitate in its getaway. Today it sits on top of the bucket with easy self-assurance, and wears a sophisticated look. The amused, tolerant glint in its eye suggests that it is reflecting impersonally over something ludicrous.

Is it possible that it is thinking, in its black mind, that in the past thirty years it has witnessed the gradual taming and civilization of one who was a robust young barbarian?

SLEEPING BIRDS

The cyclone that visited the Southern coastline recently announced itself with a sudden storm past midnight. Continuous downpours followed, and fitful gales at intervals, but it was the initial storm that caused the most damage.

The morning after, I went around in the thick grey rain, looking for signs of how the lesser life had fared. There was nothing on the roads except the litter of wrecked trees: whatever had been drowned had been removed by the turbulent drains. But nearer home I found strange sights. Two crows were roosting on a bracket beneath my neighbour's terrace eaves, fast asleep at 9 a.m.! Their slumped, almost confluent bodies and bedraggled plumage suggested a rough time in the stormy night; perhaps they were a nesting pair that had found refuge from the elements at last on that bracket. And on a gliricidia bough in the shelter of my own roof, I saw something I had never seen before, five White-headed Babblers huddled in a row, like birds in a Japanese woodcut, sleeping in exhaustion. That morning I observed more birds sleeping than I had ever before, some of them so heavily that I could have reached out and grabbed them had I wished to.

Birds and beasts, of course, need sleep just as we do—like love and hunger this is one of those deep needs 'that makes the whole world kin.' But their sleeping habits may be very different from ours, governed by different periodicities and conditions. Roosting birds like company—it is thought they find a measure of safety in close numbers; many animals sleep on a full stomach, ignoring the maxim 'After supper walk a mile,' and have almost different views from us on bedroom ventilation. What interests me is not their diverse habits of sleep so much as the question, does sleep come to them with sensations similar to the ones we feel? Any answer to this must be highly speculative, but even to indulge in such speculation we need to know quite a lot about how animals drowse and how we do—and how little we seem to know about our own repose!

Sleep can be an intensely beautiful experience. Others may think me naive, but it is the most complete bliss I have known in life, more rapturous than love, more deeply satisfying and exquisite than the slaking of a long thirst or childhood discovery of Turkish delight. It is the only sensual joy to which a man can abandon himself utterly, without self-conscious effort or any vague qualms of guilt or gluttony. And still there are people who do not realize the joy of sleep—perhaps because they woo it with pills and potions or take it too much for granted. Searching through anthologies for some passage that will express what I wish to say, I can find nothing adequate in English literature! Wordsworth's sonnet is insomnious, Coleridge too insistent on comprehensive simplicity, and even Shakespeare's celebrated lines seem too pat and encomiastic. It is with scientific unawareness of the bathos of my attempt that I tell you of sweet sleep.

It is not of the healing void of slumber that I write, but of its analgesic, sharp brink. On this thin rim, at times, the senses are clarified remarkably—the normal perceptions are inspissated, and a volatile consciousness that is objective and all-absorbing covers their thick residue. It is then that sleep is wonderful. One is no longer aware of tired, aching limbs, and sounds and smells that are utterly lost on one when alert and visual, come through with delightful ease. I think one must be dog-tired, physically, to attain this state, but perhaps I say this from an idiosyncrasy.

The commonest sounds are refined, soothing and clear just before sleep drowns them—the cawing of crows (everyone who has had a siesta in India will know just what I mean), the far-off bark of a village dog, the creaking of bullock carts. I do not mean just this, but the increased acuteness of perception that supervenes, at times, just before sleep, when the faintest of smells and sounds is clear and identifiable, and there is a certain selection of them from out of the much louder normal noises of the environment, which are not heard at all. I do not know if you have had the experience, or if I seem just wildly incomprehensible. I can only say that there is such a superfineness of sensibilities, in sleep, that is occasional and therefore unreliable in men. Sometimes this seems to subsist through sleep: I have jumped up wide-awake from sound, fatigued slumber, hearing some slight but unusual noise.

I do not know what senses are acute in a sleeping bird, but in most mammals the ears seem receptive, half-awake, in sleep. I can say nothing positive on this issue, but a series of experiments I made with sleeping dogs suggested that dogs are less quickly awakened by smells and sudden changes of lighting than by sounds, and earth tremors sensed through the body. The only other creatures whose tired-out sleep I have studied are pigeons, and they too seemed sensitive to sounds. Perhaps someone of my readers, who is a wildfowler and has tried to steal up to duck asleep, can tell me what it is that invariably wakens them in time.

JUNGLE
AND
BACKYARD

VOICES OF INTOLERANCE

I am a good neighbour. In this overcrowded city, hemmed in on all sides with the houses of other men, I am impercipient. Especially do I take no note of the uproars that break out around me from time to time—I presume these are signs of life's onward march here, just as the grating sounds from around the corner are tokens of the progress of trams, and I am incurious. But on Friday morning, I was awoken by such a varied and sustained din that overcoming my civic sense I rushed to the backyard and looked over the wall.

The hubbub came from a cassia in the compound of my neighbour to the east. A number of crows and Rose-ringed Parakeets had assembled about the tree, and in its top branches, circling round, settling, and circling again, screeching, screaming, cawing, and demonstrating at something that sat lumped, indistinct and immobile in the heart of the tree. The something was almost completely hidden by foliage and flowers—it looked large, whatever it was, and apparently it knew there was little calm outside the screen of leaves. I took a quick census of the demonstrators, since the object of their attentions was invisible. The crows (mainly grey-necks) kept flying in and out and were too numerous to be counted, but there were about two dozen of them, and there were seventeen parakeets. A surprising number, for although parakeets visit the neighbourhood, they do not roost here, and I had not thought the locality held so many of them.

For a few minutes I had to rest content with watching the demonstration, for the cause of it all gave no clue of its identity—I thought it was a large owl that had strayed into the neighbourhood, incautiously. Then unable to suffer the prying eyes and the many-keyed curses of the birds, it broke cover, climbing down surprisingly to

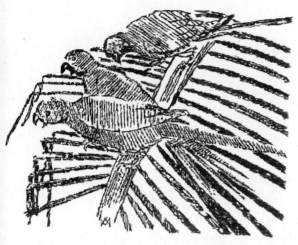

earth—a young three-fourths-grown bonnet monkey, with half its tail missing, raced across my neighbour's compound and streaked up the wall, and from it up the tall coconut tree in the corner of my backyard. Promptly the frenzied crows and parakeets shifted en masse to the coconut, and with a plainer view of their quarry demonstrated against it even more agitatedly.

There are no monkeys hereabouts—this one must have been a runaway from some gypsy's troupe. From the coconut to the great wood-apple tree in my compound, from there through a row of coconuts to a mango, and finally to the concrete parapets of my western neighbours, the fugitive took its wretched liberty, never descending to earth again, seeking the cover of foliage from the tormentors—and the birds followed every move in its progress in a vociferous mob. Only when that harassed monkey took to the housetops, abandoning green sanctuary and disappeared westwards to where there were no trees, did they stop heckling him. Then all at once the chivvying ceased, as suddenly as it had begun some half an hour earlier.

At first all this may seem trifling, and hardly worth the record, but I feel the incident is not without interest to the naturalist. For one thing, this was the first time I had seen parakeets demonstrating at a monkey, or any other creature for that matter. Dewar, I think, mentions an instance of Rose-ringed Parakeets panicking at their roost, when a hawk took one of them, but this was something quite different. Though there were many more crows there, the varied voices of the parakeets almost drowned their cawing, and the crows seemed half-hearted in their heckling, by comparison. They just flew in from neighbouring perches to the monkey's tree, and then out again; but each parakeet, before settling, circled the tree on stiff-held wings, with every long-graded tail feather outspread, heaping shrill curses on the unhappy macaque's head; they sat in rows craning over to peer through the leaves at their quarry till their heads seemed disproportionately big on the taut, thin necks, yelling vituperations, almost toppling off their perches in their excitement.

I cannot imagine why these birds were so affected by the monkey— in the countryside, where they lead an arboreal existence together, I have never seen them demonstrating at macaques. Anything out of place excites the birds of a locality, and certainly that monkey was utterly strange in that setting, but this does not seem to explain the obvious anger of the parakeets. The crows were merely a subsidiary force, drawn to the scene of action by the parakeets—they were, as I said, almost casual in their protests.

Another remarkable fact was the complete indifference of other creatures present. I noticed that the numerous squirrels of my compound, and a party of White-headed Babblers there just then, utterly ignored the monkey and its tormentors. Palm squirrels and White-headed Babblers are notoriously more given to demonstrating against enemies and intruders than parakeets, but they showed no interest whatever.

Even more remarkable was the apathy of the human population. A gardener's child threw a small stone vaguely in the direction of the monkey, as it leaped from one coconut tree to another overhead, but this was a purely formal gesture, prompted by some dim, atavistic obligation to throw things at fugitive creatures. After performing this rite, the child took no further notice of the monkey, well within his puerile range. No one else seemed even aware of the commotion in tree and air. One of my neighbours was shaving at a window seat, and got up—I hoped he would step on to his terrace to see what it was all about—but it was only to get a towel before resuming his toilet.

WHISTLING TEALS

For three days in May some years ago, I spent each day ensconced in a roomy ground hide set in the thick reeds that fringed a tal (a broad spread of shallow water) in central India; I was hoping to see the mammals that lived around there, for this was the only water within miles of that stretch of forest. Well, I did see a few of them—jackals, a mouse deer, and even a sambar hind, but what there was in plenty and there all the time, was a flock of some 150 Lesser Whistling Teals. They just stood around at ease, though their stance was semi-erect, perched on snags of dead wood or standing amidst the reeds in twos and threes, or floating on the water occasionally preening themselves but doing nothing much.

From time to time, alarmed by a motor vehicle passing with loud honks along the forest road close by, or by some visitor to the tal, they would rise in the air from the reed cover in a surprisingly large flock, in great numbers from where I had seen only half a dozen, and circle the water, gaining height with each circling, and then circle lower and lower to finally settle on the edges of the water; and all the time they were flying in a mob-formation they would keep coming out with the call which gives them their name: a rather short, cackling whistle.

The birds were said to keep to this particular spread of water almost around the year, and I wanted to know if this was true. I asked a local man who was said to know the area well and was knowledgeable in the ways of its wildlife, and he told me it was largely true: they were there all right most months, but that was not what was remarkable about them. The remarkable thing about them was that unlike other duck they subsisted on practically nothing. Surely, he asked me, watching them all day I must have noticed that they were hardly ever feeding, even when afloat on the water—they just stood around, or floated around, or preened themselves.

I said I thought they were just resting or sleeping, but he pooh-poohed the idea: it was at night that birds, excepting owls and such like, slept. It was just that they subsisted on so little—they were the poor people of the duck: drab, dingy, listless, managing with very little.

As I knew from previous conversations, this man did know the area and its animals, but he did not know these birds. I had to leave the tal well before sunset, for it was a long way to where I was staying; but elsewhere I had watched these whistling teals late in the evening—twice by brilliant moonlight, once in a paddy field. They are drowsy by day and active at night. Like many duck, they are nocturnal in their feeding, though they are more given to lethargic inactivity by day.

At sunset, before it is quite dark, whistling teals rise from the cover fringing the water in a close flock, circle their pool once or twice and then fly away to some far feeding ground—a rice field (they are much given to the nocturnal raiding of paddy) or some deep tank. They are expert swimmers and divers, and almost omnivorous in their feeding— grain, water plants, freshwater insects, crustaceans and molluscs, are all part of their diet. They seek their food zestfully, swimming and diving deep at speed, and are altogether transformed into highly active, energetic waterfowl.

During their dusk flight, too, they whistle in chorus as they fly in a flock, but their whistling then has an almost musical quality—perhaps it is some change in the temperature and humidity of the evening air that is responsible for the difference in tone of their calls.

Because they raid wetland cultivation, they are shot in places, but are 'unfit to eat' according to wildfowlers. I think it is in *A Passage to India* that there is the anecdote about an examinee who answered, briefly and to the point, 'The nightingale is not an edible bird,' when asked to annotate Keats's celebrated address to it:

Thou wert not born for death, immortal Bird!
No hungry generations tread thee down

Perhaps the Lesser Whistling Teal, too, has survived the hostility of cultivators and others for much the same reason.

THE CROW-PHEASANT

The Crow-Pheasant is an unhappily named bird, for it is neither crow nor pheasant but a non-parasitic cuckoo, the sort of cuckoo that takes posterity seriously and builds a nest instead of foisting its eggs on others. It is as big as a crow but with a longer tail, black with metallic greens and blues glossing the highlights, and round wings of pure chestnut, a bird that is unmistakable once seen or heard. It skulks in dense cover or hops about treetops, a habit not at all reminiscent of the crow, and its weak, low flight is no more corvine. But a general resemblance to a crow is there and so the first part of its name is understandable, but why 'pheasant'?

Dewar and many other European ornithologists have justified the name on the ground that, as it skulks long-tailed through the under-growth, the griffin is liable to mistake it for a pheasant. But I suspect that few novice sportsmen have bagged a Crow-Pheasant by mistake. Pheasants are not common all over India, as the Crow-Pheasant is, and moreover though this cuckoo spends quite a lot of its time on the ground it is wholly unlike any gallinaceous bird in its deportment and gait.

I have the feeling that a much sounder reason lies behind expert justification of the name 'Crow-Pheasant': the subconscious recognition of the uncouthness of the only other English name this bird has, Coucal. Incidentally, I am unable to discover the origin of the name 'Coucal'; perhaps it is African, for the African Crow-Pheasant is also called by the same name. However, it is a useful word to those planning crossword puzzles.

The vernacular names of this bird are equally incomprehensible. In Tamil names, 'Shanbakha-pakshi' and 'Sembothu' are uninterestingly causeless, but in Kannada it is called 'Sambarakagi' which, translated literally, means 'spice-crow'. Once I asked a Kannadiga why it was named so, and he explained the reason—because it looks rather like a crow, and because in cooking its flesh, which is valued medicinally, it is wise to use plenty of spices! This is the bird that comes out with a deep, solemn *whoop, whoop, whoop* from a clump of bamboos or some thickly grown corner of the compound, or even from a treetop on occasion. The call, most often heard early in the morning, at noon, or at sunset, is unmistakable but hard to describe in words. Dewar calls it a 'low, loud, sonorous *whoot, whoot, whoot*, the kind of call that one associates with an owl'—I must say that though the commas he has used to punctuate the call are more indicative of the intervals than the usual hyphens are, I have never been able to find anything owl-like in the call. Lowther gives a much nearer rendering: a deep, booming *whoop-whoop-whoop*, pleasant to listen to, sometimes mistaken for the cry of the black-faced langur monkey. The resemblance to the normal *whoop* (not the alarm call) of the langur is very much there, but no one who has heard the Crow-Pheasant is likely to mistake its voice for that of any other creature, bird, beast or reptile.

Every large, old-fashioned garden is likely to attract the Crow-Pheasant, especially the ones planted with a clump of bamboo in a corner; it is equally common in groves and large public parks, well-wooded avenues and in the purlieus of villages. As per old South Indian traditions, the bird is one of the hereditary enemies of snakes, and for once tradition is true, for it will kill and eat small snakes, besides other small reptiles, frogs and insects. I have seen it eating a banyan fig and perhaps it supplements its hunting with occasional fruit.

I know a rather curious but true story about this bird, I don't think it is one of those birds considered specially auspicious by native superstitions (such as the King Crow or the roller, the sight of which, when one sets out on an important errand, assures success). But some of us started the legend about the Crow-Pheasant in a small, illiterate rural community, purely for a joke. In a few years it had caught on and spread, and I was solemnly assured by a native that it was exceedingly lucky to see the bird when starting on any mission or quest; when questioned, he informed me that he heard about this omen from his father who, no doubt, had it from his father—which conclusively established its authenticity!

M. Krishnan

A JEKYLL-AND-HYDE BIRD

One of the most destructive bird pests of agriculture and horticulture. Keeps in small parties or large noisy rabbles which often band together in enormous swarms to raid ripening crops of jowar, maize and other cereals, and orchard fruits. The birds clamber about the twigs and gnaw into the half-ripe fruits, wasting far more than they actually eat. Or they descend in swarms upon ripening fields of food crops, biting into the ears of the grain or cutting off the head completely and flying with it to a nearby tree where it is raised up to the bill with one foot and after a nibble or two wastefully discarded, the bird soon returning to the field to renew its ravages.

That is the verdict of the best authorities on our avifauna, Salim Ali and Dillon Ripley, on the Rose-ringed Parakeet. Henry, writing on the birds of Sri Lanka, says this parakeet 'is partial to ripening paddy...biting off whole ears and wasting far more than it consumes.' And Baker and Inglis, in their old book on the birds of South India, say 'it does immense damage to fruit, as we know to our own cost, especially to guava trees, littering the ground below with half-eaten fruit.'

Bunched Pods

I have just looked up these citations, after spending half an hour closely watching a pair of Rose-ringed Parakeets feeding off the bunched pods of a cluster-beans plant in my neighbour's kitchen garden—everything was in sharply revealed detail as I watched through my binoculars, with the birds only about twenty metres away. They ate only the seeds within each slim, green pod after deftly splitting it open along its length into two halves, not wasting even a single small seed. After they left, the clusters of pods on the bush remained intact, but suddenly doubled with each pod split neatly into two along its seams. I have noticed the same painstaking method of feeding when these parakeets feasted on the seeds of the pods of the flame of the forest trees along the Kachida Valley road in the Ranthambhor Tiger Reserve.

There, the two halves of the split pod, being broader and thicker, soon withered and fell away, so that only a month after the trees had burst into prodigal red bloom not a single pod could be seen on them, and there was no natural regeneration. How can one reconcile this meticulously tidy mode of feeding by this bird with its frantic and extravagantly wasteful ways, testified to by such eminent authorities?

The clue, I think, lies in the fact that my neighbours have gone away on a holiday and there is no one there to look after the kitchen garden. With no risk of human hostility in their backyard now, as in the Kachida Valley, the parakeets take their time splitting open each pod methodically to get at the seeds within. However, even when no man is near, they do waste more than they consume, feeding on guavas and similar fruits, or when (as in a field of ripening grain) there is so much in abundance that there is no need for thrift.

Not for a moment do I suggest that these birds are not the pests that others have so emphatically asserted they are, but on occasion they can be remarkably tidy too in their feeding, even delicate. Anyone who has kept a parakeet as a pet will know that when the supply of food is well chosen and rationed, little is wasted, and that when offered something the bird specially fancies (such as a ripe red chilli) every little morsel is consumed. The truth is the Rose-ringed Parakeet is a Jekyll-and-Hyde bird.

Dual Personality

Its voice also offers another instance of its remarkable dual personality. In most Indian languages, poets describing feminine charm have often endowed their heroines with voices 'as sweet as a parakeet's'! I could never understand why our poets, so responsive to the importunate,

M. Krishnan

mounting yearning in the calls of the Koel and the papiha, had been so deaf to the screechy shrillness in the voice of the parakeet that they could think of such a simile. An acquaintance of mine who had a pet parakeet, a man who was something of a poet himself, once disputed this point with me. He argued that our poets had in mind not the uninhibited shrieks of wild parakeets, but the sweetness of the words that a captive bird had been taught—an unconvincing argument, for the only words his own pet could articulate, in a rasping, challenging tone, were 'Who the hell are you?'

Then, one summer I stayed for a fortnight in a first-floor room outside the window of which there was a great pipal tree, with a Rose-ringed Parakeet's nest-hole in its bole at the level of the window. There were two nearly full-fledged nestlings in it, and periodically the parent bird would arrive to feed them with regurgitated fruit pulp, and perching on a twig just above, summon its young to the mouth of the nest-hole with a low, long, tremulous, ineffably sweet call—hiding behind the window-curtain, I have heard that call many times and can find no words to convey its tender sweetness. Maybe our poets knew a thing or two that we, prosaic naturalists, do not realize they knew.

THE PECKING ORDER

Around eight in the morning, when the early birds are no longer vocal and the sun tops my roof to hit the coconut palms in my backyard almost at a right angle, I hear harsh, cackling laughter and know that the woodpeckers have arrived. These are the familiar Goldenbacked Woodpeckers, the commonest of woodpeckers, especially in and around human habitations, and they are in a pair: the male with a flamboyant crimson crown and crest, and the female with the crest red but the crown black, minutely speckled with white. Incidentally, there are less common Goldenbacked Woodpeckers of a different genus altogether, but those are forest birds.

My Coconuts

For two weeks now this pair has been visiting my coconuts regularly, late in the mornings and usually again an hour before sunset, their arrival invariably announced by their unmistakable cackling laughter-like call. They settle on the upright boles, their strong, sharp-clawed feet well apart and the stiff, pointed shafts of the tail feathers bracing the wood behind them in a tripodal support. They go up the vertical trunks with quick, jerky movements, often in a somewhat spiral ascent, halting every now and again to peck at something or to scrutinize narrowly a crevice or a protrusion in the bark. At times, they indulge in an amazing movement in reverse gear, descending a short distance in a deft, downward slide—I have not seen any other woodpecker doing this.

Last September, too, they were much in evidence in my backyard, and in summer this year. Were the birds the same? Unless they had been caught, banded and released, one could never be sure of such identification—but it seemed to be the same pair: the birds seem so set in their habits. Why are they visiting the coconut trees so regularly, soon after the sun was on them? At first I wondered if they were seeking to site their nesting hole in a coconut bole, as they often do, making a neat, circular hole in the wood with their chisel-tipped wedge-shaped bill, and then boring a downward tunnel to the nest-bottom.

But this cannot be the motive, since it is in summer that these birds begin to propagate their species. I think it is the ants that are the draw. Like most woodpeckers, these are also much given to feeding on ants, and all over my house and grounds there are ants now, many kinds of them—big and black, small, black and swift, and red—and given to biting fiercely. The nights are humid and it is only after the early morning sun dries up surface moisture that the ants begin to run all over the ground and up trees.

In a park featuring many small, woody trees I have closely watched these woodpeckers hunting ants. They come down to the ground, and their legs being adapted to an arboreal, not a terrestrial, life, hop along somewhat gawkily. But they are able to pick up the ants before ascending the base of the slim trunk from which they have descended; going all round it and capturing the fleeing quarry.

In summer, the attraction in my neighbourhood is obviously something else: the coral tree in my neighbour's territory, overhanging his terrace and heavy with sprays of big, scarlet flowers early in the hot weather. Once I spent a whole morning in an improvised hide on that terrace, and had a good, close look at the many birds that visited the coral tree to feed on the nectar in the big, red flowers—bulbuls, babblers, Black Drongos, a Golden Oriole, sunbirds, mynahs, even a crow and a pair of Goldenbacked Woodpeckers. The woodpeckers with their tapered beaks and highly extensile tongues seemed far more adept at getting the nectar from the flowers than the other birds.

Summer Visits

It was during their summer visits, I noticed, that these woodpeckers indulged in short bursts of tapping on the trees (including the coconuts). Now, while the way in which woodpeckers drum on wood, and the different patterns of the drumming and the duration of such noise production have been observed and noted, the precise motive that makes them drum is not clearly established, and there seems to be more than one motive. Obviously, the drumming of some of the larger kinds is for communication—advertisement of the presence of the bird indulging in the activity. For instance, the Great Black Woodpecker, as large as a crow and vividly black, with white in a patch just above the tail, a white abdomen and a flaming red crest, comes out with a long-drawn spell of powerful drumming which has been aptly compared to 'a burst of machine-gun fire', and which sets the hill forest vibrating.

This does serve effectively to announce the bird's presence and may well be, during the breeding season, a means of establishing territory. But other woodpeckers, such as the Goldenback, do not drum in this manner, but only indulge in a brief tattoo—a quick, rhythmic tapping of the surface on which they are—which probably serves to dislodge or bolt the insect prey sheltering under the bark or in a crevice. The same action can have different connotations with different animals, even with the same animal, when it is varied in a manner that we, human observers, cannot readily appreciate.

M. Krishnan

PIED KINGFISHERS

Kingfishers are another highly specialized family of birds, adapted for a particular way of life. With an exception or two, they subsist mainly on fish and other aquatic prey, even diving right into the water to secure their catch. There are a baker's dozen species in India, varying in size from small birds no larger than a sparrow to the Himalayan Pied Kingfisher which is as big as a House Crow. However, all of them have the same distinctive build: big-headed, short-necked and top-heavy, with a prominent straight, long, stout, pointed beak and quite small legs and feet, with the front toes more or less joined together.

They are brilliantly coloured in blues, blue-green, purplish violet, brown and white, or else pied black-and-white. Their beaks and feet are deep red in some kinds, black in others. The Lesser Pied Kingfisher is widely distributed over India where there are rivers, streams and lakes. It is the size of a mynah, speckled black-and-white on top, with a double gorget of black across the white breast in the male, and a single gorget in the female: the tail is black with a white tip, and the beak and legs black. Even apart from its distinctive looks, it is readily identified even from afar by its mode of hunting. When seeking prey, it usually flies over the water at a height of about six metres; on sighting its quarry beneath the surface, it halts in the air on hovering wings, like a kestrel, holding itself upright with its beak pointing downwards, and making sure, dives headlong right in, emerging with its catch in its beak, to fly to a perch on the bank and batter it to death before swallowing it head first. It is often seen in a pair, a little distance apart, and when fed and not hunting, the pair stay together perched on the bank.

As its name suggests, the Himalayan Pied Kingfisher (the largest of the family in our country) is a bird of the submontane Himalayan

Lesser Pied Kingfisher

Himalayan Pied Kingfisher

range. Apart from being much bigger than its lesser cousin, it is also slightly different in plumage. Both birds have a thinly white-streaked black nuchal crest, but the Himalayan lacks a black gorget across the breast and on top it is barred black-and-white. It does not hover over its prey. But it keeps a sharp lookout from a convenient perch and plunges in at a slant to secure its victim.

Like other kingfishers, both kinds of Pied Kingfishers nest in earth banks, digging a long horizontal tunnel into the bank, enlarged at the end into an unlined egg chamber.

WINGED PIRATE

Every morning, on waking, I hear the somewhat weak, unmistakable trilling of a White-breasted Kingfisher. There is a well with an electric pump outside my bedroom window, in my neighbour's backyard, and the kingfisher sits on a pipe above the cistern and greets the risen sun with its tremulous song. At other times, too, I hear it, especially before sunset and while in rapid flight, but its voice then is quite different, a series of grating calls—the early morning performance is its song, sustained and very subdued by comparison.

I think it is a very old bird, going by its looks and colour. It is squat, with a conspicuous spread to the white of its shirt-front, and the blue of its back has a faded, Prussian-blue tinge—in young birds, I have noticed, the blue is warmer and much brighter, deep cerulean or new blue, the deep bay of the head and neck has a decided maroon shade, and the beak is Indian red or redder; this colouring is typical even of quite adult birds. But in my bird the head and neck are a deep burnt umber, and even the beak is a dark brown, with its tip alone pale. I think it is an old cock, for on several occasions I have seen it chasing away a younger, brighter White-breasted Kingfisher which also lives in the neighbourhood.

It is what the bird eats that interests me specially. Everyone knows that this kingfisher is much less dependent on fish than others of its tribe, and is often to be found far from rivers and broad sheets of water. Not that it cannot plunge into deep water and fish like other kingfishers, but while not averse to water (it loves a good splash when bathing), it is far more cosmopolitan in its diet. It loves a perch overlooking a well, or a puddle, or an open gutter, and will freely take tadpoles, small frogs, earthworms, crickets, and other moisture-loving small fry: it also hunts dry-land grasshoppers, mantises and similar insects, and only yesterday

I saw this old pirate of my neighbour's well leave its perch, dart straight into a hibiscus bush, pluck a gecko from a twig without alighting, and return to its pipeline to swallow its catch.

I have also seen this bird carry off a centipede, a young skink, and some tiny, squirming, hairy something that looked suspiciously like a caterpillar. However, when the termites swarmed after the first rain of summer, I noticed that it was practically the only predatory creature that was not hunting. One curious habit of this bird that I noticed was that after swallowing sizeable prey it often jerked its entire body and head stiffly up and down in a rather reptilian movement.

Kingfishers are exceptionally keen-sighted, and can see quite well even when the light is dim, as in shady locations. But I suspect that the birds are not able to see when it is really dark—an illogical suspicion, for they nest in deep burrows in the earth where it is quite dark.

I remember climbing softly down a well at night when I was a boy, to capture a dozing kingfisher perched on a projecting ledge; I also remember how surprisingly light the bird felt in the hand, and the painful swiftness of its jabbing beak. Perhaps it is that kingfishers sleep heavily at night as many birds do, and not that they cannot see well in the dark. Unfortunately, I do not know and cannot find out where this musical pirate next door roosts at night. Otherwise I might be able to conduct some tests to verify my suspicions.

LONE SENTINEL OF THE PUDDLES

Life has grown wet and plastic during the past week. Visitors bring in footloads of mud which they scrape against the stone steps or distribute over the veranda—being given to petty joys, I note with satisfaction that when they go away, the sodden gravel leading to my gate shakes off at each step from their shoes, and that I have gained soil. The ditches flanking the road are turned into brown rivulets, and the dip in the field beyond, hardly perceptible in September, is now a miniature pond.

All this wetness is different from the somewhat formalized depictions of wetness that we are so used to. There would be white glints and dimpled blue patches in an artist's picture of these October puddles and flooded drains, and turbulent streaks of red, perhaps, to denote the freshets. Actually, the lowering skies yield no highlights; everywhere the water is a torpid, deep umber, thick with mud and squirming with infant life. Almost as if by magic, innumerable mosquito larvae and tadpoles have appeared in the pond in the field, even little fish. Life began in the slush, according to biologists, and the slush is very fecund still. As I bend over its squelching rim to peer into the pond's teeming depths, I am conscious that I am not alone.

Another huddled watcher is on the other side, acutely aware of me. My cautious advent has driven it several yards away, and now it seems on the point of flight. I retreat to the roadside and squat immobile, and the Pond Heron returns to the water, step by deliberate step, its apprehensive head stretched out in front on its long neck. It stops at the water's edge, and is immediately harder to see. The extended neck is doubled up and drawn in between the shoulders, so far in that the bird is neckless; the streaked brown of its humped back and the yellowish greys of its legs and beak blend with the muddy background. It walks carefully into the water, lifting each foot clear of the surface and carrying it forward through the air before immersing it quietly again, and now its neck is again outstretched—it is withdrawn once more as the bird halts, and takes its stance in the shallows.

For two long minutes it stays—utterly still, only the hard, yellow glint in its eye betraying the avid life in the dull, slumped body.

While fish that pass pass by,
till the destined fish comes in,
Great is the heron's dejection

—says a cynical couplet, in Tamil. Presently, and without the least warning stir, the dagger-billed head shoots down on the extensile neck, a tadpole is lifted deftly out of the thick water, and swallowed in the same movement. At once the neck is drawn in, and the morose, huddled pose is resumed, so quickly and completely that I could have sworn that its waiting had been unbroken, had I not watched the movement.

The Pond Heron or 'paddy bird' is probably the most familiar of our waterside birds. Wherever there is not too rapid water, a puddle or a pond or any shallow stretch, you will find it there, an unmistakable little heron with dingy plumage, a humped back and sulky habits. When alarmed it emits a harsh *kra-ak* and is instantly transformed into a dazzling creature on broad white wings—its pinions and underparts are white, but hidden except in flight by its earthy mantle, and in flight it seems an all-white bird. Americans in India used to call this heron the 'surprise bird', from the sudden contrast between its drab, unobtrusive repose and the flashing whiteness of its flight; I believe the name is no longer in fashion.

Though roosting and nesting in company, Pond Herons are unsociable by day. They are lone hunters; occasionally you may see three or four near one another, but they never seek prey in common, and even when going home to roost do not join together in large flocks. They are strong fliers, and though they look rather like Cattle Egrets in size and whiteness when on the wing, it is easy to tell their firm, quick wingbeats from the lubberly action of the egrets.

M. Krishnan

Incidentally, all herons fly with their necks tucked in. Wordsworth's—

And heron, as resounds the trodden shore,
Shoots upward, darting his long neck before.

—might be quite true of a heron shooting up into the air in alarm, but once it settles down to flight the neck is not darted before, but is doubled up and drawn in—that, in fact, is the token by which one may know members of the heron tribe from other waterside birds on the wing.

THE INDIAN TREE PIE

The Indian Tree Pie is an attractive-looking bird, though it sports no brilliant blue or green in its plumage, or a bright red or yellow beak, like its cousins, the magpies of the sub-Himalayan North and of Sri Lanka. It is the contrast of sober, soft colours and its long tail that endow it with looks: the head, neck and upper breast are sooty black, and the body a light brown on top and a lighter brown below, the pinions are black and the top of the wings looks conspicuously white in flight—the long, graduated tail is grey and broadly tipped black, with the central tail feathers whitish above their black tips.

It is a woodland bird with a very wide, almost ubiquitous range in India, though it is not found outside. It especially favours deciduous forests. In its habits, its relationship to the common crow is evident on a close look. It has the same stout, convex beak and strong-toed, curve-clawed feet, which it uses much like a crow to hold down small prey and peck and tear it to bits. In its hunting it is as alert and persistent as any crow, and it has the corvine habit of tilting its head sideways to scrutinize objects. Perhaps because of its long tail, it is not so much at home on the ground as crows are and keeps mainly to the trees, though it does come down to the earth when it has to and can hop about.

In its flight, however, it is wholly unlike a crow. Its wings are shorter in proportion, lacking the spread and length needed for air-mastery. Crows are strong and expert on the wing, covering considerable distances with a rhythmic, rowing action, and can twist and turn in the air dexterously. The tree pie seldom indulges in a long flight, and in its passage from one treetop to another it dips and rises in the air, alternating a quick flutter of its wings with a short sail.

It does feed on wild fruits, but its food consists mainly of insects, caterpillars, tree-frogs, lizards, the eggs and nestlings of other birds and similar high-protein fare.

Mynahs, Cattle Egrets and King Crows follow grazing animals, not only cattle but also deer and even rhinos and wild pigs, for the insects they flush from the grass when they move on, and they often perch on grazing animals; some, even crows, pick ectoparasites like ticks off these herbivores. But the tree pie goes further. When deer, especially sambar, are in the last stages of antler regeneration and the velvet is coming off the hard-horn in shreds, tree pies pull off and consume these shreds.

Salim Ali once wrote a diatribe on urban and suburban crows, suggesting that they should be shot down because of their persistence in seeking out the nests of smaller birds in gardens and parks and devouring their eggs and young. The tree pie is seldom to be seen in towns or populous villages, but as a woodland egg-stealer and baby snatcher it is no less persistent and painstaking.

In jungleside settlements, and in the interior rest-houses of some wildlife preserves, tree pies often take the place of crows as scavengers of kitchen refuse. It is remarkable how shrewdly they pick out small bits of cooked meat or eggs from the vegetable scraps thrown out along with them. Once, to test the bird's selective skill in this, I wrapped up pieces of an omelette in the skins of cooked tomatoes, and stuck the tiny packages on the spiky twigs of a dead and dried-up tall bush that stood outside the kitchen of the forest rest-house I was staying in. Sure enough the visiting tree pie turned up a little later, and inspecting the stuck titbits first with its head tilted to one side and then to the other, picked them up one by one and deftly unwrapped the tomato skins and gobbled up what was inside them.

Not the least remarkable thing about this perky bird is its voice. It does not croak or caw like a crow, but has a number of harsh rasping calls, varied from time to time with a musical, metallic *ting-a-ling-a-ling* as of struck bells. And though I cannot be sure of it, I suspect that it can, on occasion, also imitate the calls of other birds. There was a tree pie haunting a forest lodge I was in some years ago, and I often heard the mellow, liquid whistle of an oriole from a tree just outside, but could never find any oriole anywhere around—only the tree pie!

AMATEUR ASSASSIN

In a world where life depends so frequently on lesser life, the killers usually know their job. Their methods are swift and efficient, not out of self-conscious mercy but because by quick killing they avoid many risks to themselves. Sometimes there is hardly any killing—with a lizard or bird feeding on small insects it is just stalking, seizing and swallowing. And even where a killer takes on sizeable prey, too large and strong for instant dispatch, there is no intentional cruelty, and possibly, in the excitement of the fight for dear life, less pain than we imagine.

Many cynical naturalists have pointed out that it is only man that inflicts pain with the will to hurt. I will not repeat that; we are also sensitive to the suffering of others in a way that few animals are, often with a superimposition of sentimentality over deeply felt sympathy. I only wish to say that there is not much scope for sentiment in any study of the murder technique of animals.

Most killers are efficient but a few are not; these latter are usually creatures that have taken to a predatory life for which they are not fully equipped by nature. Among these is the Jungle Crow, which was named long ago when it was less common in urban areas than it is now.

It is a bird equipped for a life of scavenging, plunder, theft and insect hunting; intelligent, long-lived and capable of much individuality. It is not such a dexterous flier at low elevations as its grey-necked cousin, though Whistler comments on its aerobatic skill. It is big and black and has a wicked bill, but lacks the talons of the true killer; in fact, it never uses its feet for seizing anything in the air.

It is given to carrion feeding in the countryside, and is an inveterate egg thief everywhere. It has long been known to attack maimed birds and fledglings, but I do not know whether it has always been an amateur assassin as well, a role in which I have known it many times.

When I was a boy I was a tumbler fancier. I learned, then, that it was necessary not only to protect eggs and unfledged squabs from these crows, but also to shut in young and inexperienced birds before dusk. Such youngsters were chased by the crows into the gathering darkness and as night approached the pigeons could no longer see their way about while the crows could; they were apt to panic and get lost. I do not know whether the crows actually got them in the end, but they never came back.

Jungle Crows kill bloodsuckers in a particularly revolting manner, by slow torture and paralysis of the hindquarters. The bird looks sufficiently big and powerful for a forthright attack, but always uses the utmost circumspection. It comes in from behind and tugs at the lizard's tail, avoids the open-mouthed rushes of its victim by hopping aside, and tugs and pecks at the base of the tail repeatedly—unfortunately for itself the bloodsucker has not the fragile tail of the geckoes. Slowly the lizard loses the ability to pivot around on its hind legs, and is then pecked from nearer till it sinks; it is then carried away.

Sometimes two crows take part in the killing, so that when the lizard turns on one adversary, it exposes its hindquarters and tail to the other—it is the grey-necked House Crow, rather than the Jungle Crow that hunts in pairs like this.

People do not realize, quite often, what is taking place when they see crows hopping around a bloodsucker and tugging playfully at its tail. Such a close observer as 'Eha' was misled into thinking the birds were having a game with the lizard—it is no game, but cold-blooded murder. When cover is handy the bloodsucker may escape, but usually the birds wait till it is well in the open before attacking.

A pair of Jungle Crows that live near me are much given to baby-snatching. I have seen them hunting baby squirrels among the tiles and eaves of roofs, and recently I saw one of them abduct and devour a fully fledged White-headed Babbler. This was at sunset, as the light was just about to fade. It held the youngster by the nape in its beak and flew off to a parapet its victim squeaking loudly all the while. There was a full contingent of grown White-headed Babblers close by but none of them went to the rescue of their abducted child—an amazing reversal of their normal behaviour. The crow sat on the parapet, right in the open, and killed its prey by repeated blows of its heavy beak. When I went near, it carried the little corpse away, plucked almost clean of feathers.

M. Krishnan

THE GREATER OWLS

In our classical traditions, the foe the crows fear is the owl, and last week a classical scholar came to me with a doubt over this age-old tradition. Crows are diurnal and owls, as everyone knows, are nocturnal: so how could their paths cross, and anyway how could an owl kill a bird as big, brisk and blackguardly as a crow?

This seemingly logical objection is fallacious. Nocturnal predators will certainly take prey that is diurnal by nature if they come upon it in the dark. It is true that wholly diurnal prey species seek a safe retreat with sunset to escape night hunters, but this prudent habit does not always save them. All our monkeys are wholly diurnal and roost high up trees at night, but, on occasion, the leopard does get them, by panicking them into leaping down to the ground to bolt to some other tree.

Moreover, the scope of the predator is far greater when a nocturnal bird of prey hunts a roosting diurnal bird. Actually, crows are not strictly diurnal: they do roost close together at night, foregathering at some chosen tree from all around, but when the moon is bright they are still active flitting from tree to tree—and even when they are together and still on a treetop nothing prevents a big owl from taking one of the roosting crows, an outlier that it can grab and throttle.

The power of grip of an owl's talons is formidable. Once when a superstitious and trigger-happy neighbour shot a Spotted Owlet (no larger than a mynah), I picked up the fallen bird. With its last breath it clutched my thumb in one foot and died immediately thereafter, and long after I had extricated my thumb from its unrelaxing grasp, it still felt numb.

I explained all this to that scholar and assured him that our largest owls were twice the size of a crow and could kill prey even heavier than themselves, but he remained sceptical. The way to convince a scholar is not by reasoning or the authority of one's own knowledge—it is the printed word that he respects and accepts. So I hunted up an old ornithological treatise, and showed him two passages in it about our two largest owls. The first was Stuart Baker's account of the Forest Eagle-Owl in which he says—he 'saw one bring down a roosting peafowl and another feasting on a big civet cat.' The second was about the Dusky Horned Owl, equally big but less purely nocturnal and less limited to dense, dark forests: this citation was conclusive on the point referred to me, for it said that this owl 'feeds principally on crows, but also on animals of some size.' I pointed out that both the peafowl and civet must have weighed considerably more than their killer, and he went away satisfied, happy that the natural history of his ancient texts had been proved correct.

I have little personal acquaintance with the Forest Eagle-Owl but have long known the Dusky Horned Owl, and also the third and last of our biggest owls, the Great Horned Owl (which, in spite of its name, is actually a shade smaller than the other two). When I lived in the Deccan, I often saw a pair of Dusky Horned Owls that haunted a precipitous, rocky gorge, bush grown on top. Late in the evening, they would perch on the boulders above the gorge, squat, grey, cubist shapes (the thin, black vertical streaks on the breast are visible only when the bird is seen close on hand, even by good lighting) with the 'horns' silhouetted against the paler grey of the darkening sky.

And coming home from that gorge along the six-kilometre avenue closely flanked by tamarind trees, I have sometimes heard their love song. A sudden series of banshee shrieks and demoniac groans would shatter the darkness overhead, to be answered no less startlingly and diabolically from another tamarind top farther away, and though I knew it was only these courting owls, the experience was always blood-curdling.

The normal reaction of big owls to close human approach is to indulge in a threat display, fluffing out the soft, lax plumage till they look half as large again as they were, half opening the wings over the flanks, in the attitude known to falconers as 'mantling', and clicking the tips of the beak together. The bold, black streaks over the breast and the finely barred plumage below the breast are characteristic of the Great Horned Owl. Its eyes have orange irises—the iris is yellow in the Dusky Horned Owl and dark brown in the Forest Eagle-Owl.

All these three big owls belong to the same genus *Bubo*, though formerly the Forest Eagle-Owl was classed apart. All have conspicuous 'horns' and legs feathered down to the toes: all are powerful predators that can, and do, kill sizeable prey, but usually feed on smaller and more readily available creatures like field rats and mice, small snakes, lizards, and even crabs and beetles. These big owls can come zooming into their perch at high speed, dexterously avoiding twigs and branches in the way, and in silence, for their pinions are soft and flexible. They will not hesitate to attack men who intrude on their nest—it was to an owl that the well-known bird photographer, Eric Hosking, lost an eye.

THE SENTINELS OF DEATH

There are no vultures in Sri Lanka. In the course of the past century, two or three White Scavenger Vultures (the smallest of the clan) have been recorded, but were obvious vagrants. They never bred there, nor has any other vulture been even sighted in that country.

Considering the superb air mastery of these birds and their ability to cover great distances on the wing, it is strange that they have not crossed the narrow channel to Sri Lanka from South India, when other birds have done so. No explanation of this paradox seems to have been advanced. Vultures soar for hours at great heights on thermals—is it possible that over the sea such hot air currents do not obtain at heights? I do not know but I have never seen a vulture soaring over the sea, and probably others also have not: further, when two countries are separated by an ocean, the same species of vultures are not to be found in both. Not knowing, I consulted an oceanographer, and he dismissed the idea rudely and summarily as just so much hot air. I noticed, though, that he said nothing about oceanic air currents. Perhaps he, too, did not know.

Main Concern

This speculation is not as idle as it might seem. The main concern of vultures is dead meat. Though so big and equipped with heavy, hooked, flesh-tearing beaks, they do not hunt living prey—the few rare instances of a vulture attacking some small disabled creature are not relevant in this context. Their survival depends on their ability to spot a carcass from high in the sky, and they scour the heavens vigilantly over vast distances seeking such subsistence. Most vultures keep together in groups and reside within an extensive home ground, and when one of them spots food and descends, the others descend along with it, and demolish even a large carcass in an incredibly short time; frequently, more than one group of vultures of more than one kind associate in this gruesome orgy, and there are timed records of even a dead bullock being picked clean to mere bones within forty minutes!

After gorging themselves, sometimes to such repletion that they are unable to rise in the air and stay sprawled on the ground with outspread wings, the birds can go without food for days on end, something essential for survival when the finding of carcasses of any size is so chancy a matter. But on occasion, when food becomes scarce within their beat or is more freely available outside it, they may shift ground. Writing of the commonest Indian species, the Whitebacked Vulture, Salim Ali has this interesting information: 'Where absent or rare in pure desert facies a few years ago, e.g. Sind, Punjab and Rajasthan, now well established and expanding with advent of river barrages, canal cultivation, populous villages with livestock, and trees for nesting.'

Such shifts would, naturally, depend not only on the increasing availability of food and amenities outside an established territory, but also on the dwindling of these same resources within it. Note that unlike some other scavenging animals (such as crows and jackals), vultures have no use for food in garbage heaps or abandoned in the open when it is of a vegetarian nature. They are the sentinels of death, and must have dead flesh to live.

In the historic past, when internecine wars were not uncommon in our country, vultures were the chief means of disposal of the dead in battlefields, as classical literature bears testimony. Even today, their names in some Indian languages refer to their feeding on human corpses, names such as 'corpse-eater' and 'battlefield kite'. The practice common all over the country of abandoning dead livestock where they have fallen around human settlements, and the remains of the kills of wild predators in the jungles are their sources of sustenance today, and both seem to be dwindling.

Around large cities where there are sizeable vulture populations (Delhi is a good example), the risk to aircraft from the birds is a major problem, and the authorities have advised the disposal of dead animals and slaughterhouse refuse in such a way that the vultures cannot get at them. In some locations I know, of which Whitebacked Vultures were quite a feature, they have almost vanished today, apparently having shifted. But where have they shifted to?

Few Records

From the few records of such shifts available, the shift will be to towns and cities where there are slaughterhouses and where the disposal of animal remains is indiscriminate, or else to dry, open countryside where there are human settlements and, inevitably livestock, especially cattle. Whitebacked Vultures may not cross the seas, but they can and do fly over hill ranges, even elevated ranges. Therefore they will not be hampered in their shifts by the peninsular hills, but the Himalayas (which have their own high-elevation vultures) are a different matter altogether. The Whiteback, which has been such a considerable help to man and wild beast for centuries by its swift disposal of dead flesh before it became putrid and harmful, seems unlikely to be able to emigrate to countries beyond ours, and, within, it is apparently on the decline now.

M. Krishnan

THUGGERY IN THE TREETOPS

For the past month I have been hearing the thin, high, petulant *ki-kiyu* of the Shikra, and occasionally I have seen the bird in the dazzling midday sky—whirring along on quick, blurred pinions, then sailing in an ascending circle on still, round wings, the long tail spread like a half-shut, banded fan. There are two of these hawks about, that call and answer in the same querulous tone, though they seem to keep a certain distance apart. By these tokens I know they are a courting pair that will later nest somewhere near, probably in the clump of mangoes a quarter-mile away.

Ordinarily the Shikra is not given to high jinks and public appearances, for it lives by thuggery and thugs do not proclaim themselves. It lurks in obscuring foliage, waiting for the unsuspecting victim to approach before pouncing down on it, and when it goes from tree to tree, its passage announced by the shrill twitters of little birds and the alarm *cheep*s of squirrels, it keeps low and flies direct and fast. Even when it goes coasting the fields, as it does at times, it hugs the contour of each dip and hollow and takes good care to keep below any line of trees, so that it may arrive unexpectedly at the next field. It is capable of determined pursuit and speed over a short distance, but furtive means and attacks from ambush are what it favours.

But just before it pairs and breeds, it takes freely to the air and goes soaring on high. Its harsh, grating voice then changes to a high, frequent *ki-kiyu*, a call that is exchanged all day from the wing and even from perches between the courting pair. To human ears few bird calls are more expressive of tantalized impatience at the slow, tedious progress of love imposed by nature! However, the call is also used at other times. I have heard an angry Shikra, attacking crows, repeatedly indulge in this

call—it seemed louder and less plaintive then, with a challenging ring in it, but this was probably because I heard it from so near.

When the sun sinks behind the trees and night is imminent, sparrows and other small birds flock to their roosts, and the Shikra is well aware of this opportunity. It lies in wait, huddled, in some thick-leaved tree, and if a little bird alights nearby it makes its plunge, flinging itself bodily through twig and leaf. Often enough the quarry escapes, and then the hawk may fly swift and low to another tree, or lurk on in the same ambush. There is no rule governing its behaviour on such occasions, except that it fails quite frequently in its dusk hunting. One February evening, I followed a Shikra from 6.25 p.m. till close on seven o'clock— it made three attempts to snatch its dinner in that time, and having failed, flew away over the horizon when it was almost dark.

The Shikra is capable of a fine courage, too, when there is need for courage. It can tackle mynahs and birds almost as big as itself, as the old-time falconers knew well, and it will fight even larger birds on occasion. Once I was watching a Shikra eating a bloodsucker on the branch of a neem, when first one Jungle Crow, and then another, came up and settled on a branch close by. The hawk resented their covetous glances and their sidling closer, and abandoning its prey it flung itself at the intruders with a torrent of *ki-kiyus*—I was amazed at this onslaught, for the crows were larger birds and by no means incapable of fighting, moreover there were two of them.

So impetuous' was the attack that all three birds came tumbling down in a frantic ball of black and barred feathers, that rolled about on the ground below for a moment before resolving itself into two crows that fled for dear life and an angry, open-beaked hawk. Both crows must have been grabbed simultaneously, one in each taloned foot, for this to have happened, but incredible as it may seem, it did happen. I would much like to tell you how the victor returned to the hard-won meal and consumed it in triumph, but, in fact, this incident ended even more like a story. For, while the hawk was routing its enemies, a third crow made an unobtrusive appearance on the scene, by a rear entrance, and flew away with the dead lizard even more unobtrusively!

THE CRESTED HAWK-EAGLE

The term 'hawk-eagle' naturally suggests a raptor that combines in itself the characteristics of the short-winged hawks and the big, long-winged eagles, but is not quite applicable to a few members of the tribe which, though comparatively large, are falcon-like in their hunting. However, the Crested Hawk-Eagle does have both the short, broad wings of a hawk and the size, strong build, and powerful beak and talons of an eagle.

It is not slim, but not stout either. It is noticeably bigger than a kite, a mottled brown on top and pale fawn or near white below, darkly spotted and streaked over the breast. At the back of the head four or five long, thin, black plumes (usually tipped white) form a lax nuchal crest, and the legs are feathered down to the toes, not luxuriantly as in many eagles, but with a tight 'stocking' of close-set white feathers. Young birds are much paler, with the neck and underside white, sparsely marked with thin dark streaks on the breast, and with the brown of the back flecked with white. Some adults retain this pale, juvenile plumage to a large extent. The beak is not long, but is deep and strongly curved, and the feet

are a slightly brownish yellow, with black, sharp, well-developed claws.

The Crested Hawk-Eagle is a resident forest raptor with wide distribution across India, where there are deciduous hill forests and foothill forests. Except when nesting, it is usually seen by itself, and is much given to sitting on some commanding branch in a treetop overlooking a clearing, keeping a sharp lookout. On spotting prey beneath, it swoops down on it and clutches it with its talons, killing it. Some ornithologists have said that it subsists mainly on lizards, small birds and such easily overpowered prey, but no doubt that is because they had observed it only in locations where only such prey animals were common. Actually, the Crested Hawk-Eagle is a bold and formidable predator and hunts junglefowl, young peafowl and, on occasion, even hares—and a grown hare, which this raptor has killed, would be about twice its killer's weight.

It flies swiftly, with strong flaps of its broad wings, but seldom soars. Its voice is a high-pitched staccato squeal, usually repeated a few times, and while most of the time it is silent, on occasion it is quite vocal.

RESCUE OF A FLEDGLING

After a solid breakfast I smoked my favourite pipe, and while my table was being cleared and dusted, had a nice, cold wash. Then I had a cup of strong, hot coffee. I was preparing to work.

By two o'clock I had decided on the plan of work—before tackling hard jobs it is wise to spend a moment in planning the attack. And as I sat down at last to the hateful, necessary thing, a commotion broke out in my backyard, a series of high, thin squeaks and quivers, like the 'ghosts that did squeak and gibber in the Roman streets'. White-headed Babblers are excitable creatures, and there is a clan of them living in and around my compound, sounding the alarm at each passing cat and human. However, there was a sustained hysteria in their alarm now, something in the way their *cheee-cheee-cheee*s and tremulous *chrrrrrr*s rose in outraged pitch till they were choked altogether, that called for immediate investigation, and I stepped out to the corner of my backyard.

Frantic Voices

On the clean-swept ground beneath the mango tree was a fledgling babbler, just out of the nest, fluttering weakly against the corner of the compound wall and the bathroom, falling to the ground after each futile attempt to gain the top of the wall. Two adult babblers were on the

ground beside it and three more in the boughs above, all encouraging the premature adventurer with frantic voices and quick flirts of their round, half-spread wings and loose-feathered tails. And strolling along the top of the wall towards this domestic group was a small, grey cat.

The cat was the first to see me. It froze in its tracks, gave me one intense, green-eyed look, and disappeared down the other side of the wall into my neighbour's territory. The birds flew into the tree at my approach, but when I was right under the tree and just a step from the fledgling, they flew away in a loud body to a drumstick tree some twenty yards away, and there continued their alarm even more agitatedly than before—I noticed that not one of them was facing me and that some hopped down to the grass beneath the drumstick tree, as if what excited them lay there.

The moment its elders left, the infant babbler crouched low and was instantly turned into a small, grey, shapeless, immobile lump; it did not move or bat an eyelid even when I touched it. Here was an intriguing situation! The fledgling on the bare ground was exposed to every passing enemy, and the older birds would not come to its rescue so long as I was near; they would persist with their instinctive demonstration at the grass beneath the drumstick tree. Should I move the youngster beyond the drumstick tree, where it would be safe in the innumerable bolt-holes offered by a pile of broken brick and scrap, or should I leave it where it was, keeping an eye on it from a distance and watching further proceedings? There was also the question of my pressing work, already mentioned, but I am a man of principles and on principle I think a man shouldn't work when there are other things to be done. Finally, I retreated to a point equidistant from both trees, after taking a photograph of the fledgling, and sat down to watch.

Baby Snatchers

Till five o'clock I sat stolidly on, observing happenings. First, all except two of the babblers (the parents of the grounded youngster?) left ostentatiously, whirring and skimming on weak, blunt wings over and beyond my roof. The birds that stayed behind stuck to the drumstick tree, twittering feebly from time to time. Next, a pair of ill-assorted baby snatchers arrived on the scene, a Jungle Crow and a House Crow; they perched on the compound wall and cocked their heads from side to side, looking at me and at the ground beneath them with sly, sidelong glances. After a while they hopped towards the mango tree.

This was the signal for the waiting pair of babblers to fly headlong into the mango tree, yelling blue murder—and the rest of the clan was there at once, as if by magic. Routed by the pack of yelling, gibbering babblers, the crows fled to a coconut top some distance away. This performance was repeated several times, the babblers leaving the mango tree and even my compound, the crows approaching furtively, the babblers returning in screaming force at once to mob and drive away the enemy. The grey cat, which appeared on the wall again, was also mobbed and chased away, but the passage of a Shikra low overhead was marked by silence.

Into The Crevice

All the time the little one stayed put. I doubt if it as much as lowered its bill by the fraction of an inch in all those three hours. But it closed its eyes and did not open them except when the crows, whose proximity was proclaimed by the furious babblers, were near. It was evident that no attempt to induce the youngster to move to safer quarters would be made so long as I was there. The sky was darkening, and rain imminent. I decided I had watched long enough, and taking the fledgling gently in my hand, deposited it on the scrap heap, and it promptly disappeared into a crevice.

In a moment the adult babblers had joined it and, the new ground being sufficiently far from me, vociferously encouraged the fledgling to essay flight. However, in the further fifteen minutes that I watched, it did not succeed in getting out of my compound—the babblers have no nest here, but probably have one in my neighbour's compound. Next morning they were more successful, and the youngster cleared the wall after a few tries. Apparently, a day and a night make all the difference in development to a fledgling learning to fly.

M. Krishnan

THE NEST BY THE NEST

Enormous patience is required by any person who desires to make a success of his liking for photographing birds in their nests.

A feature of bird photography in the past few decades is the amount of work done at the nest from a hide. While accurate statistics would be hard to gather, it would be a fair assessment to say that 70 to 80 per cent of bird photography is done at the nest and that this is true not only of our country but of most other countries as well. I refer, of course, to serious and pictorially advanced work; the amateur, who is content with tiny specks which he identifies as particular birds, never bothers with the elaborate ritual of putting up a hide and then waiting patiently within for opportunity—in fact, he seldom goes in for bird photography of any kind.

The reasons for birds being photographed so very much at the nest are not hard to comprehend. They are, as a rule, smallish subjects, and snapped from fifteen feet away or so, the image on the negative is a mere speck that cannot be enlarged to yield an adequate portrait. True that with lenses of extended focal length and genuine telephoto objectives, the image size can be considerably improved, but with such equipment one is set up against the peculiar set of mutually antagonistic factors that makes photography such a fascinating medium and a true art: with the increase in image size the depth of field is proportionately reduced, which necessitates stopping down to the smaller apertures for sharp details; this, in turn, calls for a longer exposure, thereby requiring a tripod or other support to eliminate camera shake, and bring in the almost insuperable element of subject movement—for birds, though often placid at the nest, are fidgety when openly approached. Try getting to within fifteen feet of the bird in the bush with a camera with a 12-inch lens mounted on a stout tripod, and you know the difficulties of this method immediately.

A generation ago, when splendid work was turned out in India by photographers like E. H. N. Lowther and R. S. P. Bates, there were other difficulties that made work at the nest appeal powerfully to the serious bird photographer. For one thing, equipment then was much more cumbersome, and again the emulsions available were considerably slower; exposures of from one-tenth of a second to one full second, with the lens stopped down to f:11 and beyond were the rule then. Today, with equipment available in much more compact form, emulsions fast and not too grainy, processing generally easier and more certain, and the great advances in the use of flash as a fill-in (or if one can get near enough as the main illumination), freelance bird photography is much less of a wild goose chase. But even so, the same old methods will have to be used, that is, positioning oneself in the likely path of birds and keeping very still, and occasionally stalking them. The main chance would still be to try for opportunist flight pictures with a long lens. Personally, I know of no game that is more fascinating than to lurk in the probable line of flight of some bird and to snap it when it seems in focus—or a game that is less rewarding.

No wonder, then, that the bird photographer goes in for a hide which may be anything from a bamboo 'thatti' overlaid with straw to a trim little prefabricated affair of green canvas, and erected on the ground or on a machan put up to reach a towering treetop. The size and furnishing of hides will depend, naturally, on the photographer's preference and purse, but it may be said that those who go in for this mode of photography usually spare neither pains nor expense. The ultimate object is to get within ten feet of the sitting bird (sometimes nearer), and wait for one's opportunities for real close-ups, showing every feather in sharp detail and the pupil of the eye.

This note is not about the technique of getting pictures of birds from a hide, which presents no insurmountable photographic problems, once the desired position is attained. This is about the ethics of such photography, about which little has been said in our country and

M. Krishnan

less generally understood. I dislike the word 'ethics' and am alive to its pomposity. Few words have been more used and abused in recent times. The unsuccessful candidate questioning the methods adopted by his rival at an election uses the term as frequently as those engaged in an abstruse discussion of social morality, and it is freely used by the pharmaceutists in describing chocolate-coated laxatives. However I can find no other word. This, then, is about the ethics of photographing birds at the nest from hides. The popular belief is that this is a wholly harmless pursuit, indulged in by the eccentric rich; even photographers have somewhat similar notions, for so many nature photographers talk of shooting with the camera instead of the gun, as a humane and harmless pursuit. However, nest-side photography can be and is at times, quite as lethal as shooting the nestlings with a gun.

Let us first distinguish between the photography of birds at the nest, and of other animals, from hides. Some wildlife photography is done from hides at water holes and other likely places, but most of it is opportunist, done from some transport or on foot. There can be no question of harming the beasts in such work: actually, it can be quite risky—to the photographer—and provide real or realistic thrills. Unquestionably, the finest nature photographs in the world, and some of the most convincing examples of the use of the camera for the purpose of record, are the wonderful pictures obtained by adventurous photographers—of a man-eating tiger carrying away its victim, of elephants fighting and antelopes in flight. The risks the bird photographer runs—which can be real if his elevated stance is not too secure—are very different, and his pictures are rarely spontaneous records. In fact, the risks are mainly run by the birds.

Birds disturbed at the nest will desert their eggs and young—that is the risk. On second thoughts, I feel it would be truer to substitute the 'will desert' with 'may desert'. We must realize that birds are not intelligent in such matters—they are moved by dominating instincts which, being instincts, are quite unreasoned. They are unable to appreciate the fact that the photographer intends them no harm, or that he is a very distinguished and experienced nest-side worker who will take every possible step to assure them, and himself, of comfort during the few days he proposes to sojourn in his nest, beside their nests. Strong instincts bind them to their eggs and young: the instinct of self-preservation is no less strong. Desertion will depend on the mutual conflict of these two instincts.

It is often said that some species are more prone to desertion than others, and on the whole it is true, but the behaviour of birds in a given circumstance is difficult to predicate, for they are more complex in their behaviour than is usually realized, even by careful observers. For example, it is well known that the confiding Tailorbird that enters our verandas so freely, will not stand close scrutiny of its nest, and will desert, at times, even if one just takes a peep at the nest. I knew a Tailorbird which had its nest in a hiptage bush that allowed me, then an ignorant and insatiably curious boy, to actually take the fledglings out of the nest and then replace them, and to watch by the nest, squatting on a parapet a yard away, and which still reared its brood to maturity! The reverse may be equally true. Birds like the iora, which are normally close sitters, may quit on the slightest of provocations.

The earnest bird photographer usually takes great pains to avoid such happenings—remember, he cannot get his hoped-for picture with the nest deserted! However, that is not the only reason; no doubt he is also influenced by humanitarian considerations. Men internationally famed for their bird pictures, like Eric Hosking, are strong in their condemnation of any method of bird photography at the nest that will lead to desertion. Such a thing is not only defeatist, but also utterly needless, for it can be anticipated and avoided. As the noted British bird photographer, A. Faulkner Taylor, says, every precaution must be taken to start the hide on a modest scale and at a considerable distance from the nest, gradually moving it nearer, watching the reaction of the nesting bird carefully through binoculars from far away, and abandoning the attempt at the least sign of alarm. Birds sitting on eggs are more apt to desert than those feeding young.

Patience and a slow approach, coupled with some knowledge of avian behaviour, will usually suffice to avoid desertion. It may be thought that the setting up of the camera on a tripod by the nest and the taking of the actual picture by remote control is a safer method, than the erection of a huge, intimidatory hide, but in practice it does not work that way. No doubt some wonderful pictures have been obtained by the remote control method, but a suitably camouflaged and carefully introduced hide has every chance of being accepted, and at the times the mere sign of the camera is sufficient to scare the sitting bird. I have very little experience of photography from a hide, but for years I have studied the reactions of birds at the nest, to disturbances by natural and unnatural forces (including photographers), and though a properly introduced hide has good chances of being accepted, I know at times nothing will induce the bird to return to its nest till it is removed—on such occasions, they sometimes permit an undisguised man to approach fairly close, and if he moves very, very slowly, even as close as within five or six yards! The sudden intrusion of a hide, however well camouflaged, will frequently cause desertion.

Much the best way, where it is feasible, is to put up a hide by the known nesting site of a bird before the breeding season. This will generally be accepted, but if it is not, it can be removed before any damage is done. Naturally, it is only where a bird is known to nest in a particular tree or other place year after year, that this can be attempted. It is also possible at suitable localities where waterbirds breed in numbers annually.

That brings us to the most objectionable use of the hide by the nest, its sudden erection at an active nesting colony. This invariably leads to a percentage of the birds deserting—practically all the birds sitting on eggs will leave, as also a percentage of those feeding young. Of course, much will depend on the way things are done. Where a hundred birds are nesting in two or three contiguous trees standing in water, the sudden erection of a hide close by the trees, if done sufficiently clumsily, may lead to wholesale desertion. However the point is that even when it is done most skilfully and unobtrusively, a percentage of the breeding birds will desert. Naturally, the species breeding will determine the extent of desertion in some measure. Night Herons, Little Egrets, Spoonbills,

Openbills and cormorants will be less prone to abandon their young than Grey Herons, ibises and Darters at a mixed heronry. However, nothing can be stated as an absolute prophecy, except that however cunningly the machan and hide are put up, however quietly and under cover of darkness, a percentage of the birds will desert, and there will be some loss of young life. Nestlings, particularly the young of waterbirds, consume great quantities of food and grow rapidly: even if their parents, alarmed by the sudden appearance of a large, green tent besides their nests, are only a few hours late in returning, the hungry, clamouring young struggle to the edge of the nests and often topple down into the water, to be drowned or washed irretrievably away.

Recently, a certain official advanced the argument that the very fact that the photographer at a mixed heronry got his pictures, proved that there had been no disturbance! Of course some of the birds, tied closer to their nests than the fear of the suddenly intruded hide can break, do stay behind and accept the hide—they provide the photographer lurking within with material for superb pictures from nearby. Nor are these birds, which return to their nests after the men who put up the hide have gone, frightened by the unseen photographer inside—except when he shows himself. But about the birds that do desert, what about the number of young that die of starvation and drowning? This man had every opportunity to study these things for himself, and yet he argued that no harm had been done. I declined to discuss the issue with him, for there have been only two causes for the line he took, both of which were beyond the conviction of facts and logic: either he knew better, but sought to justify an action already perpetrated, or he was inspired by invincible ignorance. His second line of argument, that there was so much loss of young life at such breeding sites in any case that the death of some more young by photographers did not matter, was not a reasonable thing to say. I was surprised to find that he did not approve of my suggestion that sportsmen should be allowed to do a limited amount of shooting at the place to keep their eye in.

BIRDS FROM
THE
COUNTRYSIDE

QUAIL IN THE GRASS

In November the grasses come up with a rush. Right from September onwards they grow, rejuvenated by the rains into fresh, green, spreading vigour, covering slopes and clearings with their lush carpets. Some of them continue their vegetative spread longer, but many are already in seed by the end of November. That is true not only of the wild grasses, but of cultivated varieties in these parts like jowar and bajra. In fields fitting together along their bunds to a geometrical jigsaw puzzle, along the banks of paths and in jungle clearings beyond, the grasses stand high or less high, offering cover for squat little things. Now is the time to look for quail in this cover.

Of course those that look for them with a gun will look later, when the crops are harvested and the birds gleaning grain in the stubble are easier to flush. Moreover there are too many young about now. Practically every bevy of quail that I see now consists of a parent pair accompanied by the young, miniatures of the old birds no bigger than a breakfast egg on red legs, marvellously assured in deportment and finished in plumage.

Even a full-grown quail is wonderfully dainty and richly marked, to those to whom its plump body has not only edible virtues. But perhaps these little ones represent the most perfect miniatures in barred and speckled beauty that can be found among birds. I have always been fascinated by the sight of a family party of quail.

They have many enemies, these baby quail, and so have their parents. I am writing mainly of Rain Quail and bush-quail, but I suppose it is true to say that the entire quail family means juicy meat to all hunters in the scrub, besides men. It is by wariness—the ability to run swiftly in the cover of grass and low shrubs or squat tight in a thorn bush—and the sure instinct of obedience in the young, that the tribe survives. A baby quail is strong on its legs within a surprisingly short time of its genesis, and very soon it is able to whirr low on its tiny wings, but it is the watchfulness and craft of the old birds that saves them most often.

Recently I watched the escape of a quail family from a purposeful hunter. I was sitting immobile behind the screen of a lantana, watching a pair of bush-quail and their three tiny progeny. They were pecking at an anthill some twenty yards away, in the middle of a grassy field (incidentally I think young quail, like many other young birds, depend quite a lot on termites and other soft-bodied insect prey). A prowling cat saw them and walked away, very casually, and disappeared in a dip beyond. Presently I saw that cat come creeping in from an altogether different direction, taking advantage of a hedge to approach the quarry. The predator was barely visible from where I was, but well hidden from the quail by the mound of the anthill. However, one of the parent birds saw him when he was just three yards away, and bolted with a hurried whistling call, running fast to the cover of the hedge on the other side of the field. Had the rest of the family scattered the cat might have had a chance, but they too made off in the same direction, running smoothly and instantly away from the threat, the young ones invisible in the cover of grass. As everyone who has been present at a beat knows, bush-quail when flushed are apt to disperse suddenly in different directions. I was surprised at the orderly method of this escape.

And I noticed that that cat accepted defeat with philosophical calm. It made no attempt to get at the quail again, with another flanking movement, but just walked steadily away, to 'fresh fields and pastures new'.

THE BUSTARD-QUAIL

Bustard-quail and button quail do not belong to the vast and varied family of partridges, quail, spurfowl, junglefowl, pheasants and peafowl, but only to the next family; but since they are so quail-like in size and appearance, they may be noticed here. Like the much larger bustards, these little rounded birds have no hind toe: their feet have only the three forward-pointing toes, a peculiarity by which they may be distinguished from quail at a glance.

Apart from this, as a family they are notable for a life history which will delight the hearts of all militant feminists. In them, the female is larger and more showy in appearance than the male, and takes the dominant part in courtship: the female is polyandrous, and leaves the taxing duty of incubating the eggs and rearing the hatched young to successive males.

The Indian Bustard-Quail, typical of its tribe, is a small, plump bird the size of a Jungle Bush-Quail, with a more pointed tail. Both the male and the slightly larger female are brown on top, mottled with buff and black; the chin and throat are pale, and the underside buff, banded on the breast with black in the male. In the female, which is richer in colour, there is a black longitudinal patch over the breast. In both sexes, the iris is white, giving the bird an angry-looking, or sometimes a furtive appearance.

This bustard-quail has a wide range over the country, but is by no means common, for it does not congregate in numbers in any area as quail do. It favours grassland in the plains and lower hills. It sticks to ground cover and is not readily seen, but the female's challenge to rival females often betrays its presence—a long, reverberating call extending over nearly twenty seconds, remarkably like the sound made by a small

FEMALE BUSTARD-QUAIL.

FOOT
OF QUAIL & BUSTARD-QUAIL.

motorcycle going uphill half a kilometre away. This call is evidently sounded as an assertion of territory, to warn rival females not to encroach into the area and, according to C. M. Inglis, is always sounded with the bird sitting down on its folded legs.

As said, the female is polyandrous, establishes breeding territory and takes the active part in courtship. The four grey eggs, heavily blotched with brown, are laid in a scrape in the ground, usually well screened by bushes around. Once they are laid, the female abandons them and goes away to seek another mate. Successive mates are found in this way, but whether the female is promiscuous or sticks to the same partners is not known.

M. Krishnan

PLUMES IN THE WIND

I was surprised to find peafowl in the place. There was a tortuous 'nala' here, full of a coarse, buff sand—an old riverbed along which no water flowed even in heavy rains, though it held subterranean stores and basin-like pools. Clumps of trees dotted its course, and in places bushes and the wild date formed shelving banks, but otherwise it was flush with the flat red fields around and the flat black fields beyond. Only grasses and weeds grew besides the sprouting corn—the country was so dead level and open that one could motor right across it at a fair speed. It was almost like some gigantic map rolled smoothly out, with a tree here and a clump there sticking out of its flat spread in dark green marking-pins. However, there was a breeze moving the grass tops. It was a steady, low breeze, not balmy, not gusty, but always there with a palpable pressure.

The fauna was typical of this open spread, capable of long speed. There were herds of blackbuck in the black-cotton soil, and a few buck in the red fields, foxes had their hearths in the sand of the 'nala', and many of the birds belonged to the bare, brown earth—larks, the Tawny Eagle, the doomed Great Indian Bustard, partridges where there was cover of bush and arid sandgrouse where there was not. I had seen peafowl in scrubland before, but never in such naked, even country.

At first I was sure they had been introduced, that by some unlikely feat of adaptation these peafowl had taken to an exposed life. But inquiry soon disproved my theory. There had been peafowl here always, not just a few along the wooded parts of the 'nala' as now (where there were roosting trees and safe water), but in abundance, all over. What remained were survivors of a once plentiful tribe, too trustful of humanity. Furthermore the vague, blue, undulating ridge on the horizon marked solid peafowl ground, broken, bush-clad hills, and though this was far away it was not so far that trekking peafowl could not get to it from terrain they disliked or feared. It made no difference to the remarkableness of finding them here whether or not some ancestral pairs had been introduced.

Man seemed to be their chiefest enemy here. The greater cats shunned the flatness of the place—I did not even see a Jungle Cat here. Foxes do not attack such big birds, and I doubt if the mongoose would; even stalking the sharp-eyed, absurd-looking chicks would be a job with no cover. Still, I could not help thinking that a peacock out in the open, say, a furlong from the nearest tree, ran exceptional risks in this breezy, flat country.

I chased a magnificent cock and three hens upwind, across four fields, just to see what they would do. They preferred to run in the young millet, straight towards a thick clump, and had no trouble at all in keeping well clear of me at first, in a tight bunch. Then the hens drew ahead, leaving the plume-laden cock yards behind. The wind, with no bush or hedge to break its insistent push, seemed to bother them considerably. When pressed, the cock crouched lower, depressed his bobbing, flagged head till it was almost horizontal at the stretch of his neck, and ran in a slewed rush, on high-stepping, labile legs—the wind against his splendid train pushed him bodily to one side. None of the birds sought flight, and when I stopped to recover my nicotine-undermined breath on their entering cover, the cock seemed quite as

M. Krishnan

badly blown as I. Peafowl fly farther and faster than most people think, but they take time to get going in the air, and in such open country I think a determined hunter could run them down.

Incidentally, I was puzzled to read in a standard book on Indian birds that the caterwauling scream of the peacock is its alarm call. This call, with which it greets the sun each day, may occasionally be used as a warning when the enemy is far away and clearly visible. But the typical alarm call is a harsh, grating, quickly repeated *crank-crank-crank-crank-crank*—a sure indication that this vigilant fowl has sighted a prowling predator.

THE COMMON KINGFISHER

Migratory birds, like many plovers and sandpipers, cover thousands of kilometres twice every year, in winter from their snowbound homelands to distant countries where food is less hard to find, and in spring back home to breed. Such birds may be common, at different times of the year, in countries far apart. As distinct from these, the identical bird, or a regional race of it (a mere subspecies), may be resident right round the year in widely separated countries, having a very wide distribution—familiar examples are the Night Heron, the Little Egret and the Barn Owl.

Less Cosmopolitan

Kingfishers, as a family, tend to be less cosmopolitan in their distribution. The kinds of kingfishers of a country usually belong only to it and to adjacent countries. The kookaburra is so very distinctive of its country that its long-drawn cackling, laughter-like call has been adopted as the signature tune of Radio Australia, and most of our own kingfishers are there only in India and near around. But one of the smallest, the Little Blue or Common Kingfisher, has an extensive range, which is why it is termed 'common', not because this bright little bird with a Prussian blue back and orange-chestnut breast is undistinguished and 'ornery' (as the Americans say), but because it is common to many countries—South Africa, much of Southern Asia and Europe.

It is the only kingfisher of Britain, and naturally there it has no adjectival prefix to its name (like 'little blue' or 'common'), being just 'kingfisher'. In an authoritative modern treatise on Britain's avifauna, it is described as 'the most brilliantly coloured of British birds.' Elsewhere, as in India, there are far more colourful birds, more colourful kingfishers, such as the much larger White-breasted Kingfisher with its dazzling new blue back and heavy, long, dark crimson beak, and the tiny, flashing purple Three-toed Kingfisher. In temperate countries, birds tend to be less arrestingly plumaged than in ours, and are usually a quiet grey or brown, or mottled and blurred, and when one is, unusually, bright blue like the kingfisher, it is enthusiastically acclaimed. Poets in England have been moved to ecstatic lines by the bird—here are fair samples:

> brilliant, clear, and broad,
> Forty-two yards up the middle of the river
> Under my eyes shot the turquoise unflawed!
>
> —A.Y. Campbell

And,

> It was the Rainbow gave thee birth,
> And left thee all her lovely hues
>
> —W. H. Davies

Our own poets have written of brilliantly plumaged birds, like the parakeet and the peacock, but I doubt if there is even a line in the poetry of Indian languages about the kingfisher.

An interesting thing about the brilliance of plumage of the Common Kingfisher is that ornithologists cite it as an example of warning colour—it is said that 'predators have learnt to leave the bird alone, because its flesh is foul-tasting.' True, birds do have a sense of taste and decided preferences in food, even among birds of prey: true, also, that their vision is far more acute than ours and that it is colour-perceptive. But on this basis can we presume that it is the kingfisher's blue colour that keeps predators away?

The lesser falcons and other birds that hawk their prey on the wing take bright blue and blue-green dragonflies and other similarly coloured insects, and the larger birds of prey take blue-coloured birds. A roller in flight is a flashing contrast of dark and light blue, and I have seen a Peregrine stoop on one and carry it away, and hawk-eagles occasionally take the peacock. Of course, it can be argued that it is not only the blue back of the Common Kingfisher, but *that* in conjunction with its orange-chestnut breast that serves to warn intending predators of its unpalatable flesh.

Raw Flesh

Being a vegetarian, I cannot verify the point personally, but I doubt if any of the ethologists who credit the kingfisher with warning colour have actually tasted its raw flesh. And even if someone has (there is no saying what one will do in pursuit of scientific knowledge), how can it be presumed that the sense of taste (especially gustatory revulsion) is the same or very similar in both men and raptorial birds? Most of us cannot eat a really pungent green chilli, but parakeets relish them greatly.

M. Krishnan

FISH-OWLS

Now that winter has set in, even in the South, darkness comes early, and the day no longer turns to night with that dramatic suddenness beloved of Anglo-Indian writers of romantic fiction. From six o'clock, till seven almost, there is a clear twilight that deepens slowly into obscure night. And now is the time to look for the greater owls, for the cool grey evenings bring them out prematurely.

Our owls do not say *tu-whit-tu-who*, nor mope and complain to the moon—the lesser ones yelp, chatter and shriek with demoniac gusto, and the great owls hoot in deep, resonant voices that carry far. None of them, I think, has a voice so unearthly as the Brown Fish-Owl. Soon after it emerges from its daytime retreat, its hollow boom comes floating down the dusk, startlingly sepulchral and near-sounding; later in the night, it sits bolt upright on its perch and chuckles in a muffled, snoring grunt. No doubt this bird is responsible for the evil reputations of certain countryside paths by night.

This is one of our biggest owls, dark and mottled, with a heavy cubist build and square, eared head. Its squat, erect silhouette hardly suggests a bird—in poor light, once, a friend and I mistook it for a monkey slumped on a rock. The fish-owl haunts ravines and watercourses, resting by day in the secret heart of some ancient clump of trees. It is no city bird, but at night it often visits village tanks or sits on rooftops staring percipiently into the darkness from enormous, round eyes.

The fish-owl is distinguished from the Great Horned Owls by its flatter 'horns' and the fact that its legs are unfeathered and naked. Its feet are strikingly like the Osprey's, covered with gripping scales and meant for the same purpose, for holding slippery prey. However, it does not plunge headlong into the water after fish, but sails over the surface

on hushed wings and lifts its prey out. Though it is much given to fishing, fish and crabs and such aquatic creatures do not constitute its sole food. It is known to prey on birds and small mammals, and I believe it occasionally hunts fair-sized quarry, like Rock-Pigeons.

I used to know a colony of Blue Rock-Pigeons that had their home in a large natural grotto in a river-rift gorge. Almost all the pigeons disappeared from here suddenly, and a fish-owl was seen about the place at the same time. I realize that this is highly inconclusive evidence, and that it might well be that the departure of the pigeons had nothing to do with the entry of the owl on the scene—perhaps others, more comprehensive in their observation, can confirm or dispel my suspicions.

I know of another instance of a pair of Brown Fish-Owls haunting the abode of pigeons, but am almost sure that in this case the racing pigeons within were not the attraction. The owls used to come and sit on the domed roof of the loft, on a level with my bedroom window, and lying awake I have often watched them flying soundlessly about in the dew-drenched moonlight, returning periodically to the loft. I think these nocturnal fishers were drawn to the place by the small tanks around it. The way they flapped their broad wings rapidly, threshing the cold, luminous air to rise vertically without the hint of a swish, was uncanny; they also used to sail around on spread wings. Perhaps they were courting, if such sapient-looking birds can descend to such frivolity, for they indulged in much pointless flight.

It is said that the silent flight of owls helps in locating the quarry by its sounds, besides providing a warningless swoop down to the kill. There seems to be much in this, for though they have marvellous sight by the dimmest light, hearing is an added advantage when the prey is in thin cover. Obviously, a bird flapping its wings noisily can hear little besides its own flight, and since all owls do quite a lot of hunting while coasting around, the silence of their down-lined pinions must be of real value to them. Perhaps fish-owls are more dependent on sight than others of the tribe, and that is why they have such big eyes—but it is a mistake to think that aquatic creatures are silent; fish break the surface of the stream audibly, and even crabs can be heard if there is hushed silence all round.

THE SPOTTED DOVE

I wish I had met Charles Darwin, and had a heart-to-heart talk with him about Evolution, about the Theory of Survival of the Fittest, in particular. I would have confronted him with the Spotted Dove, and then I think, the argument would have ended. I realize Darwin's greatness as an observer and scientist. That is why I think what I think. No true naturalist will suit facts to theories. Darwin would have seen the weakness of his thesis at once. There would have been no S of the F.

Mind, it is not as if the Spotted Dove is the only example I could have quoted against the Theory. The entire dove family disproves it. And there are other creatures. Chameleons, bloodsuckers, sloths and many others among the lower orders of the *Vertebrata*—instances among the higher orders occur to you, no doubt. But the Spotted Dove would have been the heart and core of my argument. Few other birds are so eminently unfit, in every way. Its sole purpose in life, from egg to adult, seems to be to nourish other creatures. Its nest is a few twigs thrown carelessly together across some fork, through which the eggs can be clearly seen. There is no attempt at concealment or security. Crows, tree pies, snakes, mongooses and many less-accomplished egg-stealers grow fat upon its eggs. A variety of baby snatchers help to keep down the number of nestlings that come out of the eggs that do get hatched, and the lesser birds of prey have a strong partiality for the plump adult. And still, I tell you, Spotted Doves are among the commonest of our birds! The secret of their survival is that they do not 'struggle for existence'. If they had, they would have perished incapably long ago. They breed on through the year, unmindful of loss, not courageously in the face of adversity, but just unmindful, and at last they succeed in rearing a pair of young. Persistent domesticity has survival value—'the meek shall inherit the earth.'

The Spotted Dove breeds all the year round, and in spring—that is, the hottest months of our summer—its voice is heard oftener than at other times. The best way to know our doves is to know them by their voices. The Spotted Dove has a characteristic, soft but clearly audible coo—*kru-kru-kru-kru- kroo! kroo; kroo*—the first four syllables quickly together and gaining slightly in loudness followed by the long-drawn *kroos*. Its voice is pleasant at all times, but heard in the sullen heat of noon, it has a peculiarly soothing quality. This dove has 'a miniature chessboard in black and white' beneath the nape of its neck, and a generally grey-spotted appearance at close quarters. But do not look for the chessboard in the field. For one thing, another dove also has this marking, though on the sides of the neck and in red and black in its case. And again, the most conspicuous of chessboard patterns melt into grey at a distance of twenty yards or so—watch a man wearing a loud, check sports coat and you will see that this is so. Go by the voice, I ask you, go by the voice and you will never fail to spot the Spotted Dove.

RAILS, CRAKES AND WATERHENS

Rails, crakes, waterhens and coots are middle-sized or smaller water and marsh birds haunting waters fringed with reeds and holding aquatic vegetation. They have stump tails and short, rounded wings and are poor fliers, though some of them are migrants. All have long legs and very long, unwebbed toes and swim well. They are great skulkers and expert at running through waterside vegetation, and even clambering up bushes and reeds, and being largely crepuscular are not often seen, but have loud discordant voices and are freely heard during the breeding season.

Only two members of this large tribe, the Bluebreasted Banded Rail and the familiar Whitebreasted Waterhen, are mentioned here. Both have an all-India distribution and will suffice to indicate what sort of birds these are—for the other birds of the tribe not described in this and the following notes, reference to any good book will disclose their identity.

The Bluebreasted Banded Rail is typical of the rails and crakes, a shy bird the size of a partridge but less plump, with a stub tail and long toes. It seldom ventures far from the cover of waterside bushes and reeds, and bobs its head and jerks its short tail upward at each step as it walks lightly over floating vegetation, a gesture characteristic of members of the family. At the least hint of being observed, it slinks back into cover at once. Like other related birds it is omnivorous in its feeding, taking in small aquatic insects, molluscs and crustaceans, as also some vegetable matter.

It is rather arrestingly plumaged for a rail, with the head and neck red-brown, the chin and throat white, the breast blue, the back and tail brown banded with pale stripes, and the abdomen and flanks smoky black barred with white. It is unusually silent for a rail, but during the breeding season is said to come out with muted shrieks.

The Whitebreasted Waterhen, there in every pond and large pool with vegetation on the banks, is a little smaller than a village hen. It is a smoky warm grey on top with a white face and white on the underside, and rufous under the tail, and less shy than most other birds of its family, but quick to run into cover if disturbed—it is given to clambering high in the waterside bushes. During the dry months it is silent, but with the rains begins to breed when it indulges in the most extraordinary and alarming sounds well hidden in cover—'Eha' compared the love song of this bird to the roars of a bear being roasted over a fire that suddenly change to the coos of a dove! In parts of India it is much fancied in a spicy curry cooked along with brinjals and is relentlessly hunted.

GOGGLE EYES

Throughout India and even far beyond, where the country is sufficiently dry, stony and scrub-jungly, you will find a brownish, much-streaked bird with enormous eyes, trotting over pebbly riverbeds on long yellow legs, scuttling through the scrub, crouching low and merging instantly with the earth. It is a bird of many aliases, all of them descriptive and none flattering.

It is the Stone-Curlew, the Thick-knee or the Goggle-eyed Plover, it is the 'bustard and florican' of Anglo-Indian sportsmen—I have even heard it called the 'bastard-florican'. However, it is ornithologists that have been least kind to it. Formerly it was termed *Oedicnemus scolopax*, but apparently it was felt that the second, specific part of the name was too easy; so, now they call it *Burhinus oedicnemus*!

Thick-kneed-goggle-eyed-bustard-plover-stone-curlew would be completely descriptive. The bird has the three-toed, yellow running legs of the bustards, and carries its body horizontally; when it runs, with quick, mincing steps, it holds its head low, in a line with its body. By day it is inactive, especially when the sun is bright and cover scanty, but as the light fails it emerges singly and in pairs, moving on quick, silent feet through the scrub looking for insects.

Its obliterative plumage is almost invisible in the dusk, but you may hear it for with nightfall it grows vocal and often keeps calling till quite late, especially when the moon is bright. And listening to its wild repeated *curlew,* ... *curlew,* a call suggestive of desolate, wide wasteland, you know at once why it is called the Stone-Curlew. In places it is only less common on the night road than the nightjar. When caught in the beams of the oncoming car, it scuttles to the shelter of the nearest bush and stays put beneath it, only its big, black-and-yellow eyes betraying it—or else it flies swift and low for a short distance, the white bar in each wing clearly displayed, before touching ground again and scuttling away. It never flies high or far when disturbed, for it is a ground bird that trusts its thick-kneed legs, but I have heard a pair flying fairly high and calling to each other in the cold, clear moonlight.

Often a bird disturbed at night on the road will fly alongside the car or right over it, before turning away, somewhat in the manner of nightjars. Once I caught one from an open lorry, putting up my hand as it came skimming over, and what impressed me was the way it went limp and yielding in the hand, and its surprising lightness. Most birds lack weight remarkably in the hand, but I think the Stone-Curlew (it is definitely larger than a partridge) is exceptionally light even for a bird.

I would like to know more about the courtship of this earth-loving bird, whether that, too, is terrestrial. Does love inspire its wings at any time or was it just the moonlight that exhilarated the birds I heard, more than once, flying high?

Growing curious on this point I questioned a number of people who lived where these birds were common. They could tell me nothing, but directed me to a gang-foreman whose knowledge of the fowl was said to be considerable. After missing a few opportunities, I met this expert at last, and this was what he told me:

'Yes, they can fly, but that's not the point. Sometimes they fly a little and sometimes a little further, but mostly they like to run. The point, however, is this: try them cold, in a sandwich.' Unfortunately, I am a vegetarian and can add no personal recommendation, but that was the expert advice.

THE JACANAS

Jacanas (the 'c' in the name is soft and pronounced as a not too sibilant 's') are an exclusive class of freshwater birds superficially somewhat like rails but more specialized for life on floating vegetation; for their size they have the longest and most widespread toes and nails of all birds, enabling them to trip lightly over the leaves of water lilies and other aquatic plants without sinking by distributing their body weight over a large area. In other ways too, they differ from the true rails. Among them the female is larger than the male and no less showy in plumage, and it is now established that the females are polyandrous, mating in turn with several males and leaving the responsibility for incubating the eggs (laid on a floating mass of vegetation) and rearing the young to the males.

We have two kinds of these birds. As its name suggests, the Bronzewinged Jacana has metallic glints in its plumage; the head and neck are black with a prominent white stripe running down the neck from the eye, the lower parts are a dark greenish colour and the wings bronzed, and the stubby tail reddish brown. It is about the size of a Grey Partridge, and usually found both by itself and in pairs and parties, in temple and village tanks and similar waters holding lotuses and water lilies, water chestnuts and thalloid algae. It has an all-India distribution. The spidery toes are enormously elongated and long-nailed, and cover a considerable area, so that the bird is able to walk even on masses of algae on or just below the surface. It can also swim. In this jacana there is no difference between the breeding and non-breeding plumage. Like all jacanas, it feeds on the fruits and seeds of water plants and on buds, and also small molluscs, crustaceans and especially insects.

Except for its similar legs and feet and long-clawed toes, the

Pheasant-tailed Jacana is altogether more showy and more given to short flights over the water, and its breeding plumage is quite different from its non-breeding plumage. When not breeding, the bird is olive brown on top and white below with a dark line from the eyes down the sides of the neck forming a gorget over the breast. In nuptial livery both sexes are chocolate brown in the body with the head and lower neck white, and the neck a glistening golden yellow on top, and the tail, which is not specially long when not breeding, gets elongated into graceful, curved plumes like the tail of a pheasant. The bird has a somewhat mewling call.

WAAK

In a story that I read recently the climax is reached when the narrator, in his boyhood, has to cross a pathway in dark. The suspense mounts as he nears the place, then, unable to face it, he turns away from the horror and walks backwards, his senses taut with apprehension: 'My ears were pricked up, ready to listen to the slightest rustle. A leaf dropping, the Night Heron darting into the still night with its shrill call "tweet, tweet, tweet" would have seen me drop dead on the ground.'

Having done most things the hard way all my life, I fear I will have no easy death, but even I would get a pretty considerable jar were I to hear a Night Heron rise into the obscure silence with a shrill *tweet, tweet, tweet!* But were its cry far more eerie, a sudden, raucous, floating *w-a-a-k!* from above, I wouldn't turn a hair, for that is the bird's call.

In many Indian languages, the Night Heron's name is onomatopoeic—in Tamil for example, it is called 'Vakka'. Perhaps it is the most identifiable of the lesser herons and egrets, a dumpy heron, grey above and white below with a black crown, nape and back. There is a silky crest of long black feathers drooping over the humped shoulders, but neither this nor the colour of nape or back is visible as one views the roosting bird from below or at eye level, though the black crown is prominent.

However, it is not by observing details of plumage that one knows this bird—the heavy, dark contours of head and beak, the blunt hollowed wings rowing a steady path through the dusk, and the hoarse, airborne *w-a-a-k!* are unmistakable.

Being nocturnal and crepuscular, Night Herons spend the day in heavy repose in their chosen roosts. But when they breed, they are day herons as well, for the ceaseless yickering of the young drives the parents

to seek food for their insatiable brood throughout the night and day. Breeding is a wearing pastime with most birds—with Night Herons it is positively exhausting for all concerned, including neighbours.

Usually the breeding sites and roosting trees are well away from human habitation, and often near water, but the birds do not hesitate to locate their nesting colony in a built-up area if other conditions suit them. In June 1946 a colony of some 150 Night Herons nested in mango trees in the backyard of a house in the heart of congested Madras—there was a tidal creek not far away and a sluggish canal right at the back, ample inducement to the hard-worked birds to pitch on this spot.

The sustained clamour of the young, and the continuous arrivals and departures of the adults rendered sleep almost impossible for the occupants of neighbouring houses. After futile, private attempts to move the birds, the residents lodged a complaint at the local police station. Our unsung police force, which is capable of dark feats of public duty, rose nobly to the occasion. A constable with a shotgun visited the scene of the offence and fired a few rounds into the loud, thick trees, bringing down a number of birds, and the rest of the colony took wing in a hurry, never to return to this homestead.

In contrast to this feverish whole-time activity of the breeding Night Heron, I must add that occasionally the bird sleeps soundly through the night, in spite of its name—when the hunting has been good in the evening and early hours of darkness. One of the most vivid recollections of my youth is the capture of a slumbering Night Heron on the parapet wall of my house, around midnight.

It stood on one leg, its head lost in its huddled shoulders and fluffed plumage. It was so fast asleep that when I switched on the powerful terrace lamp, right above it, the sudden glare failed to get through to its drowsing senses. Only when I took it in my hands did it awaken with a loud croak of protest. I held it as one holds a pigeon, with its flights and feet pinioned between my fingers so that it could not use them, but it got away by an undignified and smelly manoeuvre, by being abruptly and fishily sick.

Best to let sleeping Night Herons sleep.

SIESTA

When Goa was Portuguese territory, civic and official life in it followed a salutary convention. Work commenced in the morning and was sustained till the sun was nearing its zenith; then until the afternoon was well on its way, there was a break for lunch and a siesta, a most welcome break in India where most regions are torrid and tropical.

Observing wild creatures for a lifetime, I have come across none that observed the ten to five schedule. Even the most diurnal of them take a break during the hottest part of the day. With ruminants, which alternate spells of intensive feeding with periods of repose during which they chew the cud, this break for rest is not obvious, but is there nevertheless. Take blackbuck and chital, as typical examples of mainly diurnal ruminants of the arid, open scrub and of forests with green, grass-covered clearings: both do feed even after sunset for some time, then they lie down till the sun is up. Then again, there are spells of feeding and rumination till near noon, when they take a really long rest, till about 3 p.m.

Most birds, too, rest awhile at high noon, though not all actually indulge in a siesta. While this is true also of the birds of the bush and treetops, because much of their activity is obscured by foliage, the truth is often hidden. But with ground-birds and waterbirds (especially those that breed within our country), this trend is manifest. The best instance I know of this is provided by the Spoonbill at Sultanpur Jheel, about January. They do not breed here, but breed in locations around the jheel perhaps, even far from it, for a hundred kilometres or two is no distance to a bird endowed with the power of flight. By January they are all through with breeding, as shown by the adults lacking nuchal crests, and by the first-season birds still having a thin edging of black to their flight feathers. They assemble at Sultanpur in large flocks, to feed in the jheel till near noon, their feeding gradually getting more and more desultory, and later they grow positively lethargic, and assembling in a close flock more or less in the middle of the shallow water, stand on one leg, tuck the other leg well up into their abdomen, and twisting their flexible neck right round bury their long, spatulate bill into the feathers of their upper back and go to sleep—a hundred or more of them, each bird standing on one leg and at rest, fast asleep.

Sarus Cranes also take a siesta about noon, also standing on one leg and twisting their neck round to bury their beak in the plumage of their back, but they take a siesta by themselves or in a pair, not in a flock. In fact, all birds (except some ground-birds) go to sleep standing on one leg, even the perching birds atop twigs or branches. Do they shift legs during the course of their sleep? I think they do—I noticed my homers shifted legs during sleep when years ago, I kept racing pigeons—but that question is not really relevant in this context, because we are considering a noontime siesta and not the longer night sleep of diurnal birds.

What birds are active between, say, 11 a.m. and 2 p.m.? Many waterbirds soar early in the afternoon, storks, Spoonbills, even White Ibises, but that is usually well after 2 p.m. I have seen only vultures effortlessly circling the heavens on thermal currents about noon, wings unflapping, going nowhere in particular. Perhaps they indulge in a siesta airborne.

Chital and sambar usually lie down at noon in areas where they are free from human disturbance, the former in dappled tree-shade and the latter often in the open, in the burning sun. Gaur, too, take a siesta after the morning feed—one cow in the herd or two standing sentinel while the rest doze. Predatory beasts also rest during the hottest hours of the day, even dhole. And though cold-blooded animals like snakes are lethargic when the ground and ambient air are cool, and more active when it is warmer, they, too, rest during the hottest hours. One could go on and on with this inquiry, and so, to end it, let us look at the animals closest to us, the primates.

Studies of the larger apes in Africa and Borneo, of gibbons in

Malaysia, and of both Old and New World monkeys, all disclose a definite tendency to rest during the hottest hours of the day. Among Indian monkeys, this trend is probably best exemplified by the arboreal Nilgiri Langur. As noon approaches, the troop which has been feeding actively since morning takes itself to suitable trees with horizontal branches and stout forks, and selecting suitable crotches or branches takes a siesta. The langur atop horizontal branches positively abandon themselves to sleep lying along the wood on their stomach, with their limbs flung in pairs on either side of the branch, and their long tails hanging down.

GREY SHRIKE

I am now alone, in a tumbledown cottage surrounded by a vast and lifeless compound. A bent acacia spreads its flat umbrella above the barren waste outside, and the ruins of a great mansion, where men once loved and feasted, limit the view beyond. Each day I go out into the noisy world for a few hours, to return in the evening to the loneliness and calm of my cottage. I sit under the thin shade of the acacia and enjoy the utter solitude that appeals so strongly to my unsociable nature. And it is then that I notice that I am not quite alone after all, for a Great Grey Shrike, whose territory this is, sits on a thorny, protruding rib of the umbrella above me.

There are thousands of other living things around, I suppose, crawling and burrowing in the parched earth, but they do not count. I take no cognizance of them. It is only when another personality acknowledged by us obtrudes itself on our horizon, that we feel our privacy violated. We begin to feel self-conscious and at once assume those many and foolish attitudes that we think necessary to uphold our status in the eyes of others. Now this Grey Shrike has a compelling personality and we acknowledge each other, but not, I am glad to say, with any weak, friendly sentiment or desire to be well thought of between us to mar the isolation we enjoy. An armed neutrality, a tacit agreement to ignore, prevails. I am afraid I often break this understanding. I watch him narrowly though with a pretence of indifference, for he interests me. He is a pale, clear grey, with a murderous-looking hooked bill, black mustachios, a big black cheek-stripe and black-and-white wings and tail. His square, top-heavy build is balanced by the length of his tail, and he has a ruthless, efficient look. The lesser shrikes live amidst cultivation and greenery, by themselves no doubt, but tolerating neighbours. The Grey

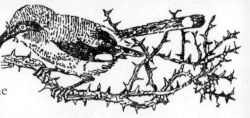

Shrike scorns company, and retires to some patch of desolate thorn where he can be alone.

He sits upright and still, and wears an air of unconcern. At times he fluffs his plumage and humps his back and seems to go to sleep—but no bird is more wide awake. Something stirs in the brown grass twenty yards away and he pounces down to the earth, to return to his perch with the prey clutched securely in his claws. He holds it down with his feet and batters it with his great, hooked bill, and then he eats, not greedily as other birds do, but bit by bit. A thin, green wing and long, horny legs drop down beside me and I know that the victim was a grasshopper. Grasshoppers seem to constitute his staple diet, but he varies this with crickets, mole crickets and an occasional lizard. And once he brought a yellow fledgling, just hatched, to his bough, which he took a long time to eat. Shrikes will eat anything they can catch and conquer. They have a habit of impaling their surplus catch on thorns, against lean times, but though I have looked carefully I cannot discover the larder of this butcher. I can well believe that he finds it hard enough to feed himself in the domain he has chosen for his own.

The call of this shrike is harsh and brief. His voice is rarely heard, but sometimes, when I grow too inquisitive and shed my reserve, he flies away with a quick, grating call. And yesterday, early in the morning. I heard a sweet liquid song from the tree outside, and a cautious reconnoitre revealed, to my surprise, that the singer was this businesslike shrike. A most significant thing, but this is not all. His plumage seems richer and fuller than when I met him first, a fortnight ago, and the grey of his back has taken on a hint of silver. I don't suppose I shall be here when he nests, but I am sure he will not enjoy his own company much longer. He will woo and win his mate, big and severe and grey as himself, and he will sing to her. But even then they will conduct themselves with a certain dignity and restraint uncommon in other birds. Afterwards, finding food for a growing family they will have little time for any display of affection, and when summer is over they will part, back to the lonely bit of waste over which each holds territory.

THE INDIAN ROBIN

The Indian Robin is a dinky little bird, bigger than a sparrow, but slimly built, with a long expressive tail. The cock is a glossy black all over—in flight each wing shows a narrow bar of white. North of the Godavari, the cock robin has a dark brown back. The hens, all over India, are the colour of sun-baked clay. Both sexes have a reddish patch under the root of the tail. This, however, is far less flagrant than the textbooks would make one think, when the bird is in the bush. The plumage lies close and sleek on the body—few birds look less like the fluffed-out Red-breast of Christmas cards. If you see a trim, small, black bird, accompanied by a trim, small, clay-coloured bird, you may safely put them down for a pair of Indian Robins.

These birds are common all over the plains, but are specially fond of suburban roads and compounds, particularly of compounds with bamboo-fencing around, over which creepers trail. Early in the morning you will see them skipping along the ground, turning over a dead leaf or inspecting some crevice in a tree trunk, looking for things to eat. In the evening you will find them still at it, getting the late worm. There is very little their casual glances miss. The Indian Robin hunts efficiently, but with an airiness that, alas, so rarely goes with efficiency. It is beautifully balanced in every movement, betraying no hint of the jerky, fidgety energy of most small birds. Only, its tail keeps fanning out, and closing, and wagging, like a thing endowed with independent animation. Give me creatures that wag their tails—they have joyous hearts.

The robin is not a gregarious bird. It is content with the company of its mate, never straying far from some chosen spot. However, no one will call it unsociable. I knew three pairs of robins that used to share in common the mean little compound of a house where I lived.

236

Evidently these unlettered birds had not read about the Theory of Territorial Claims! They would come fearlessly up the steps and even into the verandas, but no further. They like human associations, but are not parasitic on man like the House Sparrow. Very often robins build in a stable or an old shed, or even on a sheltered window-ledge. In a country where there is no scarcity of insect life, and no frosts, it is unlikely that these birds will come right in and establish themselves in the house; and they make uninteresting cage birds. But people whose liking for living things is not wholly possessive will never grudge the robin its freedom.

BULBULS' NEST

An eight-foot high kalli hedge limits the eastern boundary of my compound, and serves to keep the goats and cattle out. No beast can force its way through without getting spattered all over with the thick, white, corroding milk from the fragile phyllodes, that burns and irritates the skin, but birds with their insignificant weight and covering of feathers have no fear of the euphorbia. My neighbour's hens sit under the kalli hedge all day and scratch in its shade, dozens of sparrows roost in it each night, and some time ago a pair of Red-vented Bulbuls built their nest in it, in a green fork level with my head.

Bulbuls are not specially talented architects. Some of them nest in treetops at safe elevations, and some are careless even with regard to height. The Red-vented Bulbul is content with any site it can find, and usually nests in bushes and hedges, not far from the ground. The nest in my kalli hedge is typical of the bird—a few thin twigs and stringy roots twined together in a shallow teacup lined with fibres and grass. The nest is placed within the hedge, with a branch of the kalli overhanging it, but otherwise there is no attempt at concealment. An unremarkable nest, and now deserted and broken by the wind and rain, but it has a story to tell.

I first noticed this nest early in August, when there were four little speckled eggs in it, and by the last week of the month there were three naked, squirming squabs in it—the fourth egg disappeared, cleanly and without a trace. From the easy chair on my veranda I could see the bulbuls coming in with food for their young. Every few minutes, the intervals depending on the quickness with which they could catch an insect, one or the other parent would come flying in, perch on the overhanging bough, dive under to the nest, and emerge a moment later with nothing in its beak. The weather seemed to be a decisive factor in food supply.

High winds and heavy showers are frequent in August, and during spells of rain I noticed that the bulbuls kept to the nest. Obviously, it was futile to seek prey then, and one of the birds would stay with the young in the nest, sheltering them with fluffed plumage and slightly spread wings.

When I saw the nest it struck me that it was hardly the time of year for perpetuating the species. Mid-monsoon months, with tearing winds and downpours in the offing, is no time to rear young, especially in a nest placed in a kalli hedge. But I revised my opinion when, with each visit to the nest, I could see the young growing apace and gaining in size. They seemed to have a native hardiness that I had not allowed for, and the nest did give them a measure of insulation. Their bodies were now covered with dark, incipient plumage, though their eyes were still closed, and on sensing my approach they would open their disproportionately large mouths to the extent of their gape, squirm about and clamour for food. This violent reaction to any approach to the nest is instinctive, and I suppose it gets the young an adequate supply of food, since normally only the parents with food come to the nest. But I wonder if this does not serve, in some measure, a protective function as well. The sight of a nestful of agitated fledglings with enormous, gaping, raw, red mouths might well have a discouraging effect on a prospective predator.

Some days ago the weather took on a cold edge all of a sudden, and that night there was torrential rain, followed by a stiff wind. Next morning I noticed that the bulbuls were no longer visiting their nest with food, and when I went to it the three fledglings were lying stretched in it, cold, stiff and unresponsive. By evening some bodysnatcher had removed them.

Only the bedraggled nest remains now to bear witness to this unhappy story. The nesting pair has left the hedge and might well be one of the dozen pairs of bulbuls around my house that enliven each day with their rattling, buoyant, cheering calls. Later on, no doubt, they will rear another brood, in the milder and more even weather of November. It is not strength or wisdom or courage that survives, but persistent domesticity, and these bulbuls that breed through the year will live forever, assuredly.

COCKNEYS IN THE COUNTRY

Whoever would think that Philip Sparrow, perky, cocksure and bumptiously dominant in the city, would lose heart in the countryside and become a mild and modest bird! It is windy space that works the change. The assertive, loud chirp is toned down by open air to a weak treble, and no longer sure of themselves in enhanced surroundings, the birds seek comfort in company. They go about in tight flocks, settling in a kit on threshing yard and harvested field, gleaning the stubble together. And when they fly, high and long as they rarely do in cities, they keep together still, and cheep to one another as they go dipping and rising overhead—their voices in passage, refined by tall air, have a tinkling, almost musical quality.

Now, I know it is all wrong to judge birds (or beasts for that matter) by our experience and to attribute human motives to them. But I believe in the 'one touch of nature' that 'makes the whole world kin,' and am unaware of scientific evidence against the view that animals can experience feelings and emotions known to us. Surely a bird feels fright and joy and depression as acutely as we do—their manifestations may be very different in a bird, and, of course, it is utterly wrong to ascribe intellectual appreciation or sentiment to it, but it feels these things all the same; I think we can understand animals emotionally at times, when reason makes no sense.

Once, on a beach near Masulipatam, I realized what loneliness could mean. I was walking along a vast expanse of flat grey sand, with a flat grey sea beyond, and there was no life anywhere around except for an occasional, scuttling crab towards which I could feel no affinity. There was a level breeze blowing, no friendly bush or mound broke the dreary, grey flatness stretching away from me as far as the eye could see, and suddenly I felt puny and insignificant. My stride seemed bereft of progress and my tracks on the sand only deepened the conviction of my futile nonentity. I was a bug, crawling hopelessly on, and I was quite alone in the gathering dusk. I have often been alone, but that was the only time I felt the need for company. It seems likely, to me, that birds in open country are more gregarious from a somewhat similar cause. I think that animals, in common with us, gain confidence in restricted settings.

Naturally, all diurnal creatures grow less jaunty as daylight fails and seek safe retreats, but I think the roosting of these countryside sparrows is significant to what I have been saying. They do not retire in pairs and parties to spend the night on a rafter or a lofty bough, but crowd in hundreds in a tangled bush or some low, much-branched tree, so thickly together that the foliage seems suddenly doubled in the dark. Dozens huddle in rows along twiggy boughs, each row possessed of a confluent, coenobitic unity by the bodily contact of its birds. There is no prolonged hubbub at these roosts, as there is at the roosting trees of other birds. There is a confused chirping as the sparrows come in and settle, then the chirps grow thinner and subdued till they fade altogether. By the time it is dark there is hushed silence, and the birds are huddled and immobile—but many of them are awake still.

Other birds also roost thickly in bushes, in the scrub. Mynahs, bee-eaters, munias, Grey and White Wagtails, all crowd into bushes or trees at sunset, often in hundreds. These same birds in the less open habitat of cities and towns, are less massively sociable when roosting: there are exceptions, but on the whole they are definitely less sociable in urban settings. I believe it is the too open, limitless expanse of the countryside that makes all these birds pack solidly together, as night draws in. There is safety in close numbers—or a sense of safety. However, the fact remains remarkable that sparrows, the most self-assertive and cocky of cosmopolitan creatures, should be so diffident, tentative, and constantly together in the scrub.

THE EAR
THAT HEARS

'SUMMER IS ICUMEN IN'

The last days of February were unusually warm and dry in Bangalore. Old residents are hoping that the weather will turn cooler soon, and less uneven, for the rare early summer in Bangalore endures and is warm. In this salubrious climate the hot weather begins about April, and soon after the 'mango showers' arrive to tone it down. This year, I am afraid, they are in for a long, hot spell, for I have been hearing the Coppersmiths lately and at the beginning of this month I heard them calling steadily through the noon, announcing to all that summer had opened formally.

The Coppersmith may be justly called the voice of summer. Not only in Bangalore, but all over India, this little, vivid barbet grows vocal as the hot weather sets in, and then, till it is cool again, you hear its metallic, monotonous *tonk...tonk...tonk...* right through the fiercest hours of day. Summer has many voices in our country: the Koel (though this bird is more typical of midsummer spring), the brainfever bird, the ardent roller, palm squirrels, even the Coppersmith's larger cousin—the Common Green Barbet—which says *kutur...kutur...kutur* instead of tonking and says it later into the evening. But none of them, I think, is so sure a sign of summer's onset as the midday voice of the Coppersmith. Of course, any bird may be deceived into a false start by capricious weather, and a succession of summery days may start Coppersmiths calling, but birds are conservative in such matters and their perceptions are sound—when these barbets are calling steadily at noon, a sustained *tonk...tonk...* that goes on unfalteringly down to the foot of this page, it is a reliable indication; and that is why I am confident that summer has arrived to stay in these parts.

The Coppersmith is a gaudy bird, green above and yellowish below, with a crown and bib of true scarlet, crimson feet, a black-bordered

yellow patch around each eye, and a thick dark bill. As if to compensate for this exuberance of colouring, it is remarkably squat and economical in build, with no plumes and appendages beyond a bristling moustache. 'Coppersmith' describes its voice admirably, but its other name—the Crimson-breasted Barbet—is inadequate. However, the official title *Xantholoema haemacephala* does justice to its colouring and bloody crown.

Figs of various kinds have an irresistible appeal to this bird, and it is fond of the shady sanctuary of fig trees. It has been rightly said that in spite of its vivid patches the Coppersmith's colouring is assimilative—in its favourite haunt, the banyan in red fruit, its plump silhouette is almost invisible against the broad green leaves and bright, rounded fruit. The bird throws its head about while calling, and it is true that because of this habit it is hard to say from which tree it is calling when one is at some distance, but from near or under its tree it is easy to spot the Coppersmith from its voice.

Like all barbets, the Coppersmith is strictly arboreal. I do not think it ever comes down to drink. Often, in the blistering heat of a Madras April afternoon, I have wondered how it can call so persistently, with not a drop to ease its parched throat. A vendor of dried figs once told me that the fruit was excellent for summer heat and cooling in the extreme—I have the uncharitable feeling that had I met him during the rains, he would have assured me that a diet of figs was the thing for the wet and cold; but perhaps there was truth in what he said.

M. Krishnan

MARCH ROLLER

The March Hare, my dictionary tells me, gets its name for madness from its 'gambols during the breeding season.' I wonder what the sedate scholarly men who made the book would have said, when confronted with the March Roller. Perhaps, for all their words, the sight would have left them speechless.

For the roller is a sedentary bird at other times, respectable, even gentlemanly in a lazy sort of way. All day long it sits on some exposed perch, drab, squat and inert, indifferent to the blazing sun and the breeze that ruffles its plumage. I have seen a roller knocked off its balance and post by a gust of wind, pick itself up in the air and resume its seat in the open, in the most offhand manner. From time to time it comes out with a deep chortle (not a specially refined sound, but guttural enough to have tonal strength), but nothing breaks its bored, slumped repose otherwise. Even when it sights some passing insect and gives chase, bursting into dazzling blues with the spread of its pinions and tail, there is nothing hurried or undignified about its movements—it flaps lazily along on broad, sapphire and azure wings, like some gigantic butterfly, takes its prey casually from the air, and then flaps its way back to its pole. What is gentlemanliness, after all, but a superiority to crude emotional displays (or its affectation when others are looking)? The roller has it even when feeding. Till late in March.

Then, all at once it sheds its reserve, and becomes a thing demented. Love is a powerful influence; even in the highest animals it has been known to induce a sudden, abandoned silliness. In birds, however, whose emotional lives are not screened by reason or self-consciousness, it often reaches its climax of expression in aerial displays and melody. There is a quickening pattern leading up to a grand finale in their courtship displays, or else an undercurrent of audible, welling fervour.

But the courting roller goes plain crazy, abandons its perch, and flies about with manic energy and aimlessness. It scours the heavens, not in soaring circles, not in steep, acrobatic loops, but just anyhow. The broad wings lose their good-natured flapping action, and beat a pathless course for the bird through the air. At times it flies high and wild, when the colours of its flights and tail grow invisible and dark against the sky. So lost are its blues in the distance, so unlike its lubberly self is it on the wing now, that one who has not seen an ardent roller before could mistake it for some other bird.

And not content with this exhibition of incoherent flight, the roller sings—all the time it is flying—in an incredibly hoarse voice. At no time has it a pleasant voice, but usually it is discreetly laconic. In March, however, it sings as it flies, and its song is even more pointless than its flight; but fortunately confined to a single note, a long-drawn, grating shout. It climbs into the sky and dives recklessly earthwards, singing its harsh song unceasingly—on a still day you can hear the courting roller from half a mile away, and the increase in volume of the song alone is sufficient to tell you of its headlong descent. There are many unaccomplished musicians among birds, but few with such a raucous or persistent voice. However, it is the voice of love, inspired by the same feeling that prompts the nightingale and the lark.

Luckily, the inspiration passes. Once it mates and nests—the event varies with place and climate, but is from April to July—the roller settles down to the business of perpetuating the species, a thing that it does with its usual sang-froid, and it has no time for giddy flights and song. Later still you will find it on some pole in the sun, so staid and sober that you would have passed the bird by, but for a deep-throated chuckle.

M. Krishnan

DID YOU DO IT?

'The winter is past, the rain is over and gone; the flowers appear on the earth,' but the official opening of the vernal season is still months away. And when it does open, it will be very unlike what English poets say it is in England.

> *In the Spring the wanton lapwing gets himself another crest…*
> *In the Spring a young man's fancy lightly turns to thoughts of*
> *love.*

It is not at all like that here. There is no seasonal limit to the fancy of our young men, and our lapwing has no crest, not even in midsummer when it is the peak of spring in India.

It is different altogether from the English lapwing though related in a cousinly sort of way. Birds of the same English name in diverse countries are not necessarily of the same feather. The robin, for instance, is a wholly different bird in England, in America and in India—in fact, most countries have their own distinctive robin. The sparrow-hawk, the Grackle and the chat may be only distantly related, or even unrelated, to their namesakes in other lands, and I mention these three merely in an illustrative manner. However, lapwings everywhere belong to the plover group.

All of them are long-legged and light-footed, and broad and lazy of wing, though capable of strong flight—it is from their flapping, lubberly wing action that they get their tribal name. But there are several kinds of them in India. The one I term 'our lapwing' is the Red-wattled Lapwing, commonest of the tribe, the handsome, familiar *Did-you-do-it?* that is one of the few birds to figure in our legends.

Its call, admirably rendered by the words *Did-you-do-it?*, is quite distinctive, even when the black-and-white head and neck, red wattle and yellow legs are unseen. The only other bird for which it can be mistaken from a distance is the Yellow-wattled Lapwing, its younger brother, but the latter does not ask the querulous question *Did-you-do-it?* as it rises into the air in alarm.

The Red-wattled Lapwing is not a specially sociable bird (incidentally, there is a Sociable Lapwing); it is usually by itself or with its mate, though as many as six may be seen together on occasion. It is essentially a shorebird, fond of the shingly margins of lakes and drying riverbeds, but equally at home on plough land and in jungle clearings. It runs easily about on its neat, yellow legs, looking for its living in the sand and shingle and clods. And its knowledge of human intentions is uncanny.

It is noticeably less distrustful of humanity when on plough land or the bare, pathless thoroughfares around villages where men are on their own ground, but nowhere does it permit a near approach. Sitting in the open, in a dry nullah, I have watched this bird for quite long periods—it would invariably take wing in loud alarm at my approach, but soon alight some distance away. Any furtive movement, such as the creeping behind cover of a man with a gun towards duck in a lake or some other quarry, is instantly detected and blatantly advertised—the bird circles above the lurker, brandishing the white bar in its slow wings, as if to add indicative direction to its strident alarm. I may be imaginative, but when a lapwing proclaims the stalker in this manner its call seems to me slightly longer and more insistent in each syllable and definitely more urgent—a *Don't you see him?* rather than anything else. Naturally, shikaris have little love for the bird, and its Tamil name, 'Aat-kaattikuruvi', is remarkably descriptive—'the bird that points out men,' literally translated.

When you see a pair of lapwings on a pebbly shore or field, and one of them flutters right in front of you, be sure the eggs are somewhere near, a clutch of three or four pointed eggs, pointed ends inward in a scrape in the earth, and so like the pebbles in their mottled indetermination that you are not likely to see them till you step on them. Incidentally, you need not look for them where the fluttering bird was—they are likely to be near where its mate was.

Countryside legend credits the lapwing with the habit of sleeping on its back, so that it may catch and hold up the heavens in its feet should they collapse and fall while it is asleep. The legend has been interpreted by scholars as one illustrative of grotesquely exaggerated conceit; their comment is to the effect, 'As if such a small bird could hold up in its feet something so huge and heavy as the firmament!' But I believe the legend could be more truly taken as one symbolic of the bird's wariness.

No naturalist can assert that the lapwing does not sleep on its back, for who has caught it? At night the bird is but even wider awake than by day, and I should think its sudden call is one of the most reliable of nocturnal alarms, telling the listener that something is moving nearby, unless, of course, he himself is the cause. I have rarely heard the bird when it was quite dark, but when there is moonlight it calls frequently and I have heard it by such faint light that though I knew from the sound that it was flying directly overhead, maybe twenty or thirty yards above, I was not able to see it.

A MIDDAY CHORUS

About one o'clock it came on to rain. It began gradually and mildly, with a great pearl-grey cloud spreading itself across the sky, rendering the midday light wonderfully soft and clear. There was a refreshing coolness in the air, but no palpable breeze. In fact, it was as if the hot, sweltering jungle had been magically air-conditioned and furnished with diffused artificial illumination and a mother-of-pearl ceiling.

I was lying on my back in a sandy riverbed, in the shade of a tall tree. I had gone to sleep dog-tired and feeling ill, and woken up only minutes later to find the sky and air and jungle transformed, and a euphoria in me. Almost a hundred feet above was the top of a giant culm of bamboo, leaning over the nullah from a great clump on the bank; a pair of Grey Drongos were perched on that swaying bamboo-top, and all at once they burst into song, a series of trilling, wildly sweet calls.

Immediately, as if this were the signal for which the other birds had been waiting, a medley of musical bird voices filled the air. It was a chorus such as I have never heard before—and I have heard the exhilarating chorus of White-bellied Drongos in the cold greyness before dawn, the Racket-tailed Drongo's ecstatic song to the rising sun, the welling rhapsody of the Shama at dusk in the bamboo jungle, and many mixed dawn choruses, but this was something different, differently compounded.

A tree pie, nearby, joined in with almost-chimed metallic calls, varied from time to time with its familiar *ting-a-ling*; the loud melody of a party of Hill-Mynahs came through clearly, and nearer at hand some other drongos (probably White-bellied) were singing; the cadenced *broken pekoe* of the Indian Cuckoo, a call that I love, was so pleasantly repeated from behind the bamboo clump, and less musical voices, the distant screams of parakeets, the jabber of Jungle-Mynahs and even the faintly heard axle-creak call of a serpent-eagle circling high overhead, somehow did not seem out of place in that chorus. And dominating everything was the insistent, never-ending *papiha, papiha, papiha!* of the hawk-cuckoo—the bird was some distance away, but its call cuts through distances effortlessly and has a peculiar penetration that gets through nearer bird voices.

A great black woodpecker almost the size of a crow (this was the Malabar Great Black Woodpecker) was hammering away at a dead limb of the tree above me, providing the throbbing drum-accompaniment to the many-voiced chorus. The hammering of this bird is sustained over a length of one and a half to two seconds, and I have often timed it with a stopwatch. I had often tried to count the number of evenly spaced bill-strokes within this period, but been unable to get a precise count. This time I had no difficulty in making the count several times. There were from fifteen to twenty 'beats' in each long-drawn throb of hammering. Since these were evenly spaced, each impact and interval must be about one-twentieth of a second long. I had thought it would be much shorter.

The chorus was sustained and continuous and ended as suddenly as it began. I heard the mahout and his assistant summoning the elephant, browsing at a nearby clump of bamboo, just before the drongos burst into song, and since it takes about fifteen minutes to get a reluctant elephant to abandon its lunch and lie down, lay the pad on its back and tie it down securely, probably the chorus extended over that space of time. A lazy drizzle arrived with the elephant, and gradually the rain gathered momentum. The bird voices were stilled the minute the drizzle grew brisk.

We reached the shelter of a permanent observation platform just as the rain came down in earnest. For two hours, it rained heavily without a break, the long, vertical streaks of water coming down relentlessly all around us. Visibility was very poor, and no sound came through the dreary noise of the rain. But when the rain stopped abruptly and the sky began to clear I saw a curious sight.

There was a great mango tree close by, and two Hill-Mynahs and a Jungle-Mynah were practising a remarkable exercise right at the top of its towering bole. There were some holes in the wood high up in the tree, and when I saw them first, through the slackening rain, the birds were sitting in these holes, ruffled up and sheltered from the downpour.

Then they came out, and clinging to the bark with their claws, slithered down a few yards, and then climbed up the bole again using both feet and violently flapped wings to propel them; then they slithered down again and flapped their way up once more. I thought there was a definite purpose in this game to dry the flight feathers before the birds dared to take wing again. They flew away after five minutes to another tall tree where they went through the exercise again thrice or four times, and then they flew away for good.

VOICE OF THE DUSK

When the sun has set and the outskirts of the village are lost in the gathering darkness, the nightjars wake up from their daytime repose and bestir themselves. There is much *chuck-chuck-chuckurring*, calls melt together as the birds begin to answer one another, and ghostly forms circle around on wings that are soundless whether sailing or flapping. One evening last week I sat in a clearing outside a village, still as the rock beneath me, watching the circling and settling nightjars, almost invisible in that light even on the wing, and listening to their voices.

Those who associate fluty tones with birdsong will be pleasantly surprised at the soft rhythm of these voices of the lonely dusk. There is no resonance or 'full-throated ease' in a nightjar's call; it is a subdued *chuck-chuck-chuckurr-r-r* that has been justly likened to the sound of a stone sent scudding across ice. But it has a sure rhythm in it that is all the more enchanting for its lack of emphasis, it is so much and so naturally the voice of the uncertain greyness. He who has not been alone and listened to the chorus of nightjars and has not inhaled the sudden perfume of the wild night-flowering jasmine does not know the charm of dusk in the Indian plains.

Crepuscular birds, nightjars in particular, greet the coming darkness as diurnal birds greet dawn, with wings and voices. More strictly nocturnal birds are vocal and very active for a brief spell after emerging from their daytime retreats; and gregarious day birds, like sparrows and mynahs in September-October, are specially noisy and keep shifting around till it is quite dark when roosting; some, like crows and lapwings, invariably call and fly when the moon is bright. It was such things that I thought of that evening.

When it is quite dark and night has definitely arrived, the chorus of the nightjars dies down and the birds appear to drift away from the

open gathering ground. Their huge eyes are admirably suited to seeing through the dark, just as their softly barred plumage and owlishly silent wings, and the ear-to-ear gape of their mouths, are suited to the hunting of night-flying insects. However, as anyone who has travelled across country roads at night knows, quite a substantial part of the night is spent by these birds on the ground, squatting in the dust of the roadside.

You see a pair of ember-red eyes in the glare of your headlamps, eyes that seem buried in the dust of the road, then you see the mottled, indistinct form of the bird squatting low, and then, as the relentless tyres are about to crush it under, it rises on soundless wings to go floating ahead of the car or low overhead, the sudden white bar on each wing proclaiming its identity.

Sometimes it flies so low overhead that you feel you can reach up and pluck it out of the air—in fact, I have known a nightjar so captured. And not always is its last-second swerve infallible; once I saw the bird hit the side of the mudguard and fall back on to the road.

Motorists who know only the hard-surfaced and tarred main roads will probably be less familiar with the bird, but sometimes it is seen even on such roads, when the scrub adjoins the roadway and there is dust enough at the sides. Why it sits so constantly on the roadway I do not know; other birds, like the finch-larks, also love the earth-road, and perhaps the loose-plumaged nightjar likes a frequent dust-bath—or perhaps it finds the road convenient for its hawking of insects. The only thing I can say is that if I had to spend much time reposing on the road, I, too, would prefer the cushioning dust to the metalled surface.

MYNAHS EN MASSE

I remember an evening in Bombay, many Januarys ago, when I was shopping in a hurry in a particularly crowded bazaar. The rest of the world also seemed to be in a hurry, and as it grew darker, the frantic hustle and enquiries and jostlings of the almost confluent crowd of shoppers drowned even the noise of traffic. But above it all, clear above the confused hubbub of human voices, hooting motors and grating trams, I could hear hundreds of mynahs, roosting close on roof and rafter, telling one another excitedly of the day's doings.

I had seen mynahs roosting in the heart of a city before, in Mysore and elsewhere (I do not know why it is, but they seem to have a penchant for the main bazaar), but nowhere had I heard louder evidence of their vocal superiority over the utmost that man (and woman, even) can achieve.

However, if you want to know how loud these birds can be in company, you should visit the roosting sites of mynahs in the countryside, for here they foregather in larger numbers than in urban places; and with no competing human noises, you can appreciate better the carrying power and fervour of their late evening tumult. About this time of the year mynahs roost together in the countryside, flock after flock coming in from all around to the chosen site as darkness sets in. Our birds are generally more congregational during the cold weather than at other times, from a variety of probable causes—I am speaking of resident birds, of course, and not of migrants. And, of course, I write of the Common Mynah, the loudest and longest of the vociferous mynah clan, when it really gets together.

The roosting site is often near a piece of water, and while there seems to be no preference for particular trees, I have known a clump of acacias (babool) to be favoured. The roosting trees are usually and fortunately some distance from human habitation, but it requires no great effort or cunning to locate them. All that you have to do is to go out into the evening and listen. Presently, a distant but audible clamour breaks in on you, which gains in volume and clarity as you walk straight towards it.

At no time is the Common Mynah soft-voiced, not even when it is decorously parading your lawn, reducing the grasshopper population. The voice of this bird is naturally robust, and harsh, and it loves to hear itself. But a mynah by itself, or with a mate, hunting prey, is a comparatively silent creature. When the day is done and there is no longer the preoccupation of the chase, when the oncoming night limits conversation to a few brief, insufficient minutes, it is then that the mynah feels the urge to tell its fellows all the news, and to be first with the gossip. Like all good talkers it finds company stimulating. The din at its rural roosts is indescribable.

However, what impresses me at these communal roosts is not the vocal ugliness of these birds, but the thought of the solid good that they must be doing us. They live mainly on insects and worms, and by a not unnatural association of voice with mouth, I have always been reminded, as I retreated from the clamour of the roost and the voices of the mynahs would grow less and less discordant, of the untold numbers of harmful insects that go down these mouths each day.

OF BIRDS AND BIRDSONG

Some time ago I heard a caged Shama sing in a bylane of one of the most congested parts of Madras. Its owner, a Muslim artisan, had built his pet a roomy bamboo cage, considerately provided with two perches. He was careful to give it the kind of food it should get, and though he could afford no luxuries, he had made a cover of fine, loose-woven green silk, spangled with tinsel stars, for the cage; he explained that this served to keep the bird relaxed and quiet at night, and saved it from being frightened by passing cats, while still letting the air in; moreover, for some reason beyond him, it made the bird sing more freely.

In the close confinement of that tiny room, cluttered up with broken chairs and an assortment of tin trunks and gaudy cardboard boxes, with children shrieking and playing in the lane outside and an altercation between two women literally next door, the Shama's sustained, liquid melody was as surprising and lovely as anything could be, but it did not delight me. Not that an anthropomorphic, sentimental feeling for the prisoner dampened my spirits. It was only that song, at all times and of whatever kind, is as dependent on the environment and the musical experience of the listener as it is on the singer, and that I had heard the Shama many times in the dark, cool jungles that it loves.

In particular, I remember a few days in the forest block of Supa in Karwar. The great deciduous forest was all around our camp, and not far away there was a patch of giant bamboo, and a pair of Shamas had nested in one of the clumps. Every morning and evening, before sunrise and at sunset, I would go over to the bamboo patch to hear the cock's song. The Shama's song has been extensively studied by experts like Dr Thorpe, both from its live voice and from recordings (to borrow terms from broadcasting), but few of these men have heard the bird in the jungles where it lives, and I think that the appeal of birdsong, in particular, is much dependent on its setting.

Would Keats have written—

In some melodious plot
Of beechen green, and shadows numberless,
Singest of summer in full-throated ease.

—if he had only heard the nightingale singing from a cramped, shrouded cage in the smoky murkiness of London? Very likely he would. The much-vaunted Keatsian sensuous imagery has always seemed to me wholly independent of experience or recollection, and entirely the product of imagination conditioned by a feeling for euphony. The man was a songbird in a sense: he could sing from a cage.

However that might be, the Shama should be heard in the deciduous forests that are its natural home. The feathery, cool green leaves and intricate tracery of the bamboo branchlets provide

a fit auditorium for its welling melody, ineffably sad to the human ear at one moment and cascading with liquid delight the next. We know, of course, that birdsong is more an instinctive proclamation of territory and part of courtship display than anything else, and we do not know for certain what moods the avian mind can sense. But then I am writing only of human apprehension of birdsong, and nothing that I have ever heard has affected me so spontaneously and deeply as the Shama's song.

M. Krishnan

THE BIRDS OF PEACE

A pair of Ring Doves perched placidly on the top twigs of a twisted, villainously thorny tree might suggest the hopes of peace in a world torn by hatred and intolerance to most people, for doves are the accepted symbols of peace and goodwill, and specially noted in poetic traditions for their gentleness. Such a thought will never cross the mind of a naturalist because, as many have pointed out, from 'Eha' to Konrad Lorenz, few birds are more quarrelsome or intolerant of others. An excerpt from a recent ornithological text on the Ring Dove seems indicated at this juncture. Here is what Salim Ali and Dillon Ripley have to say on the bird in their weighty tome: 'Very pugnacious when nesting, chasing an intruder in its territory with vigour and determination, literally from "pillar to post", accompanied by the strident challenging *koon-koon* as "war cry", until driven off. On the ground the rivals sidle up to one another rather surreptitiously, then suddenly jump up and lash out viciously with the wings…'

Prey Species

So much for the territorial possessiveness of the bird. Its extraterritorial acquisitiveness is no less remarkable. As a class, pigeons and doves (the line of demarcation between them is thin and almost invisible at times) are the prey species of a great many different kinds of predators, but being fecund have generally managed to survive, though now, with human invasion of their haunts, some are on the decline. Not so the Ring Dove. It favours dry, open scrub jungles (though it is also there in the forests of Assam) and is very much a bird of such tracts in many oriental countries, but in recent years it has made a conquest of foreign lands, and is now breeding in Britain and Scandinavia. That, of course, is quite in keeping with the popular attribute of meekness to it, for does not the good book say 'the meek shall inherit the earth'?

Doves do form gregarious associations at times, as when feeding on the ground, gleaning a harvested field or a patch of short grass that is in seed. At such times, even several Ring Doves may feed amicably together, sometimes also in association with lesser members of their tribe, such as Little Brown Doves. Moreover, if gentleness and a peaceable disposition are to be judged by wholly non-violent means of procuring food, doves are gentle all right. Many seed-eating birds, like sparrows and their kin, feed only on purely vegetable fare when adult, but their nestlings are provided with a high-protein diet of insects actively hunted and killed, and then dismembered, by their parents. The squabs of pigeons and doves are fed softened, part-digested grain from the parental crop, the semi-liquid sustenance termed 'pigeon-milk.'

Part of the reason for the dove being chosen as the emblem of peace probably lies in its modest, sober but most comely looks. Doves do not sport crests and combs, flamboyant tail-plumes and hackles, and as a rule their plumage is not brightly colourful. There is an Emerald Dove, it is true, that does have an authentic emerald sheen, and there are other doves that have flashes of colour, but these are not the birds featured in the emblem, which shows a modestly pale grey dove with no frills and fancy touches—only a delicate vinaceous bloom to its grey in places.

And doves have soothing voices. They do not chirp and cheep or whistle boldly, or caw or scream or even indulge in a song. Their voice is repetitive and crooning, but highly distinctive. In fact, one can spot the identity of a dove from its calls, even if one does not see it. Not all doves, it is true, have pleasant voices—for instance, the Rufous Turtle Dove has a high, somewhat nasal and querulous call, the same phrase reiterated with the repetitions running into one another monotonously. But even the Ring Dove has a deep, pleasant, repeated trisyllable call, with the middle syllable much prolonged, in addition to its 'war cry'.

Soothing Voices

One of the pleasantest bird voices I have heard is the *kruk-kruk-kruk: kroo, kroo, kroo* of the Spotted Dove, a bird common enough where there are trees and clearings. I seldom sleep by day and not much at night, but in summer sometimes indulge in a brief siesta. On such occasions, I can hear Spotted Doves from a clump of trees in a neighbouring compound. On the brink of sleep, one's hearing becomes highly selective; I can no longer hear the lorries on the road outside the gate, but the voice of the Spotted Dove comes through, clear if progressively fainter—a lullaby sweeter than any I have ever heard.

BIRD LANGUAGE

In the tales of Vikramaditya, you will remember, there was a talking parakeet. A happy choice, for it is true that parrots and parakeets, like mynahs, Hill-Mynahs and certain other birds, can be taught to mimic human speech. In Tamil poetry, parakeets have often been the chosen messengers of lovelorn maidens—this has no value as evidence, creatures that are usually silent, or even quite mute, like swans (which, incidentally, do not occur in Tamilnad) and storks and bumblebees, are among the traditional carriers of love messages in classical poetry. However, the point of this note is not whether some birds can be taught to imitate human speech and other sounds, or learn to do so for themselves—that they can, undoubtedly—but whether birds have a language of their own.

Of course most birds do, if by 'language' we mean sounds through which communication of some sort is effected. Personally, I would go further, remembering the time I lost my way in Banaras, and define language as sounds through which communication can be effected. The difference between the 'is' and the 'can be' of the two definitions may seem trivial at first sight, but it is vital. That time in Banaras, finding myself in an unfamiliar and thinly peopled lane, I asked half a dozen passers-by the way to the main bazaar, in two South Indian languages and in English, and what they said in reply I do not know, for it was in a dialect of Hindi that baffled me completely. Tamil and Kannada are two of the most ancient of our languages, English (as many have pointed out recently) is the tongue with the widest reach in the world today, and Hindi has been declared the national language of India—there can be no question of the claims of all these to the most eminent status as languages, but for all the communication then achieved I might have been the Man from Mars. Finally I was reduced to pantomime, and uttering the one word 'bazaar' clenched my fist into a visible interrogation—the man of whom I asked this, who evidently found my bewilderment amusing, burst out laughing, then pointed helpfully towards the heavens. Yes, language can be a means of communication all right, but need not necessarily serve that purpose every time.

Having warned ourselves of the ease with which language can be misunderstood, or even seem utterly meaningless, we are better placed to comprehend such languages as obtain among birds. We should also realize that much avian communication is effected through visual means, through attitudes and gestures, and that birds are unintelligent compared to the higher mammals (though I am convinced their lack of intelligence has been overstressed in modern popular science) and much more governed by dominating instincts and reactions. Their distinctively or colourfully marked plumage, with its wonderful capacity for erection and depression, and their quick ability to spread or close wing, tail and crest, lend themselves to a fluent diction of signals and displays. Since we have defined language as something uttered and heard, these visual communications which substitute or accompany sound production, and which play such a large part in the parental relationships, courtships, social life and responses of birds, cannot be detailed here though they must be mentioned.

Birds do not produce sound from a voice box in the throat, as most mammals do—their voice box is placed much lower down. Nor is all bird-sound cogent or produced only by the syrinx—some waterbirds, such as ibises, egrets and Spoonbills, have no call beyond a grunt or a hiccuping noise, and most storks (at least when adult) are dumb except for a clattering together of the mandibles.

Birdsong is, of course, part of avian language. It has been widely recognized among men in all countries, for the welling melody of birds like the skylark, the Magpie Robin, the Shama, the nightingale and the blackbird, has always impressed human ears with its notational purity and seeming ardour—the restive, repetitive call of the Koel, justly acclaimed as the 'voice of spring' by our poets, does suggest the fervid unrest of the vernal season. However, we should realize that the grating, far-reaching croak of the March Roller, zigzagging through the skies in its crazy courtship display, is no less the voice of love, and that many birds indulge in spectacular courtship displays without any accompaniment of song—the peacock, for example. The uses of birdsong in claiming and holding territory, in warning rivals and in courtship, have been so well established by careful study during the past few decades that ornithologists are apt to look askance at anyone who imagines that the song of a bird can be spontaneous expression of elation—though they would do well to think twice before they come out with the ugly-sounding word 'anthropomorphic', for many naturalists in different countries (among them the most eminent of our generation) accept that boredom, elation, and similar feelings may serve as impetus to birdsong. And we do know, just as we know that birds are governed by powerful instincts and responses, that they are highly emotional as well, and that to think of them as automatic, vivid little repositories of a series of conditioned reflexes would be every bit as unscientific as the worst flights of anthropomorphism. It may be argued that since, anyway, courtship, territorial proclamation and the inspiration of moods are all personal, birdsong has no meaning outside a limited domestic circle or except to the individual bird, that it has no social significance. That would be to ignore the well-known phenomenon of the dawn chorus, and the less celebrated but equally interesting roosting choruses of many birds.

It is the call-notes of gregarious and highly vocal birds that have been closest studied by men. Some of these calls have a significance outside the species and genus, and even the avian class. For example, many avian alarm calls are recognized by other animals. Even we can comprehend these alarms provided we have heard them before and listened carefully. The quick brief *'ware hawk!* call of small birds seems to be well known to squirrels and other small mammals. The jabbering of babblers or mynahs when a cat or snake enters their ground, and the 'swearing' of bulbuls are all distinctive alarm calls.

Crows and their cousins are among the most sapient of birds. Being long-lived, they do learn by experience to some extent, and their instinctive responses are strongly patterned. Ernest Thompson

Seton claimed to understand crow-language after a fashion, and has described the calls and typical call-attitudes of the American Crows he studied. Konrad Lorenz has gone one better—he has succeeded in imitating some corvine calls sufficiently well to be comprehensible to his pet raven! Much interesting work has been done on the calls and social behaviour of crows, but still we have much to learn. In recent experiments where French and American naturalists collaborated, it was found that the tape-recorded alarm calls and gathering calls of American Crows produced no response when broadcast to French 'crows' (rooks, jackdaws and carrion crows), and that the recorded calls of French crows seemed equally meaningless to their American cousins. The question whether this non-response is due to genetical or environmental factors has been asked, a question to which the answers can be rather complex and partial. I should add that the recorded alarm call of a species of bird has often been used to stimulate the very pattern of behaviour that a natural alarm call would induce.

While such scientific and properly controlled experimental work is most revealing and valuable, it can never completely substitute authentic field observation, and, to yield reliable results, must be most carefully assessed. Fieldwork can, of course, produce quite as many problems as experimental work. In Madras, I have repeatedly observed a Jungle Crow coming out with what sounds, to my ears, identical with the assembly call of its tribe—the bird sits on a bough or other perch and assumes a horizontal attitude when calling, the wings are frequently half-spread and fluttered, and the call is a reiterated, long-drawn *craaaa*. No Jungle Crow in the neighbourhood ever takes any notice of this display!

One circumstance that sometimes needlessly complicates the study of bird calls is a tendency to assume that every bird-sound must have some significance, or serve some purpose. When I read the dissertations of ornithologists on the possible purpose of some avian call, I feel thankful at times that these learned men are concerned solely with birds. How insufferable life would be if we did not have the freedom of loose speech, and a body of savants sought to discover meaning and purpose in every syllable that we uttered!

BIRDSONG IN INDIA—THE CUCKOOS

I sleep on a first-floor veranda, with a roof overhead and a wall to one side, but open to the air on all other sides, which give on to tree-filled backyards with no obstructing buildings.

Every morning an hour before daybreak while it is still dark and cool, I am awoken by Koels. The air around me throbs with their fervid voices till sunrise, but with the light getting stronger they move on to unseen trees beyond. Till 8 a.m., I can still hear them, but with the fervour and excitement in their voices rarefied by distance and overlain by other bird calls and human neighbourhood sounds.

Koels are a feature of the locality I live in. This part of the city is not wholly choked up with construction and holds some trees—birds still come to it. Actually, except during the Northeast Monsoon, Koels can be heard in every month, even at night when there is a moon. They begin calling early in the year, practising their crescendos, some cocks (first season birds?) with sudden cracks in their voices that gradually acquire the fluid continuity of their tribe. But only for about three months, to the rain in August, am I roused from sleep each day exhilaratingly in this manner by their predawn tumult. I can recognize three cock Koels by their voices, but cannot place the hen-calls, the sudden shouts, the quickfire stutterings and the high, thin *kekarees*.

Why do they indulge in this torrent of crescendos and calls, so long before the light? No comprehensive explanation seems possible, but then a likely one, even a possible one, will suffice. After all, with the vast and varied differences in sense perceptions and emotive expressions that exist between ourselves and the bewildering diversity of the rest of life, we will realize in due course that the current anthropocentric trend of

Song-birds
of India

natural history, to try and explain everything in logical terms, is only a little better than the earlier anthropomorphism it displaced.

The *Reader's Digest Book of British Birds* has an excellent section on why birds sing and call, which sums up current theories on the subject. 'Naturalists are not as quick as they were only a few years ago to dismiss the idea that birds may sing from sheer high spirits,' says the book and goes on to add, 'It is often difficult to draw a precise line between a song and a call. But song is concerned primarily with defending a territory or attracting a mate, whereas the function of calls is to pass on other kinds of information, such as the fact that a predator is approaching. Songs tend to be complex arrangements of notes, uttered rhythmically and in most cases by the male; calls are generally short groups of up to four or five notes…'

The cock Koel's crescendo is unquestionably a song, and can have no possible function in defending nesting territory, for like many other cuckoos, Koels build no nests. But probably it serves to attract the hen, perhaps even to challenge other cock Koels. It is significant that it is in these very months when Koels are at their loudest that the crows nest. Incidentally, Koels may be promiscuous in their mating (as other cuckoos are) but in my locality a pair often stays more or less together for weeks on end. Ornithologists have said that the persistent, loud song of the cock Koel induces crows nesting nearby to chase the intruder, enabling the hen Koel to lay its eggs in the unguarded nest; that may well be so but has no significance to the babel of Koel voices around my veranda, for no crows nest anywhere within half a kilometre of it.

Granted that the purpose of the cock Koel's song is to attract the hen, what is the purpose of the many quick urgent calls of the hen and why do the birds keep both singing and calling before and well after they are through with breeding?

The Koels in my locality may be more or less resident, but the other cuckoos that also foist their eggs on avian foster-parents are birds of passage over a vast tract of peninsular India, and breed during their transit of the area. The most familiar of these are the Pied Crested Cuckoo, considered the harbinger of rain in many places, the Indian Cuckoo (*Cuculus micropterus*) and the Common Hawk-Cuckoo.

All three are woodland birds, though the Pied Crested Cuckoo favours open scrub jungles. It has no melodious song, but an abrupt metallic call and a longer polysyllabled phrase that is also somewhat harsh, though it resembles the Indian Cuckoo's call in its pattern. One of the pleasantest bird voices to be heard in our forests is the Indian Cuckoo's four-syllabled *broken pekoe* (rendered *bau-kotha-ko* in Bengali), never in a crescendo but repeated at brief intervals in a descending cadence from a treetop.

The Common Hawk-Cuckoo is the 'brainfever bird' of Anglo-Indians, and the 'papiha' beloved of Hindi lyricists. In our lyrics it is the voice of love, and the voice of love, you comprehend, is not placid, sweet and low, but plangent with unrest and desire. Not even the Koel's tireless voice can rival the papiha's crescendo, shrill, urgent, rising to an almost hysterical climax and then ceasing abruptly to begin all over again, and again, and again.

BIRDSONG IN INDIA—OTHER BIRDS

What is a songbird? Naturally, the answer depends on what we term birdsong. Song is generally considered a sequence of integrated notes, as distinct from a call of just one, or a few notes. Further, this sequence must please our ears, for we have no conception of how a bird hears the voice of another. What seems strident and staccato to us may be divine music to avian ears, and contrariwise the songs of many nesting birds rapturously acclaimed by men (Wordsworth, Shelley, Keats, Hardy et al) have an intimidatory 'keep away' significance to others of their own kind.

Furthermore, there is the factor of difference in the apprehension of bird voices by different people. W. H. Hudson calls the shrill, harsh trill of a kingfisher a song. Salim Ali thought the Greywinged Blackbird our finest songster. Others may award the palm to the Shama. Because of this, perhaps the criterion should be the opinion of that non-existent being, the average Indian citizen—and also that of some who are anything but average, the poets. Our poets have praised, besides the Koel and papiha, the voices of larks, drongos, bulbuls and parakeets! Finally, it is no average citizen or poet but I that am writing this note, and my personal fancies will also colour the writing.

Bulbuls have cheery, rollicking, many-syllabled calls, but as 'Eha' pointed out long ago, they do not sing outside lyric poetry. The related chloropsises do sing, but their song is freely interspersed with faultless imitations of the ditties and alarm calls of other birds and even mammalian sounds. They are unsurpassed natural mimics. Male ioras and chats have a long, modulated whistle, that some may term only a call. To me, the ditty of the cock Pied Bush-Chat that ends on an ineffably sweet, ecstatic note has always seemed most evocative.

The Shama is the most gifted of our songbirds. I have heard the nightingale only from a sound record, but have listened to the blackbird and thrushes in the wild. The blackbird is peerless for the richness and fluid flow of its song, and whistling thrushes sing with verve and abandon so peculiarly in keeping with the wild, unfettered setting of the fast-flowing mountain streams they haunt. But for sheer sustained tamed melody, and swift change of mood, few birds can rival the Shama. Years ago, for three days in Karwar, I got up at four in morning to steal a ride to a forest some six miles away, where a pair of Shamas had nested in a clump of dry bamboo. The cock would begin to sing before sunrise, a welling, liquid flow of cascading delight and sudden, deep pools of sadness; exquisitely refined in tone in a passage, and full-throated the next.

The poets regard these as songbirds—(r. to l.) bulbul, parakeet, mynah, dove, Koel, papiha and oriole.

Though it has a wide range in India, the Shama is a forest bird and both uncommon and shy. Not many would have seen or heard it. But its poor relation, the dapper little Magpie Robin must be familiar to most people, for it frequents gardens and parks. Early in the morning the cock perches on top of a post or a bough, and puffing out its breast bursts into impassioned song.

For those who like their birdsong less unrestrained and passionate, there are the fantail-flycatchers. Theirs is a pretty little ditty of a few set phrases, and as they sing it they fan out their tail and pirouette.

Drongos dominate the dawn chorus in woodland settings, and in the cool freshness of the early morning their uninhibited, high, harsh whistles are remarkably exhilarating, but still constitute no song. However, the most magnificent of them, the Racket-tailed Drongo, does have an authentic and highly individualistic song, a high, clear paean to the rising sun that is one of the most memorable musical sounds to be heard in our hill forests. At other times, too, it indulges in short snatches of its distinctive song.

Orioles are notable for their mellow richness of voice. The forest-loving Black-headed Oriole has a brief but clear-fluted song. Grackles (Hill-Mynahs) are perhaps the most celebrated of talkers among cage birds, but in the wild they are notable for the full-bodied sweetness of their high whistles.

Wordsworth has the word for lark-song—ethereal. Perhaps even when heard from near and on the ground, larks have exceptionally pure-toned voices, but usually one hears them only when they are airborne and on high, some two hundred feet above one. There are larks in India, in no way inferior to the much-sung-of European skylark, and they sustain their melody for almost two minutes, a shower of crystal-clear notes that come tinkling down from the heavens in what is almost a spiritual experience.

Some doves have crooning, soothing voices. The Pied Wagtail has a gay little song, and there are quite a few others that may be reckoned among our songbirds. And the night has its voices too, the rhythmic, churring voices of nightjars and the rousing resonant repeated *Tuk-Tok-Torrock!* of the Little Scops Owl. But I shall mention only one other bird much praised by our poets, the parakeet, if only to point out that the poets were not so wildly imaginative and innocent of natural history as might seem. Parakeets have remarkably penetrating and unpleasant calls, a variety of shrieks and yelps, but the hen calling its nestlings has a different voice altogether, a long, low, sweet trill, tremulous with tenderness and affection.

BIRD
FLIGHT

THE GREEN BEE-EATER

An oblong of lawn, some thirty yards across, lay between the barbed wire on which the bee-eater sat, and the foot of the parapet I sat on. Every blade of grass, each leaflet and blushing flower of the tiny wild indigo that grew amidst the grass, stood out in sharp relief viewed through my binoculars, for the sunlight was cloud-filtered and there were no highlights and shadows to confuse the eye.

The bee-eater sat hump-shouldered on the wire, sideways to the lawn. A needless, secondary line of barbed wire, two inches below its perch, lay across the pin feathers of its tail, further suggesting the fixation of its inertia. The plumage of its back, though, was slightly ruffled and it seemed lost in unseeing introspection as if chasing far memories.

Suddenly it launched itself into the air and came sailing over the lawn on acutely triangular wings, chased an insect on quick-beating pinions, caught it and returned to the barbed wire again, to resume its slumped vigil. In the half-hour I watched it through the glasses, it sallied out twenty-one times from its perch to catch prey, mostly over the lawn, right under my nose—and not once did I, with that hunting ground so clearly in magnified view, spot its prey before the bird.

It was only by following the bee-eater's line of flight that I could spot the insect each time, though I was watching the lawn from above all the time, rather than the bird. The prey consisted mainly of some minor sort of bee, but it took two small white butterflies (patently clear against the grass to me—after my attention had been drawn to them by the bird!) and once a dainty, green dragonfly.

After each successful sally (there were a few misses) it returned to its perch to take up the same, contemplative, sideways attitude. No doubt it watched the roadway with the other eye, the eye away from me, for sometimes it took its prey across the fence, over the road. What surprised me, even more than the quickness and certainty of its sight, was the fact that each eye covered territory so unerringly, independently of the other.

I have seen this bird take large, red dragonflies, darting about at dizzy speed near electric supply wires. These were the fierce-looking orange-vermilion dragonflies, some three and a half inches long, clear against the sky in spite of their erratic speed—I have not seen any other bird hunt them, though I have seen them when rollers and King Crows were near. The bee-eater had no difficulty at all in catching its speeding quarry. It sailed out to meet the ill-fated dragonfly at a particular point in its headlong flight, as if by punctilious appointment, plucked it casually from the air, and returned to its perch.

The bird had some difficulty, though, in killing and devouring its considerable meal. It held the insect by the base of one pair of wings, and dashed it against the wire with quick, lateral jerks of the head to kill it, swallowing it when quite still with obvious effort. I noticed that after it had eaten three dragonflies in this manner, it showed no further interest in the circling insects.

During the cold weather (right now, in fact) bee-eaters roost in close company. I used to know such a roosting place on top of a hillock, where two large, spiky, much-branched bushes with little leaf on them and sheltered from the wind by green cover beyond, provided all that the birds wanted. Each evening some hundred bee-eaters would assemble here, and roost thickly on the bushes, endowing them suddenly with lanceolate, living leaves.

It was pleasant to climb that little hill at sunset and to rest for a while in that sheltered clearing on the top, listening to the trilling voices of the bee-eaters.

GREEN BEE-EATERS

WHITE WINGS

Every evening, at half past six, the Cattle Egrets fly southward over my roof to their roosting trees by the water. They go past in a broken string, five or six first in compressed Indian file, flying low, then a long break, then five or six again following the same diagonal course over the roof and trees, picking up the threads of the flight that went before. Their flight is round-winged and leisurely, heads drawn in, yellow beaks pointing forward and black legs trailing behind, the full, curved wings never stroked in vigorous flaps but moved in an unhurried rotatory action, like boats rowed slowly with broad, bent oars.

There is grace enough in their slow white flight against the slaty sky, and a steady aim, but no hint of power or speed. Twelve hours later, soon after sunrise, they are back in the sky again, flying no longer in a set direction but circling in small parties, for they are now seeking feeding grounds. Their flight seems even weaker now, as they row around indecisively on hollowed, dazzling wings, gliding occasionally before settling in some field. They look even more like the curve-winged white birds of Japanese screens in the sun than they did at dusk.

Bird flight can be very deceptive. Butterfly-winged Hoopoes are capable of steep speed when pursued, and long distance migrants like wagtails often have a weak-seeming dipping flight. But the lassitude of wing of the Cattle Egrets is not illusory—they have not even fugitive speed. I have known this for years, from the time I was a young savage with a catapult. Among the savages with whom I consorted furtively in those days was an Anglo-Indian boy, bigger than the rest of us, and an acknowledged master with the catapult. I have seen him bring down Cattle Egrets on many occasions. His method was to stalk a flock in a field and flush it from near; the birds would fly away, then turn in a sharp bend and come back, and as they came over some five yards above, he would let fly. It was useless winging a bird, it had to be hit in the head to stun or kill it, for any prospect of recovery. Perhaps an empirical skill guided the marksman's aim a shade ahead of the fleeing quarry, but I have never seen any other flying bird fall to a catapult. There were many blank stalks, but I have also known my friend turn home with three egrets from a morning's hunting. According to him, the birds were insipid even in a curry, but not so bad as paddy birds, because they did not eat quite so many frogs.

It is true that the Cattle Egret is far less dependent on frogs and fishes than its cousins. It belongs to the tribe of egrets and herons, professional anglers, and has the wading legs and dagger bill on extensile neck of the fraternity, but it lives mainly on the insects of green fields. It is a pastoral bird, much given to following in the wake of grazing cattle; it is an adept at seizing the grasshoppers and other insects that their hooves scatter, and everyone has seen it picking ticks and flies off cattle. Still, it has not wholly lost its tribal love of water, as its nesting and roosting trees will show, and occasionally it reverts to angling for tadpoles and small fry at puddles.

One would think that the birds that seek their meat in the air, like the Peregrine, would find these slow-winged egrets easy prey, but I believe it is not often that a Cattle Egret dies this way. The Pond Heron, which flies faster and higher, sometimes meets this fate—the ancient Tamil curse 'May you fall headlong like the Pond Heron struck by the Shahin' is based on fact. For one thing, the Cattle Egret never flies far except when going out to feed and when returning to the roost, and even at such times it flies low—the hunters of the air prefer prey that will seek escape in flight, providing a depth of air below to make giddy swooping safe. Moreover, it is when the air is cold and slow, early in the morning and late in the evening, that Cattle Egrets undertake their flights—birds of prey are rarely on the wing then, for they like plenty of light, and warm air currents for soaring.

I must make it clear that I make no suggestion of intelligent apprehension, or dominant motive, in saying this, but I have been

watching Peregrines lately, and it seems to me that Cattle Egrets do choose their journey hours safely. There is no need at all to presuppose reasoning in a bird for the development of a habit that is beneficial to it, but, of course, it is quite possible that the flight habits of Cattle Egrets have nothing to do with the habits of birds of prey.

FREEBOOTERS OF THE AIR

Watching India's first historic Test victory over England, along with a huge holiday crowd, were a dozen kites. They had followed the game with unrelaxing eyes over the previous three days, and I knew some of them by the close of the opening day.

One had two forward primaries missing from each wing, one had a squarish tail, a kite was exceptionally light in colour, a bleached golden brown, another was almost black in its swarthy new plumage, and there was a bird that had lost its entire tail quite recently. I was amused by the vigilance of these birds, patrolling the sky above the ground. Whenever drinks were brought out to the players, the air overhead was suddenly thick with kites, swooping and circling low for a minute before sailing away disappointed. During the breaks for lunch and tea there were opportunist scrambles, some birds alighting on the grass to consume scraps thrown aside by the crowd, others flying away with the booty. Quite a few of the spectators, discussing the happenings and prospects excitedly, had the hurried morsel expertly plucked from their hands. Especially was I amused by a sandwich-eater who laughed uproariously at his neighbour's loss, only to have his own bread snatched the next moment—the sheepish smile on his face was worth going a long way to see.

Looting kites are quite a feature of our bazaars and city markets and I know a restaurant in a park, in the heart of a big city, where these birds have grown so audaciously slick that habitués prefer the dull tile-roofed veranda to the charm of repast in the open with colourful shrubs around and grass underfoot. These freebooters of the air come a close second after crows in the list of urban fauna, but there are kites in the country, too.

There, with no meat stalls
and crowded eating-houses, kites
work harder for their living, and are
far less offensively familiar. They take to
scavenging for their food, a more strenuous and less
fashionable profession than picking pockets in cities.
And in the remote countryside I have known kites actually hunt
their prey.

I know a lake in such a place where I have seen kites fishing. They sail low over the water and clutch at the slippery prey on the surface with their talons, often without success. Here they are awkward apprentices in comparison to the many expert fishermen around, birds equipped with long, stabbing beaks or long, wading legs, other specialized features or at least the boldness to plunge headlong into the water. Elsewhere, I have seen kites chasing maimed quarry or flapping heavily among swarming termites, which they seized ponderously in their grappling-hook feet.

Once I saw a crowd of kites on the ground, in a forest glade. They had feasted with the vultures and were preening themselves after the glut, before roosting. And once I saw a kite hopping along the grass gawkily in the wake of grazing cattle. Hunger had driven that bird into a fresh inroad on the path of degradation, but apparently a kite on terra firma can only lose its balance when it tries to clutch with one foot at ebullient grasshoppers.

That is just as well, for these birds have sunk sufficiently low. They are so common that we do not notice them, and when we do, the occasion is often too annoying for us to appreciate their air mastery. Swifts and falcons are faster and more dashing, vultures more effortless in their soaring, but for sheer manoeuvre on spread wings the kite is unbeatable. No other bird has its slick skill in theft—its noiseless descent on the unsuspecting victim and grab with a comprehensive foot. The kite has a strong hooked beak, and a powerful build—it is surprising that it has not developed beyond petty theft, to thuggery and murder, with its equipment.

But perhaps that, too, is just as well. Those who raise poultry have no love for this bird as it is, and if it took to a more adventurous and violent way of life, the hand of everyone must be against it, in city and in village. And that would be no small waste of national energy considering the kite population of our country!

M. Krishnan

THE FALCONS

The last of the raptors, the falcons, are the most specialized aerial hunters of them all. Falcons have a wide distribution over the world and are of many kinds, but none is really big, the largest not being quite the size of a Pariah Kite, and some are quite small. However, they are the boldest and most skilled of the birds of prey, and usually take their quarry in the air. The larger falcons can kill birds almost twice their size, and even some of the smaller can capture fast-flying swifts and bats on the wing.

Falcons are distinguished from the hunting hawks by their wings being longer, narrower and pointed, well suited to sustained aerial pursuit at high speed, and their eyes are always dark, never yellow: a black or very dark moustachial stripe, running down each cheek from the gape, is characteristic of them. The female is larger and more powerful than the male; but otherwise the sexes are similar in appearance. Three well-known large falcons are considered here.

The Peregrine is, perhaps, the most celebrated of all falcons. It has a wide distribution over the northern hemisphere, and as its name suggests, is given to migration. It is specially noted, even among falcons, for its dash and hunting skills. It comes to all parts of India during the cold weather, especially to waterspreads along the coast, probably in the wake of migratory duck.

It is a mottled, dark slate grey on top, darker on the head and with a prominent black moustachial stripe; the chin and throat are white, and the breast also white with a warm blush, marked with black dots on top and barred across lower down. The female is noticeably larger than the Jungle Crow and the male about that crow's size. The legs and black-tipped bill are yellow.

Few sights in nature are more spectacular than the Peregrine's stoop on a fast-flying pigeon or duck. On sighting the prey, the falcon accelerates its speed with rapid beats of its somewhat drawn-in wings, circles high above its quarry and stoops on it at dizzying speed, ripping it up with the hind claw—the speed of the stoop has been timed at over 200 kilometres per hour, and the hiss of the air rushing past the stiff pinions of the almost fully closed wings, and the thud of the strike as it hits its prey, can be heard from quite some distance away. Peregrines can kill birds much larger than themselves, like the Grey Heron and the Great Black-headed Gull.

The Shahin is the Indian subspecies of the Peregrine and a resident raptor, favouring hill forests and craggy heights. It is much the size of the Peregrine, but darker on top and with its breast and the abdomen suffused with a rich, orange-brown. Shahins are quite as bold and impetuous in their hunting as Peregrines, and were, in fact, preferred to the latter by falconers in the old days. They hunt birds on the wing in the main, but occasionally also take a small mammal, plucking a squirrel off a cliff face in a headlong dive.

The Laggar Falcon is also as big and highly skilled as the Peregrine, but favours open, dry country. It is a reddish brown in the head, and its lower breast and thigh coverts are heavily blotched in dark brown. Laggars are fairly common in the arid Northwest.

Shahin

Peregrine

Laggar

M. Krishnan

THE WHITEBACKED VULTURE

People who write about animals are fond of airing the theory that man is the only creature that has acquired the effete habit of dying in bed. The beasts of prey, they will tell you, succumb to younger rivals when past their prime, and the other animals lead fit and happy lives till they meet the beasts of prey. A most interesting theory, but these people have altogether ignored the humble but essential group of animals that subsist, almost entirely, on dead flesh. Where would the hyena, the jackal and the vultures be, I ask you, if beasts did not perish, like men, of common colds, age and epidemics? The Survival of the Fittest is all right as a theory, but it goes no further. You have only got to take a good look around to see that it has not worked. Moreover, had it worked, the world would be a less densely populated place, with far fewer deaths in consequence. And the vultures would not have survived.

The Whitebacked Vulture has survived in large numbers and is a typical representative of the tribe. It is the commonest vulture of our country, an enormous dark brown bird with a naked head and neck lighter in colour. There is a patch of white on the small of the back, another on the underside of the wings, so that each black wing is slashed with white when the bird is in flight. It is a bird that likes company— these vultures go about in teams, sometimes in large flocks. All day long they soar in the air, often at such a height that one can just see them as dark, circling specks that circle higher and disappear. From this high altitude they keep a tireless lookout for dead and dying things. In the evening they circle very low, over tree and housetop. Except during the laboured take-off and when alighting, when it flaps its huge, sail-like wings heavily, the Whiteback, like all vultures, sails along majestically on outstretched wings. The wings are stretched at right angles to the body, not rigid and flat as in an aeroplane, but slightly scooped as if they could not easily support the weight of the pendulous body. This vulture is said to be capable of a speed of sixty miles per hour, but I rather fancy the estimate was made when it was sailing in a straight line on a carrying breeze. It looks a slow, heavy bird as it circles round, each dark, unmoving feather vividly silhouetted against the sky, and a slow, heavy bird it is. However, its flight is tireless, with the inexorable, expectant tirelessness of those who wait for death.

This vulture prefers hilly, open country to forests, and no wonder, for it would stand small chance in the competition with the other undertakers of nature where trees conceal the carcass. Nothing dies in the neighbourhood of the hills without the vultures knowing about it. They swoop down on the body in a struggling, clamouring crowd—an hour later, a raw and disjointed skeleton marks the place where it was. It is amazing what quantities these birds can eat and how quickly they do it. But then they have to be grasping and quick, for theirs is a chancy life, with long fasts between meals. After they have glutted themselves, they perch on nearby trees, too full of food to move. Whitebacked Vultures in a tree look strangely out of place, even more than a party of men in a similar situation. The branches bend beneath their weight, and only their flattened casque-like faces seem to have any shape. Their great, hulking bodies are shrouded in their folded wings and their necks are drawn into their chests. And you notice, with surprise, that they have sagging paunches, unlike other birds.

BIRD FLIGHT

If Alexander Selkirk had realized his fervent wish and sprouted the wings of a dove, he would still have stayed on his desert island. Beyond the fact that he was a Scottish sailor of the seventeenth century, I can get no personal details about him, but he probably weighed around 180 pounds. But even in the unlikely event of his having been thin-boned, slight of build, and a mere 100 pounds in weight, and had he the wings not of a dove, but of a condor, he could not have flown a yard still. If one wants to fly swiftly and certainly through the air, it is useless having only the wings of a bird—one also needs the body of a bird, the hollow, light, rigid skeleton, the great muscles securely anchored to the deep keel of the breastbone, the wonderfully efficient respiratory system, and all the other things that equip a bird for air mastery.

There are many things about bird flight that are interesting, even wonderful. The mechanics of flight are not as simple as they may seem at first sight, and involve delicate functional adaptations of the wing, and even the tail, to the needs of aeronautics—as everyone knows, man owes much to flying birds for the successful designing of aircraft. Again, there are so many kinds of flight, and so many deft tricks of wing that the birds exploit in flight. And then there are aspects of flight to delight the human brain, questions of speed, and continuity, and improbable-seeming achievement—some of the long-distance migrants that come to South India from thousands of miles away and the seas, such as some of the wagtails, have a seemingly weak-winged, whirr-and-skim flight that looks as if it cannot carry the birds much farther than to the next field! There is even the mystery of avian flight: now we know very much more than we did about bird migration, but it holds its secrets still. I mention all these things only to say that I am writing about none of them—I only write of some impressions of bird flight that linger in my mind.

Thinking of flying birds, naturally, I think of racing pigeons, so 'normal' in their strong, swift wing action—for I was an ardent fancier of racing pigeons for over twenty years. One of the sights of Madras in summer used to be the kits of High-flying Tumblers in the noonday skies, so high up that they were visible only as dark and scintillatingly white stars that winked with each beat of their wings, and circled in a loose constellation. One looked for them, not up into the blinding blue sky, but in a trough of water kept in the open shade—in that glareless, inverted heaven one watched the tireless fliers. And I have vivid recollections of homers, too, of watching the birds coming in from long flights. You watch the horizon for a dark speck above the treeline, and when it is half a mile away and recognizable as a homer, it holds its wings at an angle to the body in a stiff, wide-open 'V' and volplanes in at a terrific speed, gaining size with each moment.

Herons and egrets (the Little Egret in particular) flying past with casual, almost lazy flaps of their sail-like wings, represent the poetry of flight. In panic-flight they hold themselves tighter and flail the air with their wings, achieving an uncouth speed—it is when cruising that they are so graceful, especially when flying slow against a dark sheet of water. I remember spending a delightful hour beside the lake at Siruvani, the great, verdant trees and feathery clumps of bamboos on the shores mirrored in the still water to endow it with a dark, viridian calm. It was almost a scene of idyllic quiet, except that it was all too wildly beautiful to be idyllic, too like something out of a barbarian dream of paradise, and a barbarian that I am, it held me fascinated. Then an egret came flying round the corner, flying low over the water, dazzlingly white and clear against the profound umbers and greens of the reflected forest, each slow, rhythmic stroke of the wings duplicated in the mirror below. Halfway across, the bird stalled and hung in the air, the pinions of the forwardly directed wings splayed out with the breaking action, the horn-black, yellow-footed legs dangling and almost touching their twin image on the lake's surface, the head and neck stretched sinuously forward as it scrutinized something in the water below. For a moment then the stillness was perfect, and for that moment it was no dream but paradise in fact.

Large flights have an attractiveness of their own. Quick-winged flights of migratory duck have always appealed to mankind (even when it was not waiting in a rush-hidden punt with a gun!), and the high, honking skeins of geese flying through the evening have a wild and remarkable charm. Flights of homing Openbills have a quite different and spectacular appeal—a sight that can be seen almost any day at Vedanthangal, when the weather is fine and the breeding season is advanced. The Openbills come in from their feeding excursions in large flights, and when they are near the nesting trees they soar on spread, rigid wings (all storks are almost as expert at soaring as the vultures) and gain height, till they are mere specks floating high up above the breeding colony. Then, all at once, they descend in a headlong dive, twisting and angling sharply as they hurtle downward with the wings almost closed. The dive is not straight downward, but erratically angled, and the birds shoot off at a tangent when near the treetops, then flap their way to their individual nests.

It is among the birds of prey that some of the finest exponents of aerobatics are to be found, particularly among the kites, eagles and long-winged falcons. The eagles are expert at soaring and gliding on taut wings, gaining momentum when needed with a few quick flaps of the wings. The broad-winged serpent-eagle has a peculiar trick of flight—when needing to accelerate while soaring, it does not flap its wings, but hunches its back, half-closes the wings, and lashes the air with their very tips, with a quivering action.

The common kite is capable, as those who have watched it will know, of an astonishing sleight-of-wing speed and deftness in the air. But probably no other bird can equal the Peregrine's dizzying stoop. I have, unluckily, seen this breathtaking spectacle only too often, resulting usually in one more loss to my loft. Peregrines do not always attack their prey from high above in the air. They are remarkably versatile in their hunting, and will suit their mode of attack to the situation—they have even been known to carry away sitting birds. But as a rule they seek their prey in the air, and stoop on it from above.

When it has sighted its prey, the Peregrine climbs high into the heavens, till it is well above the quarry—which, incidentally, may be much larger than itself. The success of the stoop depends upon maximum momentum being attained precisely when the falcon strikes its victim, all this momentum, the keen sight, and the powerful muscles of the Peregrine directing its murderous, long, ripping hind claw.

It is not only the force of gravity that propels the falcon as it hurtles down on its prey from high above—in the first few yards of that dive, the long tips of the almost closed wings quiver in quick beats, guiding and speeding the descent. Once it is fairly launched at its prey, the Peregrine cannot halt its terrific momentum, except by opening its wings; it is for this reason that it does not attack a close-flying kit of birds, some instinctive inhibition preventing it from damaging itself badly by colliding with other birds in the kit. Various estimates of the speed of a stooping Peregrine (the maximum reached by any bird) give it as from 110 to 180 miles per hour, but it is futile assessing the impetuosity of that stoop in figures—it is something that has to be seen to be believed.

TERROR FROM THE SKIES

I know the Peregrine as an enemy, whose vivid dark appearance in the sky has often meant death to my stock. When I was a boy and fancied tumblers, I have seen Peregrines take the pick of my kit high up in the heavens; and afterwards, when I turned to homers, they killed my young birds right over the loft. Over many years of pigeon keeping, in many places, I have learned to recognize the natural foes of the birds and to guard against them. A good loft and the native wariness of pigeons do much to minimize the risk from vermin and predatory creatures. The danger is when they are in the air: only their wings and wits can save them then.

There are other birds of prey, hawks and hawk-eagles and eagles. The larger of these are rare near town and city, and homers crossing countryside fly direct and fast and get through. Pigeons have little to fear from the short-winged hawks, because they are such fine fliers, and even the goshawk does not care for the sustained pursuit of a fast-flying quarry that takes to the air. It is only the Peregrine (and its cousin, the smaller but no less deadly Shahin) that will enter into a relentless chase and claim its victim by sheer superiority of flight.

No bird is better equipped for rapine. The Peregrine is so compactly built and balanced that its power and reach are not apparent in repose. See it strike down its prey in the air, and you will have witnessed one of the most impressive sights in nature. The close-flying kit of tumblers you are watching breaks suddenly, and the birds fly wildly, with the speed and dispersal of terror. High above them you can see a slaty grey speck that circles lower, inexorably, effortlessly. The pigeons are too high up to seek the refuge of roof or loft, and the scatterbrained birds make no attempt to fly away in a beeline—perhaps that would be futile, with the falcon's far swifter speed.

Then the Peregrine descends on its victim in a breathtaking stoop, wings held pressed against its sides, diving sheer through the thin, hissing air with incredible velocity. The murderous talon of its hind toe strikes with the rending force of all that momentum and nicely calculated aim, killing instantly. The sound of the impact as it hits its quarry can be heard two furlongs away, and at times the pigeon's head is severed cleanly, as if cut with a knife.

Rarely does the falcon miss its aim, and when it does it zooms up to the clouds, or climbs on quick-beating wings, and resumes the chase. I have seen tumblers escape with minor injuries, though. In particular I remember a tumbler that jinked (yes, tumblers can jink in the air) from under the claws of doom. The Peregrine clutched sideways at it, and for a split second I thought my bird was lost—then it flew clear, and the falcon unclenched its talons to release a floating shower of long feathers. That pigeon had escaped, like Tam o' Shanter's mare with the loss of its tail!

Only after seeing the awe-inspiring spectacle of a Peregrine's stoop do you realize how perfectly the bird is made for slaughter. The big head and thick-muscled, heavy breast are suited ideally to aid the headlong impetus of its stoop; the long, curved toes can clutch and grasp killingly when the rending stroke of the hind claw cannot be used; and the long, tapering wings and full tail help in its superlative mastery of the air. Add to these an utterly fearless temperament, fierce skill and real versatility, and you have an idea of the Peregrine's equipment for its life.

Hunting birds that fly comparatively low like homers, the Peregrine adopts different methods. It takes homers when they are circling to gain height or when young birds are flying exuberantly around the loft. It does not make its attack from high up then, but steals in sideways and makes a dash at its quarry from near, like a short-winged hawk. Only, its speed on flapping wings over the brief distance is amazing, and it flies in from a slightly higher level, slanting down diagonally for the strike. The sound of the impact as the Peregrine closes in testifies to the velocity with which it strikes, even on such raids, but the prey is rarely killed outright. It is killed soon enough, though, with a quick squeeze of the talons. The victims escape with injuries more frequently in such low-level hunting, and if it misses, the falcon does not, usually, persist in the attack—this is strangely similar to the behaviour of short-winged hawks when they miss, and the hunting is also similar to their methods. Perhaps the ease with which the fugitives find cover, close to the earth, has something to do with the matter.

Of course it is not only pigeons that the Peregrine hunts. It hunts in the air, and can kill practically any bird of its size or a little larger, at times much larger birds. Strong-flying birds that keep at a fair height in the air often fall prey to it. The Rose-ringed Parakeet is often taken, and, occasionally, the crow. The Peregrine has a partiality for water and the sea coast, and many waterbirds are among its victims. It is a great wanderer, as its name implies, and has a worldwide range. The Americans call it the Duck Hawk, and even here that name has validity, for the Peregrine comes to us in the cold weather, in the wake of migrating duck. How I wish it would merit the name more literally, and confine itself solely to duck!

by M. KRISHNAN

REMEMBERING

KRISHNAN

KRISHNAN AS I KNEW HIM

My first memories of Krishnan go back to the early forties. We were in Sandur then, a princely state in what is now Northern Karnataka. It was a peaceful and unspoilt place, a modern urbanite's nightmare. Around the place where we lived there was habitation, cultivation and scrubland, with wooded hills in the distance. Krishnan made the place come alive for me. He told me of the animals that lived around us and we would go out to see them. There were birds of many kinds in the scrub. Sometimes we saw a mongoose or two. The ruling family often took us for drives into the forests. These were memorable moments for me, seeing sambar, wild boar, jackals, hares in the wild, an occasional jungle cat or porcupine, and one unforgettable night, a leopard. The odd monitor lizard was never far from the house, and snakes of several kinds made their presence felt often enough to keep us alert. For a while Krishnan kept pigeons and then goats, and a dog was always part of the family. A Poligar Hound from Rajapalayam was with us for a long time and became a good and possessive friend of mine.

Krishnan held a succession of jobs in Sandur and often worked at home late into the night, by the light of Petromax lanterns after the electricity went off at 10.00 p.m. He always found the time to round off my day with stories of animal adventures. They were delightful stories that I found perfectly plausible. He would never name the animal, only telling me what it looked like and what it did, and I had to guess what it was. I commenced my school studies in Sandur and remember finding mathematics particularly difficult. Krishnan did not mind this, assuring me that it ran in the family and I would soon get over it. This prophecy of his came true only several years later, after a long struggle.

Once at school I could not—at least to the same extent—pursue my interest in the animal world around us. Our excursions became less frequent, but Krishnan kept things going by telling me about the wonders of nature, animals and forests in distant places, when I took time off from schoolwork. This was when he introduced me to the joys of reading books and articles on subjects of interest to him: wildlife, cricket and English literature in its simplest form. He could draw, sketch and paint with an infectious ease that made me try my hand at these skills for a while. All of these interests remain with me even today and give me much pleasure.

Soon it was time to leave in order to complete my schooling. I was very sorry indeed to leave Sandur. Krishnan had made it a very special place for me. In Bangalore, where I went through the latter part of my school education, Krishnan was not with us. He came to visit us briefly at long intervals. On one such visit he taught me how to use his binoculars, a fascinating experience. When I came to Madras for my college studies, Krishnan was there, having finished his work in Sandur and in the process of coming to grips with the career he had always wanted for himself.

In sharp and singularly refreshing contrast to everyone else, Krishnan did not sit in judgement or inflict advice upon others in his personal relationships. This naturally made him the only one of my wise elders I could trust. When I finished my Intermediate (today's Plus Two), I found I had the marks to get admission to a medical college without difficulty. Only, I was not too keen on a career in medicine, being inclined towards botany instead, a preference that made many doubt my sanity. When I went to Krishnan and talked it over with him, he kept things simple and honest. Doctors, he assured me, were respected and prosperous people. Some of them enjoyed their work and a few were even quite good at it, and it was a fine profession anyway. But, he asked, was it what I wanted to do? People who had studied botany had been known to make a living of sorts, not like doctors, but good enough to keep body and soul together (a favourite expression of his). I had my answer and did not look back. A few years later, after I had finished my

M. Krishnan

university studies, I was unexpectedly selected for a career in forestry. Krishnan might have been happier to see me pursue a career in botanical research, but put aside his feelings when he saw how determined I was to be on my own.

Curiously enough, there were only a few occasions on which Krishnan and I went to the forests together. I can, in fact, remember only one, when we spent some time together in Mudumalai and adjoining Bandipur, with me on leave from my teaching assignment in Coimbatore. He was completely relaxed while taking pictures of gaur or elephants from his perch on elephant back, with the animals he was photographing going about their feeding without concern or fuss. That was because of the care and effort he put in to get them used to his presence.

Krishnan loathed exotics and deplored the craze many forest departments developed for them. He was right, of course. In the early part of my service in forestry, I differed from Krishnan, sometimes sharply, on how wildlife should be managed. Over the years, I realized he had a much more comprehensive knowledge of the dichotomy between precept and practice in wildlife management than I could ever acquire, and that his was the more sensible point of view—in fact, the only sensible one.

Some have said Krishnan did not care for recognition. They have not got it right. He was as delighted as anyone to get recognition when it came, as it did when he was awarded first, a Nehru Fellowship, and then the Padma Shri, both of which he cherished dearly. What he did not care for, was to seek recognition or to lobby for it.

Krishnan strongly believed in the need for a country to have an identity of its own. Every place, he felt, whether a country or a small part of it, made itself identifiable by all that was natural in it: hills, plains and beaches, rivers and lakes, wetlands, scrub and mangroves, and, of course, forests and wildlife. Some part of this identity was lost, he would say, if nature was tampered with. One such instance of his expression that I describe below made a lasting impression on me.

Doctors used to say it is best to be done with chicken pox in early childhood. Krishnan was not sure whether he had chicken pox as a child, and found out for himself the hard way that he had not, some thirty years before he died. It was a severe attack and I was alarmed to see how badly ravaged he was when I came from Salem to see him. Medical attention cannot achieve very much in such cases, but the doctor—an experienced and kindly specialist in infectious diseases—did his best. The rest, he said, was up to Krishnan, but he was not sure he would survive. Krishnan struggled with the disease for a long time and finally overcame it to emerge darkened and scarred, but eventually himself. After the worst had passed, Krishnan would sometimes get a high fever and become delirious. What he said at such moments naturally did not make sense.

However, every now and then, these 'bouts of delirium' were suspect because what Krishnan said about something or someone was clear and well-focused, and often caustic. Sometimes, he would wink at us to show that he was faking his illness, but often he couldn't do so because it was too difficult. One day he called me to sit near him and spoke quietly but clearly: 'Trees...not close...grass...shrubs...breeze...smell of rain...sambar and gaur...that is India.' It was a quick word picture of his favourite forest, I realized. Was he delirious? I did not think so at the time. Looking back, I am sure he was not.

M. Harikrishnan

KRISHNAN, MY GRANDFATHER AND FRIEND

Krishnan would laugh if he knew I was writing anything at all, especially about him. He knew I am no writer. I am writing this not as an objective analysis of Krishnan, but to try and convey the unique and special relationship that we shared. Krishnan was fifty when I was born and though he was my grandfather, I called him by his name. He insisted that his family and friends call him Krishnan. I remember, when some friends of mine from school called him 'uncle', he responded by calling them 'aunty' until they relented. I think that this was part of the idea he had about treating people he knew on equal terms. He also believed that you should not 'respect' someone merely because of his or her age and often joked that if someone was a fool at twenty, when he was sixty he would probably be a bigger fool, having had that much more experience of being one! Krishnan was no fool, and I respected and admired him a lot.

He was very special to me ever since I was a child. We spent a few months together every year when he visited, and again during my school holidays. When I was not with him, he wrote very regularly from Madras or from where his work took him. I first remember receiving his letters when I was about six years old. He took special care to write in legible print and would often illustrate his letters with watercolour paintings or pen-and-ink sketches. He had a way of making a seven-year-old feel important, and at the top of the page in his letter to me he would write, 'Strictly confidential and even more private!' Another similar gesture was when he custom-built a room for himself upstairs, where he lived and worked. I was five or six then and when I first entered his room, I noticed that he had fixed the washbasin at a low level, so that I could reach the tap easily.

Krishnan took me with him (after I was seven and older) on his field trips to various sanctuaries in South India, and I cherish the memories of the days spent with him in the forest. From him I learnt to love nature, something I was very grateful for, and which has given me immense pleasure over the years.

When I was fifteen years old and had finished my high school in Coimbatore, my parents decided to send me to Madras to complete my education. Both of them worked, and expected to get transferred frequently in their jobs. I went to stay with Krishnan, and this marked the beginning of eight years of our companionship. My grandmother, Indu, lived downstairs, and Krishnan and I shared the living space upstairs—this consisted of his room-cum-office, a veranda and a bathroom. We knew and understood each other very well and had no trouble getting along. Krishnan was a wonderful parent, considerate and thoughtful, going out of his way to make my stay there comfortable. He also was an excellent nurse whenever I fell sick. When I went to stay with him, he decided to move his bed to the veranda and used to say that I was like the camel that gradually drove out the Arab! He obviously indulged me a lot.

During my stay with Krishnan, I had the pleasure of watching him work. He often told me that he thought of himself foremost as an artist. He loved and enjoyed his work more than anything, the exceptions being literature, Carnatic music and cricket. It is true that Krishnan was quite a recluse and he seldom left his 'den' except on work, but he enjoyed the company of friends or relatives who came to see him. Unless he was in the middle of work in his dark room, he did not mind being interrupted at work to meet or be of help to someone he knew. In his words, he was 'the master of his own time' and, if he had lost time during the day, he would work late into the night to complete his work well in advance of the deadline.

Not surprisingly, Krishnan was a master storyteller. I remember many evenings spent listening to vivid recollections of his extraordinary experiences. His stories would be about encounters with an elephant herd or sambar in the jungle and how he photographed them, or they would involve his family and friends. Whether he was narrating a story or engaged in conversation, he would often characteristically break into verse, recalling an apt poem or parody from English or Tamil literature.

Another little-known aspect of Krishnan was that he enjoyed cooking for people and appreciated good food. He made delicious soups, curries, omelettes and other dishes for us and often cooked for me and my friends. He made what he called 'nourishing soups' if one of us was sick, made and packed sandwiches if someone had to travel. When he cooked he was very meticulous and exacting and would cut onions and chillies extremely fine—it was not easy to be his assistant when he cooked! The recipes that he gave me reflect his eye for detail and include instructions to the uninitiated on how to operate a hotplate or how exactly to orient and cut an onion!

Krishnan also had the rare quality of not giving advice to people, except when someone came to him seeking professional advice. He almost never told anyone what they should be doing with their life, be it a personal matter or a career choice. The most I have heard him say was that 'you should follow your own bent.' He had found much happiness in his life by doing exactly that, and he strongly believed that one should not be forced into any decision. I have come to value this quality that Krishnan had (which my father also shares), having had to listen to unsolicited advice from many older and therefore 'wiser' people.

After eight years in Madras, I had to move to Hyderabad to pursue my studies. I missed Krishnan very much and looked forward to his letters, with my address written in his neat hand. On the reverse of his letters was his inimitable signature—a drawing of an elephant with his initials, MK. He wrote to me twice a week, illustrating his letters, and had the knack of making even the most mundane things seem interesting.

When I decided to go to the United States to pursue my career, he was not very happy that I was leaving India. He did not like it when people left India, especially to work in the US. I, too, was unhappy about going so far away from him, especially as he was getting older. But we continued to communicate through letters and the telephone. In his last letter to me, written three weeks before he passed away suddenly in

February 1996, he enclosed his original paintings of Indian songbirds. He had painted them for an article to be published in *Namaste*. He hoped the paintings would relieve me from the pressures of my work and ended his letter saying, 'Whatever your problems are, however vital they seem, they are not worth the worry. What seems vital today is meaningless next year. ...I think and I have found...deep interests (especially in the arts), firm family ties and sincere personal relationships the only worthwhile things in life.' Krishnan lived a full and rewarding life and I am grateful to have been a part of it. He was truly unique and special and one of the best friends that I ever had.

Asha Harikrishnan

ACKNOWLEDGEMENTS

Compiling this book has been a privilege and we thank Dr Meenakshi and Mr Harikrishnan for their continued trust and faith in us.

We are also extremely grateful to Zafar Saheb for honouring us by writing the foreword for this book. He enthusiastically read the entire manuscript in less than two weeks and gave us a masterpiece!

Many thanks to Ramachandra Guha for the initial inspiration and for advice and support whenever we needed it.

Thanks also to Aasheesh Pittie for going through the lists of bird names with his usual meticulous care.

And though we have tried our best, mistakes could have crept in as far as the old and the present common names are concerned and for these we are solely responsible.

To point out problems is simple but it takes a David Davidar to offer solutions in the same breath! David, to you and to your colleagues at Aleph, sincere thanks.

NOTES

As this is an anthology of previously published pieces, the reader will spot repetitions of fact and style from time to time. For the most part we have chosen not to edit these out, but in three instances, we have excised a line or a phrase. The excisions are recorded in the notes.

We have provided updated information on bird names in order to help the reader identify the bird that Krishnan is writing about. These notes can be followed with the given legend:

Common name—Latin name—New Latin name—New Common name.

Please note that in a few cases, either the Latin name or the Common name is unchanged; in such cases we provide only the changed name. Where there is no change in the Latin name or Common name, the legend will have only two entries.

THOSE WERE THE DAYS

33 **THE POOR MAN'S DOG:** Published July 1955.

33 **Konrad Lorenz:** Konrad Zacharias Lorenz (1903-1989) was a Nobel Prize-winning Austrian zoologist, ethologist and ornithologist. He did path-breaking work on animal behaviour and described the principle of imprinting in geese and jackdaws. Among his numerous books, *King Solomon's Ring*, aimed at a popular audience, is the best known.

33 **'An extraordinarily understanding friend':** Lorenz, 'Buying Animals', in *King Solomon's Ring: New Light on Animal Ways* (London and New York, 2002), 58-59.

33 **partridge:** Grey Partridge—*Francolinus pondicerianus*—Grey Francolin.

35 **Lockwood Kipling:** John Lockwood Kipling (1837-1911) was the father of the famous author Rudyard Kipling, and a well-known teacher and illustrator. Krishnan, here, is probably referring to the chapter on animal fights in Kipling's *Beast and Man in India: A Popular Sketch of Indian Animals in Their Relations with the People* (1891).

■

37 **THE DYING GLADIATOR:** Published 1958.

38 *A gamecock clipped*: from 'Auguries of Innocence' by William Blake.

■

40 **PIGEON POST:** Published May 1950.

■

44 **THE BRAHMINY KITE:** Published March 1956.
44 **Brahminy Kite**—*Haliastur indus.*
44 **Short-toed Eagle**—*Circaetus gallicus*—Short-toed Snake Eagle.

■

47 **SEEN THROUGH A CARRIAGE WINDOW:** Published 1940-41.
47 **Dewar:** Douglas Dewar (1875-1957) was a civil servant based in Madras and an ornithologist who wrote several books on Indian birds. He was also a regular contributor to newspapers and periodicals, and encouraged field studies of birds.
47 **'should, aided by a good field-glass':** Dewar, 'The Naturalist in a Railway Train', in *Bombay Ducks: an Account of some of the Every-day Birds and Beasts Found in a Naturalist's Eldorado* (London and New York, 1906), 83.
48 **Pied Kingfisher:** Here he means the Lesser Pied Kingfisher; see note to p. 173.
49 **Ashy Swallow-Shrike**—*Artamus fuscus*—Ashy Woodswallow.
51 *Oriolus kundoo*: Golden Oriole—*Oriolus kundoo*—Indian/Eurasian Golden Oriole.
51 *Oriolus melanocephalus*: Black-headed Oriole—*Oriolus melanocephalus*—*Oriolus xanthornus.*

■

52 **THE SHAWK:** Published January 1956.
52 **Scavenger Vulture**—*Neophron percnopterus ginginanus*—*Neophron percnopterus*—Egyptian Vulture.
53 **'Eha':** Edward Hamilton Aitken (1851-1909) was popularly known as Eha. Aitken was born in India and later joined the civil services. He is known for his enchanting writing on natural history and was a founding member of the Bombay Natural History Society.
53 **Mr Thomas Atkins:** Thomas Atkins or Tommy Atkins is a generic term for a common British soldier.

■

55 **VEDANTHANGAL: OLDEST BIRD SANCTUARY IN INDIA:** Published April 1956.

58 **Openbilled Stork**—*Anastomus oscitans*—Asian Openbill Stork.

58 **G. M. Henry:** George Morrison Reid Henry (1891-1983) was a prominent entomologist and ornithologist who was born and brought up in Sri Lanka. A talented artist, he worked at the Colombo Museum for over thirty-five years, first as a draughtsman and then in the entomology section.

58 **White Ibis**—*Threskiornis melanocephalus*—Oriental White Ibis.

58 **Spoonbill**—*Platalea leucorodia*—Eurasian Spoonbill.

■

62 **Birds from a Fairy Tale:** Published January 1951.

62 **Goldenbacked Woodpecker**—*Dinopium javanense*—Common Flameback.

63 **Ivory-billed Woodpecker**—*Campephilus principalis* (critically endangered, or extinct).

■

65 **Wagtails:** Published November 1946.

65 **dachshund out for a walk:** Possibly Giacomo Balla's *Dynamism of A Dog on a Leash*.

65 **Grey Wagtail**—*Motacilla cinerea*.

65 **White Wagtail**—*Motacilla alba*.

65 **Pied Wagtail:** Large Pied Wagtail—*Motacilla maderaspatensis*—White-browed Wagtail.

■

68 **Shower Bath:** Published May 1951.

68 **'They know naught of':** Douglas Dewar and F. D. S. Fayrer, 'Birds in the Rain', in *Birds of the Plains* (London and New York, 1909), 178.

SPLENDOUR IN THE WILD

73 **The National Bird:** Published 1985.

73 **Great Indian Bustard**—*Choriotis nigriceps*—*Ardeotis nigriceps*—Indian Bustard.

73 **peafowl:** Common Peafowl—*Pavo cristatus*—Indian Peafowl.

75 **G. P. Sanderson:** George Peress Sanderson (1848-1892) was best known for developing the *kheddah* method of capturing elephants for training in forestry works. He was a keen hunter and his book, *Thirteen Years Among the Wild Beasts of India* (1879), contains personal observations and a detailed account of the modes of capturing and taming elephants.

■

76 **The Sarus:** Published January 1989.

76 **Sarus:** Sarus Crane—*Grus Antigone*.

■

100 **FORTY DAYS S.I.:** Published 1947.

100 **parakeet:** Rose-ringed Parakeet—*Psittacula krameri.*

∎

104 **LITTLE CORMORANTS:** Published April 1956.

104 **Little Cormorant**—*Phalacrocorax niger.*

105 **Fauna of British India:** *The Fauna of British India, including Ceylon and Burma* was a series of publications begun in 1881 with numerous volumes dedicated to the different kinds of subcontinental fauna.

∎

107 **ESCAPE OF AN ADJUTANT:** Published 1957.

107 **Adjutant:** Greater Adjutant—*Leptoptilos dubius.*

∎

109 **BIRD OF SURPASSING BEAUTY:** Published April 1939.

109 **peafowl:** See note to p. 73.

110 **'Her voice is ever soft':** 'her voice was ever soft, / Gentle, and low; an excellent thing in women,' from *King Lear* by William Shakespeare.

∎

112 **GREY-NECKS:** Published May 1952.

112 **Seton:** Ernest Thompson Seton (1860-1946) was a noted North American wildlife writer. He wrote extensively about nature, the outdoors and the Woodcraft way of life. He shared ideas with Lord Baden-Powell, the founder of the scouting movement, and went on to start the Boy Scouts of America becoming its first Chief Scout.

112 **House Crow**—*Corvus splendens.*

∎

115 **INDIA'S KING CROWS:** Published 1991.

115 **King Crow**—*Dicrurus adsimilis*—*Dicrurus macrocercus*—Black Drongo.

∎

118 **Pied Bush-Chat**—*Saxicola caprata*—Pied Bushchat.

BIRD LIFE IN A CITY

123 **HOOPOE:** Published January 1953.

123 **Hoopoe**—*Upupa epops*—Common Hoopoe.

∎

M. Krishnan

125 **PRETTY POLLY:** Published June 1945.

125 **Rose-ringed Parakeet:** See note to p. 100.

125 *Stone walls do not:* From 'To Althea, from Prison' by Richard Lovelace.

■

128 **FRIENDLY HOBGOBLINS:** Published February 1951.

128 **Spotted Owlet**—*Athene brama.*

■

130 **MINDLESS CRUELTY:** Published 1989.

130 **Barn Owl**—*Tyto alba*—Common Barn Owl.

■

133 **THE BABY SNATCHERS:** Published June 1953.

134 **House Crow:** See note to p. 112.

■

136 **THE NEST IN THE BOUGAINVILLEA:** Published February 1954.

136 **Purple-rumped Sunbird:** See note to p. 94—**Yellow-breasted Honey-sucker**.

■

139 **AN EXCEPTIONAL WARBLER:** Published November 1954.

139 **Tailorbird**—*Orthotomus sutorius*—Common Tailorbird.

139 **Ashy Wren-Warbler**—*Prinia socialis*—Ashy Prinia.

■

141 **SPARROWS:** Published June 1941.

141 **sparrow:** House Sparrow—*Passer domesticus.*

■

144 **MYNAHS:** Published June 1950.

144 **Common Mynah**—*Acridotheres tristis*—Common Myna.

145 **Brahminy Mynah**—*Sturnus pagodarum*—Brahminy Starling.

145 **Pied Mynah**—*Sturnus contra*—Asian Pied Starling.

145 **Grackle or Hill-Mynah**—*Gracula religiosa*—Hill-Myna.

■

147 **BIRD LIFE IN A CITY:** Published March 1953.

148 **'Eha':** See note to p. 53.

148 **Cunningham:** David Douglas Cunningham (1843-1914) was a Scottish

doctor who taught in Calcutta for many years and researched cholera. He wrote two books on animal life in Calcutta—*Plagues and Pleasures of Life in Bengal* and *Some Indian Friends and Acquaintances*.

148 **Dewar:** See note to p. 47.

·

154 **SLEEPING BIRDS:** Published June 1952.

JUNGLE AND BACKYARD

159 **VOICES OF INTOLERANCE:** Published April 1951.

160 **Dewar:** See note to p. 47.

·

162 **WHISTLING TEALS:** Published 1987.

162 **Lesser Whistling Teal**—*Dendrocygna javanica*—Lesser Whistling-Duck.

·

164 **THE CROW-PHEASANT:** Published September 1955.

164 **Crow-Pheasant:** or Coucal—*Centropus sinensis*—Greater Coucal.

165 **'low, loud, sonorous':** Dewar, *Indian Birds; being a key to the common birds of the plains of India* (London and New York, 1910), 171-172. Also see note to p. 47—**Dewar**.

165 **Lowther:** Ernest Herbert Newton Lowther (1890-1952) was a member of the British Ornithologists' Union and worked for the Indian Railways. He took great interest in bird photography working from hides 60-80 feet tall. He is famously said to have been 'a railway man in his spare time'.

·

167 **A JEKYLL-AND-HYDE BIRD:** Published 1990.

167 **One of the most destructive:** Salim Ali and Sidney Dillon Ripley, *Handbook of the Birds of India and Pakistan: Together with Those of Bangladesh, Nepal, Bhutan, and Sri Lanka*, iii (BNHS, 1969), 169-170.

167 **Salim Ali:** Salim Moizuddin Abdul Ali (1896-1987) was India's pre-eminent ornithologist, well known for his most popular work *The Book of Indian Birds*. He was prominently associated with the Bombay Natural History Society and used his influence to have the Bharatpur wetland declared a sanctuary, known today as Keoladeo Ghana National Park. He was awarded the Padma Vibhushan in 1976.

167 **Dillon Ripley:** Sidney Dillon Ripley (1913-2001) was an American ornithologist who worked closely with Salim Ali, co-authoring ten volumes of *Handbook of the Birds of India and Pakistan* with him. He served as secretary

of the Smithsonian Institution, Washington, D.C., for twenty years and was awarded the highest civilian honour in the United States, the Presidential Medal of Freedom, in 1985.

167 **Rose-ringed Parakeet:** See note to p. 100.

167 **'is partial to':** G. M. Henry, *A guide to the birds of Ceylon* (1955), 186. Also see note to p. 58—**G. M. Henry**.

167 **Baker and Inglis:** H. R. Baker was a lieutenant colonel in undivided India, and Charles McFarlane Inglis (1870-1954) was a naturalist and planter, and curator of the Darjeeling Natural History Museum for twenty-two years. Inglis's notes were published in the journal of the Bengal Natural History Society. The two co-authored a book on the birds of South India (see below).

167 **'it does immense damage':** H. R. Baker and C. M. Inglis, *The Birds of Southern India: including Madras, Malabar, Travancore, Cochin, Coorg and Mysore* (Madras, 1930), 166.

■

170 **THE PECKING ORDER:** Published 1990.

170 **Goldenbacked Woodpecker**: See note to p. 62.

172 **Great Black Woodpecker**—*Dryocopus javensis*—White-bellied Woodpecker.

■

173 **PIED KINGFISHERS:** Published July 1991.

173 **Lesser Pied Kingfisher**—*Ceryle rudis*—Pied Kingfisher.

173 **Himalayan Pied Kingfisher**—*Megaceryle lugubris*—Crested Kingfisher.

■

175 **White-breasted Kingfisher**—*Halcyon smyrnensis*—White-throated Kingfisher.

■

177 **LONE SENTINEL OF THE PUDDLES:** Published October 1952.

178 **Pond Heron or 'paddy bird'**—*Ardeola grayii*—Indian Pond Heron.

179 ***And heron, as resounds***: From 'An Evening Walk' by William Wordsworth.

■

180 **THE INDIAN TREE PIE:** Published 1990.

180 **Indian Tree Pie**—*Dendrocitta vagabunda*—Rufous Treepie.

181 **Salim Ali:** See note to p. 167.

■

182 **AMATEUR ASSASSIN:** Published January 1954.

182 **Jungle Crow**—*Corvus macrorhynchos*—Large-billed Crow.

182 **Whistler:** Hugh Whistler (1889-1943) was an English ornithologist. His *Popular Handbook of Indian Birds* was one of the earliest field guides on Indian birds and contributed greatly to Indian ornithology.

184 **clean of feathers:** After this line, the following paragraph in Krishnan's piece has been excised; Krishnan is, in fact, summarizing an earlier piece 'The Baby Snatchers' here, which is also included in this selection (pp. 133-5):

'Recently our National Committee for Bird Preservation appealed to bird lovers to help the avian population of their locality by thinning out House Crows. Commenting on this I pointed out (in the issue for 7 June 1953) that the Jungle Crow, more at home in tree-covered areas, was the more potent inhibitor of bird life. There is, of course, no question of sentiment involved, but if we want the bird life of any place to flourish, I think this clumsy, amateur assassin should be sternly discouraged.'

■

185 **THE GREATER OWLS:** Published 1988.

186 **Stuart Baker:** Edward Charles Stuart Baker (1864-1944) was a police officer in Assam and an avid hunter. He is credited for having put together a fine collection of bird skins, and another of around 50,000 bird eggs. He wrote copiously on Indian wildlife, his most definitive contribution being the eight volumes on birds in *The Fauna of British India, Including Ceylon and Burma*. Also see the 'Introduction'.

186 **Forest Eagle-Owl**—*Bubo nipalensis*.

186 **Dusky Horned Owl**—*Bubo coromandus*—Dusky Eagle-Owl.

186 **'feeds principally on':** Baker and Inglis, *Birds of Southern India*, 213.

186 **Great Horned Owl**—*Bubo bengalensis*—Indian Eagle-Owl.

187 **Eric Hosking:** Eric John Hosking (1909-1991) was a photographer who specialized in bird photography. Hosking was little known before he was attacked by an owl during a photo shoot and lost an eye. His autobiography, *An Eye for a Bird*, was published to great acclaim. He was one of the rare photographers who made a living from photographing birds alone. He was awarded the Gold Medal of the Royal Society for the Protection of Birds in 1974.

■

188 **THE SENTINELS OF DEATH:** Published 1989.

188 **Scavenger Vulture:** See note to p. 52.

189 **Whitebacked Vulture:** See note to p. 287.

189 **'Where absent or rare':** Salim Ali and S. D. Ripley, *Handbook of the Birds of India and Pakistan: Together with Those of Bangladesh, Nepal, Bhutan and Sri Lanka*, ii: *Megapodes to Crab Plover* (BNHS, 2nd edn., 1981), 308.

■

215 *It was the Rainbow*: From 'The Kingfisher' by William H. Davies.

215 **'predators have learnt'**: Reader's Digest Association and Automobile Association [hereafter RDA and AA], *Book of British Birds* (1969), 178.

∎

217 **FISH-OWLS**: Published December 1951.

217 **Brown Fish-Owl**—*Ketupa zeylonensis*.

218 **Blue Rock-Pigeon/Rock-Pigeon**—*Columba livia*—Rock Pigeon.

∎

220 **THE SPOTTED DOVE**: Published January 1944.

220 **Spotted Dove**—*Streptopelia chinensis*.

∎

222 **RAILS, CRAKES AND WATERHENS**: Published February 1989.

222 **Bluebreasted Banded Rail**—*Rallus striatus*—Slaty-breasted Rail.

222 **Whitebreasted Waterhen**—*Amaurornis phoenicurus*—White-breasted Waterhen.

223 **'Eha'**: See note to p. 53.

∎

224 **GOGGLE EYES**: Published January 1954.

224 **Stone-Curlew**—*Burhinus oedicnemus*—Eurasian Thick-knee.

∎

226 **THE JACANAS**: Published March 1989.

226 **Bronzewinged Jacana**—*Metopidius indicus*—Bronze-winged Jacana.

227 **Pheasant-tailed Jacana**—*Hydrophasianus chirurgus*.

∎

228 **WAAK**: Published June 1953.

228 **Night Heron**—*Nycticorax nycticorax*—Black-crowned Night Heron.

∎

231 **SIESTA**: Published 1987.

∎

234 **GREY SHRIKE**: Published March 1945.

234 **Great Grey Shrike/Grey Shrike**—*Lanius excubitor*—Great Grey Shrike.

∎

236 **THE INDIAN ROBIN**: Published January 1943.

236 **Indian Robin**—*Saxicoloides fulicata.*

•

238 **BULBULS' NEST:** Published September 1950.
238 **Red-vented Bulbul**—*Pycnonotus cafer.*

THE EAR THAT HEARS
245 **'SUMMER IS ICUMEN IN':** Published March 1951. The title refers to an early Middle English *rota*, a musical piece for several voices, from the mid-thirteenth century called 'Sumer is icumen in.' It literally translates as 'Summer has arrived,' and goes on to beckon the cuckoo to begin its invocatory song.
245 **Coppersmith**—*Xantholoema haemacephala*—*Megalaima haemacephala*—Coppersmith Barbet.
245 **Common Green Barbet**—*Megalaima zeylanica*—Brown-headed Barbet.

•

247 **MARCH ROLLER:** Published March 1951.
247 **Roller:** Indian Roller—*Coracias benghalensis.*

•

249 **DID YOU DO IT?:** Published February 1955.
249 **'The winter is past':** 'For lo, the winter is past, the rain is over, and gone. / The flowers appear on the earth'—Song of Solomon 2:11-12, King James Bible (1611).
249 *In the Spring:* From 'Locksley Hall' by Alfred, Lord Tennyson.
249 **Red-wattled Lapwing**—*Vanellus indicus.*
250 **Yellow-wattled Lapwing**—*Vanellus malabaricus.*

•

252 **Grey Drongo**—*Dicrurus leucophaeus*—Ashy Drongo.
252 **White-bellied Drongo**—*Dicrurus caerulescens.*
252 **Racket-tailed Drongo:** Lesser Racket-tailed Drongo—*Dicrurus remifer.*
253 **Jungle-Mynah**—*Acridotheres fuscus*—Jungle Myna.
253 **serpent-eagle:** Crested Serpent-Eagle—*Spilornis cheela*—Crested Serpent Eagle.
253 **Malabar Great Black Woodpecker:** Same as the Great Black Woodpecker, see note to p. 172.

•

255 **VOICE OF THE DUSK:** Published October 1955.

255 **nightjar:** Common Indian Nightjar—*Caprimulgus asiaticus*—Indian Nightjar.

■

257 **MYNAHS EN MASSE:** Published January 1952.
257 **Common Mynah:** See note to p. 144.

■

259 **Shama**—*Copsychus malabaricus*—White-rumped Shama.
259 **Dr Thorpe:** William Homan Thorpe (1902-1986) specialized in behavioural biology and is accepted as an eminent ornithologist and ethologist. He pioneered the use of sound spectography for analysing birdsong.

■

261 **THE BIRDS OF PEACE:** Published 1989.
261 **Ring Dove:** Indian Ring Dove—*Streptopelia decaocto*—Eurasian Collared Dove.
261 **'Very pugnacious when':** Ali and Ripley, *Handbook of the Birds of India and Pakistan*, iii (BNHS, 1969), 148. Also see notes to p. 167.
262 **Little Brown Dove**—*Streptopelia senegalensis*—Laughing Dove.
262 **Emerald Dove**—*Chalcophaps indica*.
262 **Rufous Turtle Dove**—*Streptopelia orientalis*—Oriental Turtle Dove.
263 **Spotted Dove:** See note to p. 220.

■

264 **BIRD LANGUAGE:** Published December 1957.
266 **Ernest Thompson Seton:** See note to p. 112.

■

268 **BIRDSONG IN INDIA—THE CUCKOOS:** Published 1987.
268 **Koel**—*Eudynamys scolopacea*—Asian Koel.
269 **'Naturalists are not as quick':** RDA and AA, *Book of British Birds*, 336.
269 **'It is often difficult':** Ibid.
270 **Pied Crested Cuckoo:** See note to p. 97.
270 **Indian Cuckoo**—*Cuculus micropterus*.
270 **Common Hawk-Cuckoo**—*Cuculus varius*—*Hierococcyx varius*.

■

271 **BIRDSONG IN INDIA—OTHER BIRDS:** Published 1987.
271 **W. H. Hudson:** William Henry Hudson's (1841-1922) fascination with natural history began in his native Argentina. Later he settled in England, and while continuing to publish on Argentinian ornithology, moved on to British

birds. A founding member of the Royal Society for the Protection of Birds, his works on the English countryside brought him fame.

271 **Greywinged Blackbird**—*Turdus boulboul.*

271 **Shama:** See note to p. 259.

271 **Pied Bush-Chat:** See note to p. 118.

272 **Magpie Robin**—*Copsychus saularis*—Oriental Magpie Robin.

272 **Racket-tailed Drongo:** See note to p. 252.

273 **Black-headed Oriole:** See note to p. 51—***Oriolus melanocephalus.***

273 **Hill-Mynah:** See note to p. 145.

273 **Pied Wagtail:** See note to p. 65.

273 **Little Scops Owl**—*Otus sunia*—Oriental Scops Owl.

BIRD FLIGHT

277 **THE GREEN BEE-EATER:** Published December 1953.

277 **Green Bee-eater**—*Merops orientalis.*

▪

279 **WHITE WINGS:** Published March 1953.

279 **Cattle Egret**—*Bubulcus ibis.*

▪

282 **FREEBOOTERS OF THE AIR:** Published March 1952.

▪

285 **THE FALCONS:** Published June 1988.

285 **Pariah Kite**—*Milvus migrans govinda*—*Milvus migrans*—Black Kite.

285 **Peregrine:** Peregrine Falcon—*Falco peregrinus japonensis*—*Falco peregrinus calidus.*

285 **of migratory duck:** The following words have been excised in order to avoid repetition with the last piece in the book, '—in America, it is known as the Duck Hawk.'

286 **Grey Heron**—*Ardea cinerea.*

286 **Great Black-headed Gull**—*Larus ichthyaetus.*

286 **Shahin:** Shahin Falcon—*Falco peregrinus peregrinator*—Shaheen Falcon.

286 **Laggar Falcon**—*Falco biarmicus jugger*—*Falco jugger.*

▪

287 **THE WHITEBACKED VULTURE:** Published April 1943.

287 **Whitebacked Vulture**—*Gyps bengalensis*—White-rumped Vulture.

▪

289 **BIRD FLIGHT:** Published October 1960.

290 **Little Egret**—*Egretta garzetta*.

291 **Openbill:** See note to p. 58—**Openbilled Stork**.

291 **Peregrine:** See note to p. 285.

■

293 **TERROR FROM THE SKIES:** Published July 1950.

293 **Peregrine:** See note to p. 285.

294 **far swifter speed:** The following words—'(reckoned at 180 miles per hour by competent observers)'—have been excised from this line. The speed of the falcon's stoop is mentioned in the two preceding pieces.

294 **Tam o' Shanter's mare:** 'Tam o' Shanter' is a poem by Robert Burns.

■

INDEX

271; Greywinged Blackbird 271, 272; bulbuls 271; whistling thrush 272; fantail-flycatcher 272; Black-headed Oriole 273; Hill-Mynah 273; lark 273

South (India) 34, 68, 78, 154, 304; shrines 52; literature 79, 99, 165, 217; birds 80, 108, 167, 188, 289; languages 45, 264

sparrow 94, 118, 262; size 50, 66, 173, 236; prey 131; roosting 192, 238, 255; country 240-1

Sparrow, House 115, 141-3, 152, 237, 313

Spoonbill 58-9, 60, 61, 74, 203, 231-2, 265, 310

Spotbill 84-5, 311

spurfowl 209

Sri Lanka 78, 167, 180, 188

stork 60, 74, 108, 232, 264, 265, 291

Stork, Openbilled (Openbill) 58, 59, 60-1, 81, 108, 204, 291, 310

Stork, Painted 58, 80-81, 311

sunbird, *see* honey-sucker

Sunbird, Loten's 137

Sunbird, Purple-rumped, *see* Honey-sucker, Yellow-breasted

swallow 49

swan 58, 264

swift 40, 141, 149, 283, 285

Tailorbird 139-40, 150, 202, 313

Tamil 19, 56-7, 264; novelist 16; names of birds 45, 105, 115, 164, 228, 250; literature 12, 178, 305; curse 280

teal 58, 83

Teal, Cotton 84, 311

Teal, Lesser Whistling 162-3, 314

temple 52, 102, 131, 226

thrush, laughing 92

thrush, whistling 272

tree pie 117, 220

Tree Pie, Indian 180-1, 252, 315

tumbler 183, 293-4

Tumbler, High-flying 40, 290

vulture 74, 86, 108, 188-90, 232, 283, 291

Vulture, Scavenger 50-1, 52-4, 149, 188, 309

Vulture, Whitebacked 189, 190, 287-8, 321

wagtail 65, 118, 279, 289

Wagtail, Grey 65-6, 241, 310

Wagtail, Pied 50, 65-7, 273, 310

Wagtail, White 65-6, 241, 310

warbler 25, 139

Warbler, Ashy Wren- 139, 140, 313

warbler, fantail 139

warbler, tree- 139

warbler, willow- 139

waterhen 59, 222

Waterhen, Whitebreasted 222, 223, 318

weaver bird 142

Woodpecker, Goldenbacked 62-4, 150, 170-2, 310

Woodpecker, Great Black 172, 253, 315, 319

Woodpecker, Ivory-billed 63, 310